THE TOY DOLLS
From Fulwell to Fukuoka

THE TOY DOLLS
From Fulwell to Fukuoka

Ronan Fitzsimons

Ardra Press

First published in 2004 by

Ardra Press
PO Box 78
Cottingham
HU16 4WT
United Kingdom
www.ardrapress.com

ISBN: 0-9548678-0-7

British Library Cataloguing in Publication Data
A CIP record for this book can be obtained from the British Library

Designed and typeset by Julie Martin

Printed and bound by TJ International Ltd, Padstow, Cornwall

Cover design by Ciaron Lee Marlow
www.rockers-going-starwars.co.uk

This book is dedicated to all Toy Dolls, past and present, and to all the band's fans across the world, who have enjoyed 25 madcap years of The Toy Dolls.

Contents

Introduction   9
Acknowledgements   13

History 1979-1980 – *Kids in Tyne & Wear*   15
Olga's Inspirations 1 – *The Songwriting Process*   33

History 1981-1982 – *Spreading the Word*   48
Olga's Inspirations 2 – *Personal Concerns*   58

History 1983-1984 – *Digging that Groove*   68
Olga's Inspirations 3 – *Sunderland and Durham Places*   81

History 1985-1987 – *Big in Japan*   92
Olga's Inspirations 4 – *Sunderland and Durham People*   106

History 1988-1990 – *Psychopaths and Brazil Nuts*   125
Olga's Inspirations 5 – *TV & Soap Operas*   134

History 1991-1993 – *Things Get Absurd*   142
Olga's Inspirations 6 – *Famous People*   150

History 1994-1996 – *Making History*   160
Olga's Inspirations 7 – *Crazy Little Thing Called Love* 168

History 1997-1999 – *Production and Seduction*   177
Olga's Inspirations 8 – *The Cover Versions*   185

History 2000-2003 – *Bassist for Hire*   203
The Toy Dolls – A Global Phenomenon   213
Top 25 All-time Toy Dolls Rhymes   244

History 2004 – *Our Last Chapter? The Present and
    the Future*   248

Introduction

FLASH!

20 October 1979. Millview Social Club in Fulwell, Sunderland, UK. An unknown band steps onto the stage for the first time. They blink into the lights. They've got a look about them. Something special. Something fresh and exciting. The opening guitar chords send an electrifying message to the ears of the audience. That guitarist sounds good. Knows his stuff. The band's material hovers between fast rock 'n' roll and confidently executed punk of the type that has been sweeping the country for the last three years. The turnout isn't the biggest, but everyone seems to have a good time. The Toy Dolls finish their set, grin and leave the stage. A phenomenon is born.

FLASH!

December 1984. Britain is gripped by images of starvation in Africa, and the Band Aid machine clicks into action overnight. The single 'Do They Know It's Christmas?' goes straight to Number 1, and the country feels a mixture of sadness, pride and concern as it settles down with a beer to watch *Top of the Pops* on BBC1. We know that Band Aid will be on just before the end, but hold up, who's this coming on now? Three blokes in schoolboy blazers that are far too small for them. One of them's a skinny lad with plastic sunglasses and a guitar that's nearly as big as he is. They launch into a punky version of the timeless kiddies' classic 'Nellie the Elephant'. It's outrageously good. It makes us forget for a couple of minutes that there is evil, famine and stress in the world. The nation taps its feet, smiles broadly and burps its approval. The single peaks at Number 4 and goes on to sell over half a million copies.

FLASH!

22 January 1996. Be-I, Fukuoka, Japan. The same band are now selling out huge football stadiums and more traditional gig venues (such as this one in Japan) across the world – Japan, South America, continental Europe, the USA – everywhere, in fact, except the United Kingdom, where their popularity has mysteriously waned, though a dedicated hardcore of UK diehard fans remain imbued with the spirit of 79 and continue to follow their heroes from afar. The lads now have a string of albums, singles, videos and world tours under their belts, and are going from strength to strength on the world stage.

FLASH!

March 2004. London. I'm interviewing lead singer, guitarist and songwriter Olga as part of the research for this book, the first full-length biography of The Toy Dolls, written and published to coincide with the 25th anniversary of that first gig back in Fulwell. We chat about the whole history – the ups, the downs, the touring, the albums, the themes and inspirations, the guitars, the protagonists, and everyone and everything that has played a part in 25 unforgettable years. We also drink a hell of a lot of beer.

•

This book is written by a fan, and is offered to other fans in the spirit of celebrating this quarter century of one of the finest live bands around and their zany, witty, catchy tunes that can be compared to nothing else on this earth and stand proudly beneath their unique label of Toy Dolls Music. It alternates between a chronological history of the band and a series of analytical sections detailing Olga's Inspirations: where he gets the ideas for his songs from and how he goes about writing and recording them. Toy Dolls fans from across the world have contributed their thoughts to round off the celebration.

Whoever we are, whatever we look like, wherever we live, however and whenever we first got into the band, we're all Toy Dolls fans. We love the band's music, their approachability, their professionalism, their humour, the electric atmosphere of their live performances, their durability and, perhaps above all, that special feeling they've instilled within us. Whatever happens beyond the 2004-05 world tour, all of us – from Fulwell to Fukuoka – are pleased, proud and privileged to have been part of 25 years of The Toy Dolls.

Ronan Fitzsimons
Nottingham, UK
2004

Acknowledgements

Firstly, thanks to Olga for making himself available for interviews and drinking amid the frenzy of writing *Our Last Album?* and rehearsals for the world tour, and for his accessibility and help throughout the project. Thanks also to the bar staff and waitresses of northwest London, whose tolerance and ability to decipher slurred Geordie accents could not be faulted.

Thanks to Tommy Goober for his timely intervention.

Cheers to all those who wrote in with stories and contributions during the preparation of this book (some of their names appear in the Global Phenomenon chapter). There were a large number of additional comments I've been unable to use or credit as the writers didn't leave their names – thanks to you all, anyway. Quick thanks to Cameron Borland for his help, and special thanks to Kev Miller and Koen Velleman, to whom I owe at least one pint each for their tireless help.

Thanks to Ciaron (Telly Addict) for cover design, and to Rich of RMR Digital Media for other technical stuff. Cheers to Ged Naughton for accommodation, Guinness and free bus tickets in London – best of luck with your new plans, mate.

My partner Shell has been patient and supportive in putting up with my Toy Dolls obsession. Thanks. Romantic weekend breaks loom across Europe in any number of cities where The Toy Dolls will coincidentally be playing.

Finally, back in the early 1980s, two of my mates in

particular shared my belief in the band and joined me in pogoing, drinking, laughing and singing 'She Goes to Fino's', 'Tommy Kowey's Car' and 'Deirdre's a Slag' across various parts of the UK and France. Cheers to Paddy Naughton of Consett and John McNamara of Birmingham then Sheffield.

History 1979-1980

Kids in Tyne and Wear

The industrial town of Sunderland, part of the county of Tyne and Wear on the northeast coast of England, was a grim, unlovely place in 1979. Nowadays, things are different: it received its royal charter for city status in 1992; millions of pounds (and Japanese yen) have been pumped into the local economy and boosted employment figures; the polytechnic has become a thriving, community-focused university; and the city centre has undergone something of a facelift to entice local people out of their homes. But back in 79, life was crap for much of the Sunderland area: the once-buoyant shipbuilding industry was in decline, as were the coal-mines scattered across large areas of the northeast; the local football team – which had won the FA Cup only six years earlier – was breaking its passionate fans' hearts by yo-yoing between the first and second divisions; and, worst of all, the Conservative government of Margaret Thatcher had just come to power.

What the town needed was some excitement, a cultural boost, something for the people to take their minds off the humdrum of everyday life. Step forward a number of local bands who had started to plug their energy and their guitars into the punk and new wave scene that had swept the country over the previous three years. Some of these went on to greater things nationally and internationally – The Angelic Upstarts from nearby South Shields, formed in 1977, were an obvious example. Others, such as Red Alert, The Rebels, Red London, The Cult and Leatherface, had a lower profile but were very quickly getting the sort of critical acclaim and local fanbase that hundreds of other bands would have dreamed of. The area very soon began to rock, and the excitement was all the more poignant and tangible against the backdrop of Sunderland's declining economic fortunes.

In March 2003 the Newcastle *Journal* newspaper interviewed a number of ex-punks from the northeast of England for a retrospective piece. Gaz Stoker was a founding member of The Rebels, before moving on to play bass with Red Alert (a role he held at various times, before giving up finally in April 2004):

> "Punk was like a breath of fresh air. There were songs about unemployment and I could relate to that. I left school in 1977 with no prospects and went straight onto the dole. Punk was totally new and it went against the music of the time, hippies singing about peace and love. It went against fashion. When flares were the trend punks wore drainpipe trousers; when long hair was in fashion we had short hair."

A name more familiar to Toy Dolls fans, Marty Yule, was also interviewed for the article, and offered the following views, which sum up what the punk era meant for so many thousands of us:

> "Our punk band practised in a friend's garage. None of us had ever played instruments before. The appeal was that you didn't have to have talent to be a musician. Punk was the last youth movement – there's really been nothing since."

Meanwhile, back in Sunderland, more and more bands were springing up. Alongside the more successful ones, there were lesser known groups such as The Straw Dogs, who combined a dream of playing live and making good music, with a hell of a lot of hard work. Among their ranks, alongside an increasingly charismatic singer known as Pete Zulu and a bassist named Flip, was a teenage guitarist called Michael

Algar, who had for a long time been known by his nickname of Olga.

Born in the seaside village of Marsden, close to South Shields (which in turn is only a few miles from Sunderland), Olga moved with his family (his parents and an older sister and brother) to Grangetown, a working-class suburb of Sunderland, when he was five years old. Although he did not perhaps realise it at the time, it was elder brother Ernie who had the most marked effect on young Olga's musical development. Being around 20 years older than Olga, Ernie left home as a young adult to find a place of his own (and to play in a local club band), and left his vast record collection in the house. Gradually, then, as the years went by, Olga became more and more familiar with the contents of Ernie's collection – mostly rock 'n' roll classics and a range of 1960s material – and made his mind up that, one day, he too would make music. He wasn't sure how, or exactly what type, but his dream was established, and all he needed to do was grow up and learn a musical instrument.

The key moment in determining which instrument Olga would make his own came in May 1973, when the young Olga saw a photograph of Suzi Quatro in a music magazine, then saw her perform 'Can the Can' on the early-evening UK music programme *Top of the Pops*. Anyone who could offer such stage presence and glamour, whilst simultaneously singing and playing a bass guitar, was OK by Olga. He could see that the path to credible stardom lay in being a front man, a performer, whose music was in some way linked to traditional rock 'n' roll, but perhaps speeded up and somehow updated. He continued to widen his range of musical interests – spending hours listening to Ernie's records and talking about them with his mates from school – and very soon got heavily into early Dr Feelgood stuff (his admiration for guitarist Wilko Johnson was to continue for years to come) and faster R&B. Before he knew it, the punk explosion was happening, and Olga's delighted ears were being blasted by bands like The Sex Pistols, The Vibrators,

The Buzzcocks and The Jam. This was it. This was fast and exciting. This was what he wanted to do.

By this time Olga was a pupil at South Moor Secondary School in Sunderland, where several of his friends were getting more and more interested in the local music scene. He recalls not being quite as interested as other people initially, but he was certainly interested enough to set himself some targets for how to become a musician after he'd left school. Thinking back to the Suzi Quatro moment, Olga spotted a gleaming Audition bass guitar for sale in the Woolworth's department store in Sunderland for £14.99, and made up his mind to do whatever was necessary to make it his. The only way to get the money together was to get a part-time job delivering the *Sunderland Echo* newspaper to people's homes, and he did this for a whole year while he saved up the money – spending most of his Saturdays with his nose pressed up against the shop window, repeating to himself, "I'm gonna have that, I'm gonna have that."

When the money was finally in his pocket, Olga went triumphantly into Woolworth's, only to discover to his horror that they had increased the price of the bass by a pound. Bastards. Rather than spend another 3 months carrying a back-breaking newspaper bag over his shoulder, Olga took a spontaneous decision that was to change his musical life: he bought a lead guitar that was a pound cheaper than the bass. That was it – he was now a guitarist.

The unfortunate experience of being bullied at school for being small and skinny made the teenaged Olga all the more determined to succeed at guitar-playing. But surely it must have been hard for such a small bloke – with tiny hands – to manage a full-size guitar? I asked Olga what his earliest memories were of grappling with his first guitar:

> "Trying to master that first guitar was hell … I remember sitting and learning F [Fa major, on the Do-Re-Mi scale], and it was just hell – I used to sit with rubber bands around my hands and watch a film and then take the rubber bands

off, just to be able to manage to press the strings down. But bit by bit I got there."

Among Olga's mates from school were Philip Dugdale (known as Flip) and Colin Scott (Mr Scott), with whom he was keen to put a band together. But the first real band of any note in which Olga was involved didn't involve Mr Scott: The Straw Dogs had a drummer called Mac, and featured Pete (Zulu) Robson on lead vocals. Zulu was a few years older than the rest of the lads, had already left school, and fancied himself as a charismatic front man. His instrumental skills were minimal, to put it generously, so singing was his ideal niche.

The Straw Dogs played a succession of working men's clubs – the obvious gig venues for up-and-coming local bands in the northeast at the time – concentrating on Dr Feelgood-style R&B, doing 'Lights Out' and stuff like that. The experience of playing live was invaluable for Olga, gaining confidence and stagecraft, but it was clear to him that eventually he would need to break out of that style of music and do something a bit riskier, more original. At the same time as he was playing with The Straw Dogs, Olga was also starting to try his hand at songwriting, and had already crafted 'She Goes to Fino's' and 'Tommy Kowey's Car' by the age of 17. He kept these songs up his sleeve, because they weren't quite right for The Straw Dogs' style of music.

Where he was finally able to consider using his own material in a band was when he joined The Showbiz Kids – alongside mates Phil, Pat, Bob and Rob – not long after he left school. The Showbiz Kids had a manager – actually a guy who used to do bookings for older bands like Free in the local area – and a far better profile and chance of recording anything than The Straw Dogs had had. The lads worked hard, and eventually put out a low-key recording, using Olga's 'She Goes to Fino's' as the B-side to their single 'I Don't Want to Discuss That'. Testimony to the lads' musical ability is that, after the band split up, Rob went on to greater things with Dr Feelgood, and Pat was later to feature in

Bonny Baz's band The Sun Devils. More about Bob later. However, things moved on, and in the late summer of 1979 Olga teamed up with an emerging band called The Toy Dolls as their guitarist, alongside singer Pete Zulu, bassist Flip and drummer Mr Scott. This time there was no manager, but the gigs started very quickly, and were plentiful. The first of them came on 20 October 1979, at the Millview Social Club, in Fulwell, Sunderland, and it, like the next two, was a lively affair musically, spoiled only by the smallness and lack of interest of the audience. I wondered whether being restricted to the working men's club scene in Sunderland and the surrounding area made the band despondent:

> "It's difficult to make your way in the music business, but in those gigs it was particularly hard. But you have to remember that the people in those venues – while they might not have been the ideal sort of audience we wanted to break through to – they're still human beings with 2 arms and 2 legs and a head; they're just a different kind of audience. They're Working Men's Club kind of people, but they're just people – they're no better and no worse than other people who might read the music press. But breaking through to them is just as important as – or almost as important as – breaking through to the music press readership or 'real' gig-goers."

Image was important from the very start, and ideas such as the little blazers and ties partly fitted in with the 'toy' concept suggested by the band's name, and were also a nod at smart on-stage uniforms, a proven idea used by bands such as The Jam, who had blown Olga's mind when he first saw them in Seaburn, near Sunderland, in 1977. Paul Weller, as is widely known, borrowed his stage jumps from The Who's Pete Townshend, and Olga was quite happy to join the chain and expend his energy leaping about in perfectly executed fashion at crucial points in The Toy Dolls' songs. He accepts now, all these years later, that there will

eventually come a time when he can no longer jum[
such perfection, and when sitting on the bas
shoulders and other such on-stage tricks will no l
possible, but for the moment, he'll continue to make the
shows as entertaining and tight as he can. I grin at the
prospect, and ask him about the younger generation of stage
jumpers such as Busted. We're spared a vitriolic answer by
the arrival of another round of pints.

After these first 3 gigs, Zulu left The Toy Dolls, going off
to form his own band Zulu and The Heartaches with
another group of local musical mates. This band did
reasonably well locally, but never made it nationally. Pete's
real breakthrough came some years later when he achieved
some fame – and a certain amount of local notoriety – as a
chef at the Throwing Stones restaurant at Sunderland's
National Glass Centre, and as a local TV cuisine guru. His
most famous act was getting into a protracted argument
with a customer at the restaurant who claimed that the
portion of chips he'd given her was too small to justify the
price charged. It's a far cry from the cut and thrust of punk.

However, with Zulu moving on, the remaining Toy Dolls
needed to find a new vocalist, and quickly. They hastily
brought in a local singer (with no singing experience) called
Paul Hudson, or Hud, to cover a gig at Thornaby
Conservative Club, close to Middlesbrough, further down
the coast from Sunderland. Hud certainly looked the part –
bearing more than a passing resemblance to Billy Idol – but
unfortunately, on the night, he froze with stage-fright,
couldn't face the audience properly, and that was to be his
only Toy Dolls show. Anyone who has fronted a band will
know how much bottle it takes to stand up and sing, and it's
a well publicised fact that Olga is unable to perform on stage
unless he has his sunglasses on to give him courage. How did
he feel when Hud and the band parted company so quickly,
and what are his feelings on stage-fright generally? Does it
vary according to the size of the occasion or the audience?

"Yeah, it was a shame about Hud, because he had the image

and the presence to be a great front man. But the nerves thing is a killer. I'm worried before any Toy Dolls gig – I'm retching and taking the inhaler beforehand, before every single gig. It's mostly to do with the fronting thing – with The Dickies I was hardly nervous, as the pressure was off me. I don't think it's influenced by the size of the audience – you can play in front of 200 people, or 30,000, but if your auntie walks in, you're a nervous wreck. It's the person that makes the difference, whether it's a writer from the music press, or a relative, or somebody you know, a friend. I'm sure any performer will agree with me."

It was clear that the band needed to look for someone more capable and more permanent than Hud had been, so they set about auditioning locally. Throughout the process Olga had stood in as vocalist to explain to the auditioning singers what was required, and the band found that they were comparing each candidate with Olga himself. It was beginning to look a bit like the whole Genesis story – where they auditioned about 3 million singers after Peter Gabriel left, before finally choosing their existing drummer, Phil Collins. (Sorry to mention Genesis in a book about The Toy Dolls.) So how did they get from what were apparently very promising auditions, to ending up appointing Olga as full-time singer as well as guitarist?

"Some of the auditions were really good. I remember there was one girl came along who was fantastic, and her boyfriend said he was going to kick my head in unless we gave her the job, but we didn't, and he didn't! I wouldn't say nobody was good enough, but nobody was really appropriate for the job, and we had a gig at the Wine Loft in Sunderland coming up. And so we tossed a coin and I said, 'whoever loses is going to be the singer for the Wine Loft gig.' And I lost, and ended up singing for the Wine Loft gig, unfortunately... Though, as I say, I'd been singing along to help the auditioning process, so the band were getting used to my voice, and I suppose it was probably for the best that I became the singer. I still think I'm crap, but I'm probably right for this band."

So the routine settled down – lots of local gigs, with frustrating gaps in between – and, in the background, plenty of songwriting on Olga's part whenever time allowed. It was not the case that the band (or indeed Olga) had decided that he should be the main songwriter; rather, he was the man with the ideas in his head, so the other band members trusted him to come up with the goods, and seemed to like the products. The gigs would be filled with a mixture of speeded-up rock 'n' roll standards, and early Olga ditties, some of which (notably 'Tommy Kowey's Car') were repeated as many times as they could get away with to help fill the two sets of 45 minutes each they were playing in the early days. There was no great illusion about the band lasting forever: Olga remembers sitting in a pub with Flip and saying that if they could make it to three years they'd have had a good run. But what difference did Olga feel once he'd got a few gigs as singer/guitarist under his belt?

"Well, the sunglasses helped with the nerves. Actually, I'd always worn them, even before I was the singer, because I was too scared of facing the audience. But taking over the vocals made a difference, because people then started to look on me as the singer, guitar-player, performer and leader of the band – which is so much harder than just doing one job, like bass-player, drummer, rhythm guitar-player, lead guitar-player, or whatever. You're doing everything, like the guy out of Green Day. But despite the nerves, I got into the swing of it, and I was certainly enjoying myself, yeah."

So, with 15 gigs to their name – all within the confines of the northeast of England – The Toy Dolls entered a new decade as the calendar clicked into 1980. The northeast venues were notorious at that time for being very reluctant to offer gigs to punk and new wave bands, perhaps through fear of trouble among a band's fans, or maybe because they thought these styles of music weren't suitable for a specific venue.

However, The Toy Dolls seemed to be convincing the local scene that they offered a great show with no violence and lots of sweaty enjoyment, so they were luckier than most. Throughout this year, the norm of playing local gigs continued, and they amassed 65 in total, all but 2 of which were in the northeast. The two exceptions – at the Walkerville Hotel in the North Yorkshire army town of Catterick, and at Sheffield University – represented something of a step forward, the band's first foray into alien territory. Were there any frustrations in Olga's mind at being restricted to the northeast?

"Very frustrating, yeah, but what are you supposed to do? I mean, how can you break through if the only people that know you are within a 25-mile radius of where you live, maybe down to Darlington? Nobody knew us in Leeds. How were we supposed to get a gig in Sheffield, which was like the south to us, although it's really in the north – how are you supposed to get there? Catterick seemed like a million miles away, especially at the time when we'd never played outside the northeast. But I do remember finally getting the gig at Sheffield University, too. There was partly the difficulty of playing to people who weren't our fans – they'd just heard there was a gig on and come along – and also the thing of the northeast accent, which is incomprehensible to most people in Britain... As to spreading our wings a bit, well, there wasn't a point when we thought we had the northeast thing cracked, but there was certainly a point when we knew it was right to start concentrating on a different area and try and crack there – like Manchester or Leeds or somewhere – and try and do the same there as we'd done in the northeast. Mind you, we knew that wasn't going to be possible, because to try and do every town would have taken 50 years. And you had to administer the things, drive the van, get there, get back every night..."

However long it was going to take to build up a nationwide

following, the cult status the band had by now acquired in the northeast meant that their gigs in the Sunderland and Durham areas were now getting fuller and fuller. Not only were there more people there, but the band were starting to gel musically and deliver a really tight set with all the showmanship and audience interaction for which they were to become popular worldwide in years to come. I remember the sweat, heat, light and energy of a gig in a pub in Durham in 1980, where it was nearly impossible to see the band members, but the atmosphere they created was electric.

Highlights that local fans recall from 1980 include a bizarre gig at Acklington Prison, which was booked by the prison chaplain and which delighted and shocked the prisoners in equal measure, and a lively gig in Consett, during which a load of skinheads stripped Olga bare and threw him up and down in celebration of what a great guitarist he was. There was also the band's first opportunity to play at Fino's nightclub, the venue that had inspired the song. Olga remembers nothing special about the February and March gigs there, only that Fino's was simply another place to play in the Sunderland area, which, at the time, pretty much constituted the world for The Toy Dolls. He was gratified to discover that the bouncers were prepared to let him in this time, however! Did he, I wondered, have any particular favourite among the dozens of northeast venues the band played in the early days?

"Aye, I mean we were really restricted, coz we didn't have any record deal, any national music press coverage or anything, so even to leave Sunderland was a long-distance thing. For instance I used to ring Flip and say, 'We've got a gig north of Manchester,' and he'd say he wasn't going all the way down there – I mean it was only a couple of hours away! But yeah, the Old 29 in Sunderland, that was a really good venue – The Upstarts played there, and Red Alert and so on... Then there was the Turk's Head in Darlington, the Darlington Arts Centre ... Fowler's Yard in Durham was pretty good."

I'm interested in the idea of small venues, where Olga has always seemed to thrive and to feel at home with the audience. Does he still prefer the intimacy of smaller gigs, even after he's sold out football stadiums and huge halls across the world?

"Well, my manager always complains about me, coz I'd rather do 3 nights at a tiny place than 1 night at a big place. I like to be right next to the crowd, even though there's only the front 10 people can see you. I just like it more, I dunno. But I like that close contact type of thing. I think a bit of a lift on the stage would be nice – I mean when there isn't a crash barrier and people are falling on the stage all the time, people just get cheesed off coz you have to keep stopping, but I don't like crash barriers, personally. I like it when the stage is just nice and tight. I think 600 or 700 is just right as an audience. I mean that sounds like hardly any compared to some bands, but I think it's the perfect size."

The obvious benefits of building up such a strong following were 4 in number: firstly, the band became known to bigger bands locally (notably The Angelic Upstarts, who were to invite the boys to support them at a number of local gigs, followed by national tours later on); secondly, they started to attract the interest of the local press (the *Sunderland Echo* was particularly good to them, giving them glowing reviews, and the *Sunday Sun*, *Journal* and *Evening Chronicle* also lent their support to greater or lesser degrees, before the national music press eventually cottoned on); thirdly, the time was now right to think about getting something recorded; and finally, to cap it all, they got their break on local TV.

Tyne Tees Television, the local channel which forms part of the ITV network, had proposed a youth magazine programme called *Check It Out*, which would cover various areas of interest to young people, as well as providing the ideal platform to showcase new bands from the area. Malcolm Gerrie, the show's producer, invited bands from across the region to send in demo tapes so that five bands could be chosen to appear, one on each of the planned episodes. As it turned out, of the 300 entries submitted, The Toy Dolls were miles ahead in first place – in front of the other chosen bands: Erogenous Zones, The Genes (both from Tyneside) and Basczax and Return Ticket (both from Teesside) – and pulled off an even bigger coup in that their breakneck version of 'Wipe Out' was selected to be the show's theme music. Of the various landmark TV appearances in the early years, this is the one that stands out most markedly in Olga's memory – possibly because it was the first major one and hence the most special, but also because he felt a real buzz in the whole experience. I remember sprinting in from a game of football in the park that day in order to catch the programme and see The Toy Dolls, and having to shut my mother up from talking excitedly over the lads' performance. Happy days.

Another famous incident that brought the band national recognition was when BBC Radio's indie music guru John Peel – who had nurtured the careers of Stiff Little Fingers and The Undertones, along with hundreds of other bands – decided to come up to the village of Horden, a few miles from Sunderland, to check out The Toy Dolls playing live at a pub called the Bell Inn. The television cameras were there to mark the occasion of good old Uncle John venturing up into the frozen north, and in a classic piece of grainy footage, Peel can be seen talking to local pop guru Chris Cowey (later to become producer of *Top of the Pops* and who, incidentally, went to school with Olga's early girlfriend Angela), and saying not only that it did him good to get out of London and have the opportunity to see real grassroots bands playing live, but also that he thought Olga was a real entertainer, the complete package.

An amusing footnote to this came in January 1985 when the band were appearing on the 21st anniversary edition of *Top of the Pops*, and John Peel introduced them, saying, "The last time I saw this band was at the Bell in Horden – now they're on *Top of the Pops*!" You would imagine the regular drinkers at the Bell would have been thrilled to hear their pub's name mentioned on such a hallowed programme, but unfortunately there was a pool tournament on in the pub at the time of the broadcast, so the telly was switched off.

In 1980, the lads finally got their first material out on vinyl, with the release on their own label, GBH Records, of 'Tommy Kowey's Car', with 'She Goes to Fino's' on the B-side. It famously had a pressing of just 500 copies, many of which were snapped up straight away by local fans. I remember it being notoriously difficult to get hold of, but Olga recalls trying in vain to sell copies to the audience at the Sunderland Empire. A lad who lived round the corner from me managed to secure a copy, and he was the envy of the whole estate that summer. The recording marked the beginning of a love affair with a local studio where much more action was to take place in years to come: Guardian Studios in Pity Me, just outside Durham. Clearly, cost was going to be an issue, but was there anything else that made this particular studio stand out?

"Do you know what? I think Terry Gavaghan, who produced us at Guardian, had a really special little studio there. I actually thought that studio was really good. A lot of bands said it was horrible and boxy and so on, but for our band it was special, because it had that dry, up-front, telephone-booth style of sound, which I like. I went on to use it lots of times after that. I like that kind of up-front sound – I hate that big kind of Californian, multi-layered production thing. I like the fact that it sounds right in your face, like in your sitting-room."

The project was famously financed by a local businessman who owned Harvey's Restaurant on the corner of Tunstall Road and Mary Street in Sunderland. It is usually the case, in such circumstances, that the investor is involved solely to make a quick profit, but not here: this guy was into The Toy Dolls, having seen them perform at Harvey's, and was happy to use some of his money to give the lads a leg-up in the music business. Having said that, he did receive some gentle persuasion from The Toy Dolls' friend George Bernard Haswell, after whose initials the record label was named. Little did anyone know that, 24 years later, copies of this record would be changing hands on internet auction sites for as much as £50.

Despite the success of the single, there was no money to produce any more copies of it, nor was there much money in general terms to cover the band's expenses. Essentially, they would play as many gigs as possible – usually for the handsome sum of £5 – and then find that they were spending most of that on petrol and 'refreshments'. Mr Scott was the first to crack under this impecunious lifestyle (or, the sleeve notes to *The History 1979-1996* would have us believe, his girlfriend Val was the instigator of his departure). Olga confirms that money was indeed at the root of the problem, but speaks with fondness of the contribution Mr Scott made to the early development of the band:

> "You know what? Mr Scott might still have been in the band now, because he's a great drummer, great at doing all the eight-beats-to-the-bar stuff, and he was a really nice guy – I miss you, Mr Scott, I really do – and Val is fine, but she wanted him to get a tenner a gig, when we were only getting a fiver. And where was a tenner supposed to come from?"

Mr Scott left after the gig at the Boilermakers Club in Sunderland on 11 April, and has recently got back into the music business, drumming with a northeast band called Feed the Bear, where he's apparently having the time of his life. When he left The Toy Dolls, he was replaced by Dean Robson (Toy Dolls name: Dean James), who joined from local band The Cult (nothing to do with the 1980s Bradford band of the same name, who were previously known as The Southern Death Cult). Dean stayed for nearly 30 gigs, between May and September 1980, before being replaced in turn by Trevor Brewis, who was immediately endowed with his Toy Dolls name Trevor the Frog. We've all read stories about the reason Trevor left the band after 6 weeks and 10 shows, but I wanted to know how acrimonious the parting really was. Olga fills me in:

> "No, Trevor's all right actually. I'd printed up some material with our Toy Dolls names on, at a printing shop where I had a part-time job, and he rang me and said, 'I resent being called a frog and I'm packing the band in.' That's exactly what he said. He used to wear this green top, and I thought Trevor the Frog, that sounds quite good. Actually I'm glad he packed in then, because if he couldn't face being called a frog, he'd never have got through a tour. He wasn't a bad guy, though."

Dance Class were another of the emerging bands on the local music scene in Sunderland, and Trevor soon found a musical home with them.

Straddling the period between November 1980 and March 1981, Teddy Toydoll (Graham Edmundson) stepped in behind the drum-kit, on the understanding that his involvement would only be a stopgap affair, as he was quite happy concentrating on his main career dealing in car registration plates. Teddy shared a scary coincidence with last-but-one drummer Dean James, in that they both made their Toy Dolls debut playing at the West Cornforth Club, a few miles south of Durham. Anyone familiar with the village of West Cornforth – known locally as Doggy – at the turn of the 1980s will recall its reputation for gratuitous violence and brick-eating, and the fact that taxi-drivers would refuse to go there. It was the nearest thing County Durham had to the Wild West (Olga shows his mastery of the understatement by referring to it as "a bit rough"), but seemingly The Toy Dolls survived to tell the tale.

Of course, the songwriting continued. There was a classic 'Barry Manilow' ditty, which may loosely be described as a tribute to the large-nosed singer (though perhaps more accurately a no-holds-barred and highly amusing insult).

This became something of a stage favourite over the next few years, with its looping, waltzy bassline interspersed between machine-gun-speed verses, but unfortunately it was never formally recorded. Another promising project – which I must confess I've never heard – typified Olga's penchant for writing about people and things surrounding him. 'Nelly Hogg's Dog' told the tale of the hapless little dog owned by Nelly, who ran a shoe shop in Sunderland, and contained the lines: 'It's a little prat / It walks like a rat / That's the truth, Nelly Hogg / What do you think of that?' Glorious stuff, but sadly missing from our record collections.

1980 was also the year when the local press coverage of the band started to be superseded by articles and features in national magazines and newspapers. Whilst, until that point, local support by journalists like Rick O'Shea, Paul Woods – who achieved fame in a parallel life, singing with northeast band The Kane Gang – and Alan Watson had been very welcome and extremely helpful in widening the band's appeal, far greater punch was beginning to be provided by the nationals. The influential music publication *Sounds* finally took the hint that something really special was happening up in Sunderland, and so began a long-term passion for The Toy Dolls by journalist Garry Bushell. His first major piece, published on 23 August 1980, gave the band a storming introduction, describing 'Tommy Kowey's Car' as:

> "...a thing of beauty and wonder that's already sold out its first pressing. In brief it's an uptempo burst of glorious gumbie gossip delivered at frantic pace."

Unsurprisingly there was to be a lot more input from Garry Bushell over the next couple of years, much of it helping to establish the band on the national stage, a fact for which Olga has always been grateful to the journalist. The transition from local to national media coverage was, as Olga recalls it, something of a 50-50 affair, in that just as much interest would stem from journalists approaching the band, as from Olga making phone calls with stories for Bushell et al to follow up.

1981 was beckoning, but there was still time for one final episode in Olga's musical life of 1980. Just before Christmas he got a message from Max Splodge, whose band Splodgenessabounds had just had chart success with 'Two Pints of Lager and a Packet of Crisps, Please' and 'Two Little Boys'. Max wanted Olga to go down to London and audition to be in his band, which was an incredibly exciting thing for a young guitarist to be offered, even though Olga was perturbed to learn that his girlfriend had never heard of Splodgenessabounds. He takes up the story:

> "So I left Grangetown, got on the sleeper train to London, arriving 5 hours early with my guitar, and they were 5 hours late, which was ten hours after I'd arrived. So I got to this rehearsal room in south London somewhere, which was unreal, then Max turned up and said, 'Hey, Olga, Eddie and the Hotrods are rehearsing round the corner, if you fancy meeting them, but I think we should go to the pub instead.' I would really have fancied meeting them, especially as I didn't even drink in those days. I had 2 pints or something, then we got back to the rehearsal room and he asked me if I had any songs like 'Fino's'. So I thought maybe they were more interested in the songs than in me. Anyway, we did 'Fino's', 'Tommy Kowey's Car' and the 'Two Little Boys' thing, then he said, 'We'll let you know.' And I realized I didn't want anything to do with that – it just wasn't right – they seemed to be interested in me more as a songwriter than as a musician. But I did hear from Max Splodge a good while later when I did the 'Worky Ticket' thing, which he thought was fantastic, but anyway..."

The mention of 1981 brings us to another chapter of our Toy Dolls story, but first, let's have a little look at Olga's songwriting process, the first in a series of pieces running through the book under the heading of Olga's Inspirations.

Olga's Inspirations

1. The Songwriting Process

Three things are certain in the world of contemporary songwriting: firstly, only a lucky few ever get rich; secondly, it's far from glamorous, and is more likely to involve hair-tearing hours with an acoustic guitar in a bedroom than the sort of Rick Wakeman studio scenario we might be imagining; and thirdly, no two songwriters work in the same way. Over the last 25 years, The Toy Dolls have motored on, touring countless times and bringing out all the albums and singles we know and love, but it would be wrong to think that all this has made Olga – the only surviving original member, as we know – a rich man. The band has made him enough money to keep his head above water, pay the bills and think about putting the next stage of the project together, but he has been forced to dabble in the property market, and occasionally in other areas (wedding cars; stocks and shares; guitar tutoring) to try and make any financial headway. Against this backdrop, why does he bother continuing to write songs, record them and travel across the world to perform them?

The answer lies in the band's twin central philosophies: they do exactly what they want to do, and do not take kindly to anyone trying to hinder or dilute any of their activities; and they record albums in order to promote the next tour, rather than the opposite ploy of touring with the mercenary ideal of trying to sell records. It is clear to anyone that has ever spoken to Olga, or read any of the interviews he has given over the years, that the most important thing to the band is to give a great live performance as a tribute to the fans who've supported them and who have turned up and paid money to see them play. If the live material doesn't look as if it's up to scratch, then the tour doesn't happen. It's as simple as that. Perfection (or, perhaps, perfectionism) is everything.

Perfectionism is also the key concept with which Olga approaches the task of writing new songs, which is the topic of this chapter. We'll be looking at where he gets his ideas from, what the writing process is like (with timescales, finances, physical conditions, inspirations etc.) and how this gets from scribbles on a piece of paper to a polished CD for us to drool over.

When the time comes for Olga to set about writing an album, he shows remarkable self-discipline, accepting that he will lock himself away in his spare bedroom (currently in northwest London, but the same was true of many other spare bedrooms in years past) from 6.00 in the morning until midnight, often seven days a week. If there's some other commitment he has to make, then fair enough, but every hour he spends away from the task means that the pressure is all the heavier for when he returns to it. I ask him whether he can generalise on how the first germs of an idea usually occur to him:

"Sometimes it's a catchphrase, sometimes a title, sometimes a melody, sometimes it's the guitar riff. I mean, people usually say that they do words last, and generally I would say that is the case – not all the time, though – maybe 60-70% of the time. The melody is probably the most important thing, but if you come up with a great title, you can start writing down loads of references around it, but if I'm writing an album, in general I'll sit down with the acoustic guitar and the melody for the chorus will come, and then I've already written down 1,000s of titles – I'm always writing down titles – and then I write down 3 or 4 pages of references to do with that title, and then I'll try and get the lyrics for a chorus. If I can get a chorus, then I can work with the rest of the song. That's the usual way, though it's not always like that: sometimes it's a riff, or a title, it depends. I was talking to Ginger, the guy from The Wildhearts, the other day and he was telling me about songs that just come spontaneously all the time, and he said, 'it's really good that we don't dry up, isn't it?' and I thought, 'I dry up all the flippin' time.' I do find it really hard work, especially lyrics."

Olga cites the example of 'I've Had Enough o' Magaluf' from *Anniversary Anthems* as a song whose title and lyrics came to him very quickly – the atmosphere he encountered when arriving in Magaluf, on the Spanish island of Mallorca, inspired him straight away. But generally speaking, lyrics are a nightmare to him. This surprises me, as I've always thought of Olga as someone very much in control of his thoughts and his pen, and the lyrics he comes out with – particularly the rhymes (to the cream of which I've devoted a separate section in this book) – so I ask him a bit more about how he puts his lyrics together:

"I do use things like a rhyming dictionary, plus a thesaurus and all sorts of dictionaries – generally the ordinary modern dictionaries, coz they do have slang words in and so on, but they don't have rhyming half-words, rhyming syllables and suchlike. That's where the rhyming dictionary comes into its own, but then again, you can miss out on proper nouns, people's names and so on."

The notion of the syllable rhyme is a very Toy Dolls concept, and it's one that has tickled me for the 24 years I've been a fan of the band. Not only will Olga make 'swimming-pool' rhyme with 'skinny fool' (in 'Magaluf'); he can also craft a classic spilt such as 'I took the path up to the cath- / -edral where he stood there'. For me, that's one of the finest and most entertaining things about the band's music. Not only can you bounce around to their songs and have their energy brighten your day; you can chuckle along at the words, too.

Having said that, it's important to be clear about Olga's

thoughts on the humour of the lyrics. How would he define what he's doing in this context?

"Lyric-writing is difficult, but actually the pitching of humour in the lyrics is the hardest thing of all. I've written some crap – some really flippin' awful lyrics, especially on the *Bare Faced Cheek* album. I can write songs that are really witty and good, like 'Ernie had a Hernia' and so on, and I think I've got quite a few on the thing I'm doing now [*Our Last Album?*], but it's the hardest thing to make lyrics that aren't comedy, coz it's not a joke. It's borderline – you've got to be careful not to cross the line into that comedy thing, coz you want it to be a case of 'laughing with' rather than 'laughing at' the band. It's not comedy at all. I prefer descriptions like 'zany and humorous.' And that term they use, that 'fun punk' thing, I can't stand that. It is punk, in a way, but we call it Toy Dolls Music."

Just to play the devil's advocate, I ask Olga about the fact that only a small percentage of the band's current fanbase have English as their first language, and hence a lot of the linguistic and culture-specific references might get lost by a foreign audience. What effect does this have on his perfectionism in crafting his lyrics?

"If a new audience doesn't know who Ray Langton was or whatever [Deirdre the slag's first husband], that proves how important the stage show is, the performance and the melodies of the songs. Having said that, I take more time over lyrics than over any other part of the songwriting process. I still want to have the lyrics correct, even though they can only have their fullest meaning to English-speakers."

This is commendable dedication to his art. Another noticeable – and perhaps welcome – feature of The Toy Dolls' oeuvre is that it has very little socially unacceptable material in it – sure, there are some swearwords, but they seem to be gauged so as not to offend anyone. Certainly, there are no words like 'fuck' in any of their songs. I ask Olga how deliberate this decision was:

"Yeah, I prefer not to do it with this band, coz you have got little 8-year-olds asking you to sign things and so on. You read interviews in music magazines and every other word is a swearword, which is fine, but we wouldn't do it, personally, with this band. I mean in real life the odd word slips out, like I was trying to fix the shower the other day and shouted 'fuck', but there's a time and a place. I think words like 'arse' and that are OK, but as to saying words like 'fuck' and so on in a Toy Dolls song, I've just never done it. Now I listen to bands all the time with swearwords in their lyrics, and I think that's fine, and I would probably do it with a different band, but never with The Toy Dolls."

There are plenty of mild expletives in there – 'arse', 'bastard', 'crap', 'piss' and 'tosser' are examples – but the only one likely to cause any offence, if taken out of context, is 'puff'. Despite immediate appearances, this usage is nothing to do with homosexuality. In the northeast of England – and very probably elsewhere, too – a 'puff' is someone a little bit reserved or standoffish (maybe effeminate and maybe not – that's not the issue), who shows a lack of valour or an unwillingness to interact or do usual 'male' things such as playing football or drinking heavily. Hence, in 'Chenky is a Puff', there is no suggestion that the figure referred to as Chenky is gay; he just has some elements to his character that preclude normal interaction, or that make him in some way contemptible.

Olga's singing voice is a factor that must have some bearing on the styles of songs he writes. There are issues such as what key to write the song in, and also the range and strength of notes he can reach. His speaking voice is very normal – animated and friendly, with a strong Sunderland twang, tempered on occasions when he is emphasising something or quoting someone in standard English – so it is interesting to look at how he developed the unique singing voice he uses, with its relatively high-pitched squeakiness and (frequently) more than a hint of chirpy-chappie Cockney. Firstly, what are his own thoughts on his singing capabilities?

"I'm a terrible, dreadful singer – I've got a good squeaky original voice for the lead vocal, but with my voice, you're a bit dictated, unfortunately. It's a squeaky Orville [a duck puppet on UK TV in the 1980s] voice that could never work in a band like Aerosmith. So to do all the backing you need someone good. Bonny Baz and people like that will often come back in to help out with the vocals in the studio – proper singers. On stage we have all sorts of tricks – you wouldn't believe it – I mean the drummer will start to do my harmony that I'm supposed to be doing coz I just can't do it."

I put it to Olga that he's his own harshest critic, and that he shouldn't do himself down so much. The fans love his voice, and it is true to say that, were it not for Olga's voice, there would not be such a recognisable Toy Dolls sound for us to enjoy.

"Maybe so, but it's still the case that I'm the singer in the band because nobody else wanted to be originally. When Zulu left, we did auditions, and nobody was really right for the job, so we tossed a coin among the members of the band, and I lost, so I got the job. I didn't really give the sound much thought. I'm not sure where the Cockney thing comes from. My mother was from Coventry, which is nowhere near London but she did always sound really southern to me. Probably Jilted John is the likely influence, I'd say."

That makes sense. If you can picture Jilted John standing up on *Top of the Pops* and performing his 1978 Number 4 hit 'Jilted John', you can see the resemblance straight away, both vocally and in terms of the humour (and the word 'puff') injected into the lyrics.

So much for the lyrics, but I wonder about how much effort he puts into crafting the rest of each song. We know that he's the main vocalist, the lead guitarist, and (from the Dickies and Adicts tours) that he's a demon on the bass, but does he find himself exerting control over the fine-tuning of all the constituent parts of the sound? Is it an all-round involvement?

"Yeah, I worry equally about every bit of the song. The lyrics, obviously, but pretty much everything else you can think of, too: the guitar; the drum part, down to the bass drum and the hi-hats; the rhythm guitar, the scrapes, the feedback; the lyrics, the harmonies. Everything. It's a labour of love."

For various reasons, and at various times of the band's history, Olga has gone into the studio and recorded most of the instrumental work for a project himself, with the notable exception of drums, for which session musicians have been used. It just goes to demonstrate the guy's versatility and desire for the product to be right, and I suppose it proves the old adage that if you want a job doing well, do it yourself.

We chat for a while about possible keys for songs. Elvis Costello – along with a host of other songwriters, and many guitarists – is a big fan of A major (that's La for anyone brought up on the Do-Re-Mi scale), but obviously, the singer's range has to be taken into consideration. Olga reveals that he's probably happiest in D (= Re), as that suits his voice best, but that he writes a lot of material in A too. (He doesn't fall into my trap when I ask him whether he likes E – so I can confirm that Olga is strictly drug-free.) He sums his thoughts up like this:

"In this band, the songs are usually sung in the key that's best for the guitar-player (me), coz the guitar-playing's the most important thing, really – the rhythm guitar is the vital thing. The rhythm guitar sounds and parts are the most important thing for us, the rhythm guitar's going all the time if you think about it, and it usually determines the key that the song gets written in. But by the time it comes to the demos, and the actual recording, sometimes you've got to change the key."

Of course, a different sort of key-change is the one that happens during a song. Over the years, quite a few of The Toy Dolls' songs have been subjected to this treatment (including versions of 'Nellie' and 'Fino's'). How does Olga see this issue?

"Key-changes in a song can be a nightmare on stage, you're right. It's OK for the drummer, of course – well, it's all right for most drummers, anyway, if they're any good! Yeah, sometimes we swap the parts and the harmonies around so that different voices fit them better. Or maybe you sing your new part in a different octave, or you're doing a slightly different harmony thing. It takes quite a bit of working out."

Olga has often joked about how long it can take him to write a guitar solo, but what's the truth?

"They do take a massive amount of work. And sometimes the worst songs take the longest to write, because you've got a poor song that you're trying to make better and better, and you find yourself trying to boost the solo to make it stand out. I always like the solos to complement the song and what the song's about, and I don't like them to be too long (because I haven't got the time to flippin' write them, anyway). I like a tune with a solo."

If he's pushed to name famous solos that fit his criterion for complementing the song in which they feature, Olga cites Jeff Beck's 'Hi, Ho, Silver Lining' and Gerry Rafferty's 'Baker Street' as representative of what he means.

Whether he's in the studio or on stage, Olga has to have his own guitar and equipment – that's an absolute basic. He never feels at home without his Telecaster with its Seymour-Duncan pick-ups (or a Les Paul for studio solos), plus his on-stage surroundings of Marshall JCM 800 amplifier and

Marshall 4 x 12 speakers. He mentions how his friend Paul Gilbert from the band Mr Big – and also Bonny Baz, interestingly – have been known to get up onto a stage if the spontaneous occasion arises, and play whatever guitar is thrust into their hands. Not Olga – he'd be reluctant without his own guitar, custom finger-pick and sunglasses, and I can't say I blame him.

Earlier this year, he went over to Germany to do some work with a band called Gigantor, expecting only to be doing vocals. Only when he got there did he find out they wanted him to do some guitar, too! His description of his experience also reveals an interesting alternative to the conventional plectrum:

> "I was a nervous wreck, thinking, 'I haven't rehearsed this.' So anyway, I went into the studio and I have to play with a British 5-pence coin for solos in the studio, and there weren't any 5-pence coins around, obviously. And it has to be my guitar, which I hadn't brought along, so I stayed up all night getting used to their guitar and learning, getting ready to play this 2-second guitar solo! Still, we managed it OK."

Speaking of plectrums, I'm curious to learn how Olga manages to keep up the relentless speed of all the songs (both in the studio and, particularly, on stage). A traditional plectrum would not work for him, as it would slip out of his fingers with the sweat and speed of a live gig, so early on in his career he concocted a device that, in effect, binds a pick to his fingers with gaffer tape. His hands are as small in real life as they look on videos and on stage, and they don't seem especially powerful. Yet he's saddled himself with a style of music where speed is of the essence, and where lightning-quick downstrokes on the guitar are not only desirable but pretty well vital. We could also spare a thought for the band's drummers over the years, who have had to keep the beat at a million miles an hour. How does Olga himself manage on stage?

"I don't think it's the size of your hands, or your body, or your brain or anything like that. I think as long as you've done training beforehand... and once you get into a tour it's a different thing. We're going to be rehearsing 'Sabre Dance' in a couple of weeks' time – so I got the live album out, the *Stuttgart* one, and I can't keep up with it: it sounds as if it's speeded up. I'm thinking, 'how the hell am I playing that fast?' But it's because you've got the audience, and the tour, night after night. You get into the swing of it, and it all works out. There are little tricks like damping the strings, and sometimes I'll do a massive 'kerrang!' whereas in the studio it would need to be individual downstrokes and spot-on."

And how the hell do the drummers manage?

"The hardest job is those 8 beats to the bar – du-du-du-du-du-du-du-du – for the drummer. On record you might have 8 beats to the bar on the ride, then 8 on the hi-hat, but live you would do halves on the ride, then back to the 8 beats on the hi-hat, coz you've got to think ahead. When you're recording, you've got a song to record, but when you're playing live, you've got a gig to do – what's the point of getting one song perfect and another 20 crap because you're knackered? Mr Scott, Teddy and Marty were probably the best up to now at getting the 8 beats right and keeping things tight. Mind you, Dave the Nut is proving to be fantastic, too. We've not started the tour yet, obviously, but I have high hopes."

So what about the physical environment Olga uses to write his songs? We briefly discuss The Beautiful South's Paul Heaton and Dave Rotheray famously going off to a little villa in a hot country somewhere with an acoustic guitar, and coming back with an album pretty much written. Then we come back to reality. Life in Olga's spare bedroom used to be a lot more difficult, when he just had a crappy tape-recorder to work with. This was gradually replaced by a little portable eight-track recorder, which was a great improvement, and now he's progressed to the whole Pro Tools equipment on his computer. That said, the basic songs are still recorded initially on the portable cassette-recorder, and only then does Olga start to involve the Pro Tools gear. The equipment itself has set him back quite a lot of money (and he admits he probably only uses a small percentage of its capabilities), but it's made the songwriting process immeasurably easier. It means that he can now note things electronically as they occur to him, then he can add other ideas into the mix and keep everything in order. This helps above all when he's trying to write (and then learn!) a guitar solo. His comments above about writing and keeping control over every tiny aspect of a song's creation now seem all the more plausible.

The spare bedroom in question, incidentally, doesn't have as much musical equipment on display as you might imagine. There are a couple of guitars, a tiny amp, a tape-recorder, a powerful computer and a clutch of gold discs looking down from the bookshelves to remind him of what is possible.

Inspiration for the songs themselves can come from all sorts of angles (see other chapters for sections on the main categories). Sunderland and its people were the obvious choices to get things going – writing about yourself and your environment is invariably the sort of topic that comes easiest:

> "Well, that's where we were living, in the roughest part of Sunderland. We lived on this council estate, just me, my mother and my father – he died when I was about 11. Lots of people in Sunderland or other smallish towns like that never get the money or the opportunities to be able to travel elsewhere, so you're only writing about what you know and the people around you, and the only thing that's out of the area is *Coronation Street*."

The focus soon broadened out to embrace love (or, more specifically, the torment of relationships – as we shall see,

Olga isn't a fan of the traditional, soppy love song), and an increasingly amusing reliance on famous people and TV soap operas – as hinted at in Olga's words, above – to provide sources of material. This combination has remained more or less constant to this day.

One major theme in the work of many bands – conspicuous by its near absence in the songs of The Toy Dolls – is politics. It's always struck me that this must have been a conscious decision from the word go. We can count on the fingers of one hand the songs that have any sort of obvious political leaning: 'Come Back Jackie' (*A Far Out Disc*) is about a real man called Jackie who was drowned on a trawler that went missing in suspicious circumstances having set off from Hull to go about its normal fishing business. The 1984 single 'We're Mad' and 'We quit the Cavalry' (on *Fat Bob's Feet*) share an anti-war, anti-military theme, but apart from that, there is very little allusion to politics elsewhere in the band's repertoire. Olga explains why this is the case:

> "We've always been opposed to any kind of extremist political views – I wouldn't play with anyone in the band who wasn't the same as us, really – and I think within this particular band, it just wouldn't be right. I think it's fine to have political views and so on, because if you don't then you've got no substance, but for us, an extremist political stance wouldn't be right."

We chat for a long time about bands who make a big thing of their political views, or who verge on the danger of being ostracised by sections of the record-buying public if their views either get too extreme or start to get on people's tits. I put it to Olga that his primary concern might always have been to allow people a kind of escape from their day-to-day existence; not necessarily escapism as such, but offering a kind of licence to spike their hair up, jump up and down and forget about their troubles. Surely that's why there's so much optimism and bounciness in the band's music?

"Exactly. I'm not evading anything. You can compare it to a horror writer, who wouldn't write about some kind of marriage tangle situation – no matter how much or how little he believes in that situation, his writing is about horror, and that's what he sticks to. Our music has always managed to flow without getting into any sort of extremist politics, which I'm completely against. I'm an extremist and an obsessive in terms of my songwriting: it has to be this fast – it has to be duh-duh-duh-duh 230 beats per minute – that's just the way I am. But the political thing – I think it's good to have views, and I think it's wrong to pretend that the problems of the country or the world don't exist. I'm not saying, 'it doesn't exist – forget it.' I'm saying that within our music, it's nice to have this kind of escapist thing for however long the gig lasts or it takes to listen to one of our albums. But I do like lots of bands who are political."

Several articles and interviews over the years contain mentions of Olga's nervous breakdowns. Reading between the lines, it seems that he's most prone to suffering with his nerves when he's up against a deadline for writing an album – the time factor exerting an impossible force against the perfectionism of his work ethic. In the end, the job has to be done and Olga will put 20 hours a day into the project if that's what it takes, but all the associated stress inevitably leaves its mark on him, physically and mentally. Visitors to the band's website message-board will remember a moment in June this year, just after the recording of *Our Last Album?* had been completed, when Olga wrote apologetically that he had been told by his doctor to take ten days' rest, completely away from music. Quite simply, he'd been working too hard, not only in terms of physical attendance at the studio, but also in his capacity of overseer of quality assurance. It all boils down, once again, to perfectionism, and to a desire to give the fans the best possible product. What, I wonder, are Olga's memories of his earlier nervous problems?

"I've had 3 or 4 nervous breakdowns, and to be honest I

think I'm on the verge of one now [spoken in March 2004] with writing *Our Last Album?* I've always been told by the doctor to finish at 7.00, or 6.00, and then watch *Coronation Street* and things like that to take my mind off work, and then you won't take your project to bed with you, but it's hard to stop. I've got my spare room, with the Pro Tools thing set up, and the computer and the guitars and a little 3 Watt amplifier and so on. Now the ideal thing would be for it to be in a room above your garage at the bottom of your garden – this would need you to be a millionaire if you're in London, of course – so it's away from your house. But for me it's the next bedroom, so you just automatically go in there and start work. So, yeah, I've had about 4 nervous breakdowns. One was in 1989 – changing house and writing an album and all that kind of thing – it was also to do with a Chinese girl I was going out with at the time, from Hong Kong. Then I've had 2 or 3 since then, all to do with writing albums and the build-up of things happening at the same time."

The stress seems just as likely to attack during the writing process as during the recording. For a band without a millionaire budget, the choice of recording studio and time allocation is of vital importance, not only for financial reasons, but also to try and keep Olga enjoying some form of sanity. The general rule for recent albums has been for the recording to take about 5 or 6 weeks, with a bit of time given over at the end to mixing the whole thing and getting the final sound right. This contrasts starkly with the situation for *Dig That Groove, Baby*, which was done and dusted in three days. I ask Olga to give us some detail of how he approaches the recording of an album – how long he thinks is necessary, and how strict and disciplined he has to be with the time factor:

"It takes exactly how long it takes, and not a second longer. Because that's me; that's how I am. You get loads of bands that say, 'we're going to take 8 months to record an album,' and they take 9. Why? If you only work to the time you've got ... if you're writing a book in a week, you'll take a week; if you've got a year, you'll take a year. So I always say, 'I know how much money the record company has got, but I also know our level,' so we'll take 5 or 6 weeks to record and mix an album – not a second longer. They can't afford more, and I'll not get the money anyway. So that'll be – what? 8 grand or something? – for that amount of time. I might even take less time, which is great for the record company. But why people take longer I just can't understand. For *Our Last Album?* I've got a studio itinerary, with guitar solos, scratches, feedback, guitar scrapes, 2 o'clock, 3 o'clock, and everything is written down. I did that when I was producing the Japanese group Lolita No. 18, and they said, 'what's this? We can't believe this!' Coz Joey Ramone, their previous producer, had been really laid-back with them – but everybody's different: there's no right and wrong that suits everybody. It just keeps me more disciplined, and I can still think of things in between times. I've been with this record company since 1989, and we all know where we stand with the money and time, and they're very good. We've always finished in the studio either on time or a bit early. The thing is with a studio, you should get as much done before you go in as possible."

So when we all buy our gleaming copies of *Our Last Album?* later this year, we'll know exactly how much hard work has gone into the album's preparation, and we'll love The Toy Dolls all the more for having gone to so much trouble just to keep us happy.

History 1981-1982

Spreading the Word

After only around 15 months of Toy Dolls life, Olga was chatting with The Angelic Upstarts one day about styles of music, and Mensi said to him very gently, 'You know, you've got something very special in that band of yours. Forget punk or whatever – your thing is original, it's Toy Dolls Music.'

It's clear from talking to Olga that, while the band were influenced by all sorts of music, mostly R&B, new wave and punk, the term Toy Dolls Music is the one with which he's most comfortable. But as 1980 became 1981, the UK was starting to pigeon-hole its new wave bands ever more painstakingly, and another of the categories talked about was the phenomenon of Oi. Originating as an imitation of the London skinhead chant 'Oi oi!', the term was hijacked by Garry Bushell in his music columns, and it quickly became understood as a form of music embracing bands who were skinheads, or playing fast new wave with any sort of Oi-style chanting in the chorus. It was a fuzzy definition, but as a concept it was beginning to stick.

The unfortunate side of Oi was that it became inextricably linked with the resurgence of skinhead violence that reared up in the UK's seaside resorts during the hot bank holiday weekends of 1981 (part of a burgeoning social unrest – especially in inner-city areas – which also inspired the Specials track 'Ghost Town' that year). It was readily assumed that bands playing music vaguely tagged as Oi would be violent, mindless thugs whose sole contribution to society was to incite aggro. So while Olga and the lads welcomed Bushell's coverage, there was a niggling worry in the back of their minds that they were running the risk of some negative stereotyping.

Whatever the worries, it was imperative that the band should start to capitalise on the success of their local single release, and they hit lucky in March 1981 with their inclusion on a compilation LP celebrating the best of new northeast musical talent. *NE1* – a title Olga hates – was brought out under the umbrella of the Sunderland Musicians' Collective, and was the brainchild of the Collective's founder Ann Dumble, who ran the popular young people's meeting place The Durham Book Centre in Vine Place, Sunderland. Ann had been the manager of Sunderland band Disorder, and understood the need for some sort of outlet for local talent. Recorded primarily at Guardian, it featured 16 tracks, including songs by Zulu and The Heartaches, Genocide Exit, The Suspects, Red Alert and Remnants of Warsaw. The Toy Dolls' offering, recorded by Olga, Teddy and Flip, was 'Worky Ticket', and Olga was overjoyed at having his music finally showcased to a wider audience:

> "We were completely happy about it. We needed a break – which this was – and you had to be happy about anything like that. We were over the moon, to be honest, at the prospect of an album, and there was every chance that people would buy it beyond the limits of the northeast. It was fantastic. We got no money for it, of course, but in those days what we needed was exposure, plus the childish value of pointing to an LP and saying, 'Look, that's my band on that LP.' We were chuffed to bits."

By and large, the critics liked it, though most admitted that there were some weaker tracks on it, bolstered by the better ones such as those offered by Red Alert and The Toy Dolls. Garry Bushell summed it up thus in *Sounds*, offering additional comment on the difficulties of being a promising band in somewhere like Sunderland:

> "Myself, I like the album more for what it is than what it sounds like. With the way the business is, provincial talent's got next to no chance without the odd bolt-out-of-the-blue lucky break, so D-I-Y albums exist as a necessary reminder of life outside London and that the major record companies, far from being all-knowing, aren't even efficient at what they do. The more kicks up the arse they get, the better."

Before the band could blink, another opportunity arose, for them to be included on the much more widely marketed *Strength Thru Oi* album, the second of a series compiled by Garry Bushell and *Sounds* to show off the best of this style of UK music. Featuring songs by bands such as The Last Resort, 4-Skins and Infa-Riot, plus some socially acute punk poems by artists like Garry Johnson, it was released nationally through Phonogram, after *Sounds* had fallen out with EMI for their poor distribution of the first LP. This was a chance not to be missed, whatever the consequences, so Olga, Teddy and Flip offered up 'She Goes to Fino's' and 'Deirdre's a Slag'.

What the lads couldn't know at the time of recording the tracks was what Bushell was going to do for an album cover. Actor Nicoli Crane posed as a thuggish skinhead with a threatening attitude, and the image caused national uproar, leading to the easy assumption that the record was a Nazi document that could produce only hatred and violence in its listeners. In his sleeve notes to the 2003 reissue on CD of the album, Garry Bushell cogently defends the record, admitting it was a snapshot of early-80s yob culture, but rejecting the suggestion that he was pro-violence, pro-Nazi, or pro-anything he shouldn't have been. In fact, most if not all of the material on the album is about the reality of being young in Thatcherite Britain, and in no way promotes any of the evils it was accused of championing.

Certainly, the two Toy Dolls tracks could by no stretch of

the imagination be bracketed with social malaise, and were frequently hailed as highlights on the LP, but Olga still looks back on the experience with a mixture of – not exactly regret, but a certain rueful thoughtfulness and shoulder-shrugging innocence:

> "That was a different kettle of fish entirely from the *NE1* thing. It was nationally released for one thing, and we needed the exposure. But we would never have gone on that album had we known that the sleeve was going to have such a violent message. But we didn't know at that stage, we just thought, 'it's another album, a chance to reach more people, the only chance to get out of Sunderland, musically speaking.' That was our view. I suppose there was something approaching regret, if we stopped to think about it later, but it did help to increase our national profile."

What about the critical reaction? It's fair to say it was mixed, notwithstanding bias springing from the Oi debate. But The Toy Dolls did pretty well generally. Here's Chris Bohn, writing what was quite a slating review in the *New Musical Express*:

> "Only The Toy Dolls' daft 'Deirdre's a Slag' and Garry Johnson's verse refuse to be a part of the mire. The Dolls' song is an ode to a *Coronation Street* character, and Johnson's plain poems point to a condition without dressing it up, glory-boy style. They're the only two who are willing to sidestep barriers rather than erect them."

After completing his drumming work for these two compilations, Teddy said farewell to the band and returned to his business. To replace him, the band welcomed Happy Bob (Robert Kent), whom Olga had known from his Showbiz Kids days. I wondered why Bob hadn't been involved earlier:

> "We knew Colin (Mr) Scott from school, and the band was always happy with him as the main man really, but it was just the way things worked out, really. I think the second

choice was Happy Bob, because his 8-beats-to-the-bar drumming technique was so good – which was very important. He was working at Dryburn Hospital in Durham doing x-rays, which he's still doing now, lucky swine ... Bob, I'll have to meet up with you!"

As there was next to no money coming in from the band – just fees for gigs, and zero from record sales – Flip had retained his job as a forklift truck driver at a factory in Sunderland and, as we learned above, Bob was happy with his hospital job, so Olga was the only one who was injecting more full-time energy and time into organising and promoting the band. Despite this (or perhaps because of it) he still had what he refers to as 'absolutely nothing money-wise'.

1981 had far fewer live gigs than the preceding year, perhaps because of the focus on getting more recording work done and trying to promote themselves that way, but nevertheless, interest continued to mushroom, and by late spring, with Happy Bob now behind the drum kit, the lads were ready to push on with their dream. In the summer of 1981, they launched the ambitious and impeccable *Toy Dolls EP*, featuring 'She's a Worky Ticket', 'Tommy Kowey's Car', 'Teenager in Love', 'I've Got Asthma' and 'Everybody Jitterbug'. The record was famously self-financed, and released on the band's own GBH label – just like the first single a year previously – and despite selling out its 3,000-copy pressing, it reportedly left the band £3,000 in debt. So I wondered how they'd managed to keep afloat financially, and what sort of emotions Olga had felt at the time. Wasn't it a huge stress as well as a great achievement to bring out such a successful yet financially disastrous record?

"I'm a lot older now, and I think stress is a different thing for me in 2004. In those days, to sell one copy of anything would have been a tremendous achievement, so we were chuffed to bits when it sold out. Financially and in terms of promotion, my girlfriend Angela helped a lot, and with one source and another we managed to get the money together – it was everything we had, despite being, in the wider, 2004 sense, so little. But I'll tell you what – I'm glad we brought that EP out the way we did. Sure, you can have regrets about certain things, and you can always make bad decisions, but I'd have to say that I don't regret what I've done musically if I look at it as a whole."

Life has a happy habit of bringing up little coincidences and, if we're lucky, saving graces, and the advent of 1982 brought an unbelievable bit of news to the Toy Dolls camp. Not only would the £3,000 debt from the EP be cleared immediately, but their collective bank accounts were to be healthily boosted, by the stunning news that the giant EMI wanted to sign them for its punk imprint Zonophone. How are you expected to remain calm after receiving a piece of news like that?

"It seemed like they were promising the world, and we had to accept what they were offering, because it was the only way forward. Plus it was EMI, and EMI seems massive in anyone's language. Obviously, with hindsight, it wasn't the right thing to do, but at the time, who were we to turn down someone as massive as EMI?"

It's widely known that the deal fell through after just one single ('Everybody Jitterbug', in March 1982), simply by the hugely dissatisfied band keeping quiet until the option time for contract renewal had elapsed, when they promptly signed a much better deal with Volume. I ask Olga to talk us through some of the problems they experienced with EMI:

"The main problem was that not many people in the company knew who we were, but I've got to admit that, at that time, principles didn't mean as much as they do now – we certainly had them, but not to the same extent. If EMI asked us to do a deal now, then unless it was exactly what we wanted to do, and we had complete control of things like artwork, tracks, releases and money and everything, and just as importantly, we had someone in the company dedicated to promoting our material, then we wouldn't do it. We're older and wiser now; we were kids then, and it was the only record deal – it wasn't a matter of choice. We couldn't believe it when we were offered the deal. Let's put this into perspective: I sent 10 records to some guy from EMI, having realised that sending one demo or a release was no good at all, and you had to send 10. I sent one after the other – the same record, 'I've Got Asthma' – and got negative reply after negative reply, and finally, 'this is fantastic'. It just shows you. And then in the end, well it was their option, and we just left it to die, and luckily we got out and moved on."

The *Sunday Sun* reported at the time that the band would make 'a few thousand quid' each out of the deal but, although expenses and suchlike were covered and the lads now had, in theory, a much bigger pot of money behind them, Olga recalls the actually up-front payment as being £500 shared between the three of them. It wasn't a vast amount of money – particularly coming from such a big parent record company – but money wasn't the real driving force: they had accepted the deal for the potential exposure and projected record sales.

1982 was also an important year for the chance to embark on a national tour supporting The Angelic Upstarts. The lads had known The Upstarts since the early days, and it was both a great laugh and a good idea in terms of national exposure to jump at the chance to do the tour. Mensi and the lads were very kind to The Toy Dolls, letting them sleep on the floor of their hotel bedrooms, helping them out in all sorts of ways – making contacts, passing on tips, sharing raucous nights of partying – and Olga is still gushingly grateful to them.

The tour allowed the band to showcase their talents to a far wider audience, of course, but it was just as important for them to get access to hallowed venues in London such as the Marquee and the 100 Club, where so many of the lads' heroes had played during and just after the punk era. Generally speaking, the critics loved them, often (as was the case at the Marquee) favouring them ahead of The Upstarts. But in rounded terms, it helped their performance, brought them to the attention of more public and more media, and brought them a small amount of money and a vast haul of experience and memories to draw upon.

That spring, the BBC developed an idea for a series of TV programmes based around up-and-coming musical talent – a grander version of what *Check it Out* had been two years previously. Each programme in the series was to be called by a different colour for its theme, and The Toy Dolls were invited to play 'Everybody Jitterbug' and 'I've Got Asthma' on the *Orange Programme* on 5 May. This was big-time coverage indeed, but the programme became more famous in Toy Dolls history for provoking the famous Asthma backlash (see the chapter on Personal Concerns for a full explanation).

After the 'Jitterbug' single with EMI and The Angelic Upstarts tour, the year of 1982 perhaps stands out for a series of events happening in the autumn. Firstly, the band were freed from the shackles of EMI and immediately rewarded with a much more workable deal with Volume, run by Andy Worrall and Don Pheeby, two Newcastle music obsessives. Their music shop just off Northumberland Street in Newcastle was an essential Saturday afternoon visit for young people in the early 80s, where you could not only pick up punk records unavailable elsewhere, but also chat to like-minded teenagers and get the low-down on what gigs were coming up. The philosophy of the record-producing arm of the enterprise was straightforward: give the bands free rein in terms of artistic and musical direction, and keep them happy. Only a small amount of money would be forthcoming, but that was set against a huge improvement for The Toy Dolls in terms of their working relationship with the record company.

In November, Volume launched their first Toy Dolls

single, what is now known as the 1982 version of 'Nellie the Elephant'. With an initial pressing of 5,000 copies – far more than the band were used to dealing with – the single did well in the Independent charts, but failed to make a huge impression nationwide. As we now know, that would come in time, but for the moment, the lads were far from despondent. They had a good harness for their creativity, and the relationship was working well. The song was also included, towards the end of the year, on a compilation on Abstract Records called *The Beerdrop Explodes* (a pun on the Liverpool band The Teardrop Explodes, who were doing well in the UK at the time), which did no harm whatsoever.

Perhaps the band's biggest media opening yet came on 5 November, when they were invited to perform 'She Goes to Fino's' on the opening episode of a two-hour TV music programme produced by Channel 4 called *The Tube*, fronted by Squeeze keyboard man Jools Holland and Bob Geldof's partner Paula Yates, along with Scottish cultural commentator Muriel Gray. This now was truly nationwide television, and their performance, conducted in the foyer of the Tyne Tees TV studios in Newcastle, went down a storm and won them a lot of friends (to say nothing of subsequent invitations to play on the show). In typically downbeat fashion, Olga flies in the face of public opinion by recalling that 'we were awful on *The Tube*.' An added bonus was that, together with the exposure they got, The Toy Dolls had the opportunity to meet fellow performers Pete Townshend from The Who, Sting and The Jam. Also on the bill were Bananarama, Heaven 17 and Duran Duran, but there is no official record of Olga drinking into the night with Simon Le Bon and taking Bananarama in their entirety back to his five-star hotel room. Pity, that.

The band were now looking forward to the challenges of 1983, with the promise of their first album scheduled for the spring of that year. Before moving on to the second of our sections on Olga's Inspirations, and then to a look at 1983 and 84, I'll leave you with a fragment of a feature written by

Sounds journalist Ian Ravendale for the 13 February 1982 edition, who was daring enough to look into the future of The Toy Dolls. Judge for yourselves how accurate you think he was:

> "When The Toy Dolls are rich and famous, Olga will get all the publicity, but Happy Bob will get all the girls. Flip will probably get the mothers who'll worry about whether he's eating enough."

Olga's Inspirations

2. Personal Concerns

It's the first thing that hits you when you see Olga for the first time, whether on stage, in a photo or meeting him to talk to: he doesn't weigh very much. It's become part of his distinctiveness over the years, together with the sunglasses, the grin, the squeaky singing voice, the zany stage performances and the music he writes. The whole package.

Early press reports were kind enough to supply the figure we'd all been too embarrassed or too polite to ask: Olga was, according to the *Sunday Sun*, a 'six-stone weakling'. That's just over 38 kilos. The good news is that over the 25-year history of The Toy Dolls, Olga has increased his body mass by 50%, weighing in these days at a far healthier 9 stone, or 57 kilos. The bad news is that back in the 1970s, he was bullied at school on account of his size. He tries not to make a big issue of it nowadays, but admits that it did affect him at the time. His response, however, was not to run away and hide, but to find a way of facing up to the bullies, developing some skill that would force them to look up to him. Along came the world of music and guitar-playing, and the rest, as they say, is history.

Strictly speaking, although Olga came to master the guitar quite quickly as his response to the bullies, he was far more interested in becoming a performer – up there in the spotlight where everyone could see him doing his thing and demonstrating that he had left the bullies behind. Being a front man was the mission – and guitar-playing was the means to the end.

The guitar apprenticeship was also instrumental in developing what has become one of Olga's chief characteristics. Through diverting his mind and focusing on his music as if his life depended on it, he found himself becoming obsessive, a trait he retains to this day: 'Yeah, I'm an obsessive person with music and with other things in life … especially women.' About which, more later.

Perhaps linked to his physical size was a medical condition that brought him discomfort, but also a great deal of humour and professional success. 'I've Got Asthma' is both a classic piece of vintage Toy Dolls, and also a firm stage favourite with fans across the world. It may seem odd to write about something so negative and uncomfortable, but Olga is quite candid about the state of his chest and the origins of the song.

He was sitting in his family's council house in Sunderland when, as part of the ongoing scheme to update and improve local authority homes, the council workmen arrived to install central heating. They proceeded to lift the floorboards up, sending dust flying in the process, and Olga became aware of a vicious irritation in his chest and a fierce restriction in his breathing. He recalls wheezing for three weeks afterwards – 'I sounded like the girl from *The Exorcist*' – before finally going to see the doctor to get his chest examined. The doctor confirmed his suspicions that he had asthma, and Olga's reaction was one of utter joy, not because he could feel a song coming on, but because he finally knew what was wrong with him and could get an inhaler to keep the asthma attacks at bay.

He suffers to this day, and carries his inhaler with him wherever he goes. I ask whether it helps him to combat stress, and he replies that it's invaluable when he's getting stressed with deadlines for an album, or when things are getting on top of him in general: 'If I haven't got the inhaler I'll start wheezing because I haven't got the inhaler – it's mad.'

So what about the song itself? Olga remembers feeling so

ill and depressed with his asthma that he realised he'd better capitalise on the opportunity – think how many songwriters over the years have produced some of their best work when they've been at a low ebb with depression. The theme and the title were easy enough, but what about finding words to rhyme with 'asthma'? No chance. The truth is that Olga was feeling too weak to be bothered with such banalities as rhyme, and as far as he and I can remember, 'I've Got Asthma' is the only Toy Dolls song in which none of the lines rhyme. The song certainly doesn't suffer for it.

What my mates and I liked most about the song when it first came out in 1981 – apart from its surreal brilliance and its excellence as a set-list favourite – was the backing vocals, which broke with tradition and did not just repeat the lead singer's previous line. I still chuckle every time I hear 'can't breathe at all', 'blue and it's getting worse', 'wheezing like mad', 'good i-dee-ah', 'what shall I do?' and 'dear me, dear me!'

In May 1982, after the band had played the song on the BBC's *Orange Programme* – one of a series of weekly programmes, each with a different colour in the title, that served, among other things, to showcase the best of young musical talent – the BBC received a large number of complaints from people assuming The Toy Dolls were taking the piss out of asthma sufferers. Among the complainants was the Asthma Research Society, which had failed to see the joke. (That is not to belittle asthma as a medical condition – I'm a sufferer myself, too – but a little bit of research to discover that the singer was an asthmatic, and was actually recreating his own bronchial difficulties in the song – wouldn't have gone amiss.) Maybe the moaners thought Olga's 'death' at the end of the song was in poor taste, but one of my funniest memories of Toy Dolls gigs in the early 1980s was the crowd screaming for Olga to 'die', and Olga replying in good humour that we should be patient, that he would 'die in a minute, man'. It was, at the time, an essential part of the stage show we all grew to love.

It was also unfortunate – or maybe predictable – that the scene of this controversy should have been Newcastle upon Tyne, a short distance away from the band's home in Sunderland. The city had recently accumulated two prize cock-ups relating to the Irish punk band Stiff Little Fingers: a city councillor had incorrectly adjudged the song 'White Noise', from SLF's first LP *Inflammable Material*, to have been racist (when a single listen, or glance at the lyrics, would have allowed him to see the irony) and lambasted the band; and the city's Metro Radio had blown any street cred it might have had, by going into panic overdrive when the band's singer Jake Burns used the utterly inoffensive word 'crap' in a live interview. SLF went on to create a song out of the latter incident: 'You can't say crap on the radio'.

What is less known about the asthma incident is that it actually had a happy ending. After the complaints from the Asthma Research Society, and from a Mrs Marlene Kennedy – a teacher whose daughter was a sufferer, and who got her class of 14-year-olds to write letters of complaint – a lady called Irene Taylor from nearby Hebburn managed to get Olga to help her set up a northeast asthmatic society, and was delighted at his agreeing to come and talk to young sufferers, who, she said, 'look up to him for all he's achieved, despite his illness.' As they say, any publicity is good publicity, and the incident ultimately did the band no harm.

If asthma proved pivotal in introducing us to a performer and songwriter working efficiently despite a medical condition, it's tempting to ask about other factors featuring in the songs: further medical issues, fears, dislikes, addictions, vulnerabilities. Is Olga really scared of spiders? Was he really bitten by a bedbug?

'Spiders in the Dressing Room' is a great song for a number of reasons. It tells the story of Olga spotting a spider in the dressing room after a Toy Dolls gig and feeling mildly uncomfortable – that's the true bit – and develops into a full-scale fictional battle that is crying out to be made into a short film. The nursery-rhyme style of the half-spoken introduction gives way to a bloodcurdling 'aaaaargh', then Olga puts on his Doctor Marten shoes to show he means business, and we're into the first verse at double-speed. As we listen to the rest of the song – the spider refusing to die and coming back for more and more violent engagements, even escaping from a screw-top jam jar as well as resisting the full weight of Olga's 38 kilos stamping it into the ground several times – we are reminded of Olga's love of Friday night TV horror films, especially those starring Vincent Price (who makes a cameo appearance in 'Queen Alexandra Road is where she said she'd be, but was she there to meet me? No chance').

Fans who keep an eye on (or share) Olga's cynicism regarding the commercial side of mainstream contemporary music will have chuckled wryly at the tongue-in-cheek line, 'we played all our pop records and danced the night away'. Great stuff.

'Bitten by a Bedbug' dates back to the band's first USA tour in 1984, and relates the true story of Olga being bitten by such a monster in a hotel room in San Francisco. He has actually been bitten lots of times across the world, but singles out that incident, and that bedbug, for immortality in the song. Given Olga's penchant for getting to a hotel when on tour and having a shower to wash off the grime of the journey or the gig, we can only assume that it was this particular Californian hotel room that was responsible for attracting the mite. However, Olga was still prepared to spend most of the song soul-searching, wondering whether he was to blame, for any of a number of reasons: personal hygiene, something he'd spilt on the quilt, chocolate sweets or biscuit crumbs. There is also another harrowing, Vincent Price-style moment at the end of the song, when Olga moans: 'I felt the fangs rip through my vest / the mattress monster was digest / -ing me'. What about that for a word-split at the end of a line? Pure genius. The bedbug in question was unavailable for comment at the time of writing.

Fiery Jack is a well-known (at least in the UK) brand of

cream, designed to rub heat into areas of the body suffering muscular injury. Olga's brief skirmish with a tin of the product ended in agony equivalent to that experienced by a curry virgin going straight for the chicken madras with extra chilli and a side order of dynamite vindaloo. What happened was that he jumped off the stage while playing with The Straw Dogs and twisted his ankle (rather than his back, strictly speaking) quite nastily. In an attempt to alleviate the pain, he reached for the Fiery Jack, with painful consequences. The song – which featured on the *Dig That Groove, Baby* album with the spelling of 'Firey Jack' – stands out for the excellence of its rhyme: 'it's red hot on your back / believe me, it does knack'. (For the uninitiated, 'to knack' is a northeast English verb meaning, among other things, 'to hurt a great deal'. I am unsure whether the band who sang 'My Sharona' in 1979 were aware of this.)

Anyone who has drunk gallons of beer in the company of Olga – and I count myself as a member of this privileged club – and has brought up the topic of how crap disco music is, will have witnessed a level of vitriol unimaginable in a man who seems so mild-mannered. His anger is directed not only at disco music, but also at the sort of people it attracts. Perhaps we should define here what is meant by 'disco music' in this context: not just the stuff brought out by The Bee Gees at the height of the *Saturday Night Fever* period of the late 1970s, but any sort of middle-of-the-road, commercial crap played at nightclubs by overpaid DJs, involving thumping bass-drum beats, excessive use of sampling, mindless (if any) vocals, and 'dancing' involving the construction and packing of imaginary boxes in the air in front of one's chest. That sort of shite.

Now that we've got the image sorted out in our heads, we need to move on to the 'groovediggers' who frequent such clubs. We all smiled at the mention of the term in the reproduction of *Sounds* journalist Jay Williams's review on the back cover of the *Dig That Groove, Baby* LP, but we also understood what was meant. Anyone who didn't, could simply open the sleeve, take out the precious disc of vinyl, and listen to the title track. The song talks about young people in their late teens and early 20s, who dress identically in keeping with the latest high-street fashions, and emerge from their caves on Friday or Saturday nights (after their weekly bath) to catch the bus into the nearest town or city (in this case, Sunderland) and combine worship of crap disco music with unprovoked acts of violence carried out on anyone who doesn't conform to their stereotype.

At the beginning of the 1980s in the UK – and probably elsewhere in the world, too – it became fashionable to wear trousers with a belt that had about 20-25 centimetres of excess length, and this would dangle from the waist at one side of the genitals. Its only purpose was to irritate the shit out of Olga. Young male posers wearing such a belt, and covered in Old Spice aftershave (I suspect many of us of a certain age may be guilty of having worn this in the late 1970s and early 80s, largely because our fathers would have a bottle and it was easily 'borrowed'), would prowl around the pubs and clubs of the city centre, waiting for the opportunity either to impress a female groovedigger or, failing that, to start a fight. Their behaviour is described not only in 'Dig That Groove, Baby', but also in 'Fisticuffs in Frederick Street' and 'Park Lane Punch-up'.

I wondered whether the girl and her boyfriend in the last verse of 'Dig That Groove, Baby' were based on real people. Olga answered, then warmed to the subject and spat out more venom aimed at trendy, townie, posing groovediggers:

"Yeah, they were real people. I can't remember their names now, but she existed, pretending to be a punk then turning into a disco girl, and her boyfriend was a kind of skinhead. He still is, actually. But we felt really strongly about the mindlessness of that kind of thing – all townie lads and groovediggers and disco people are mindless, I don't care what people think. And their music is not good – it's crap. It's not a different kind of music – it's crap. I don't care how pretentious that sounds – it's crap. Those people haven't got any taste. I know that sounds hard, but they really haven't. And I know that everybody who's reading this now completely agrees with me."

We certainly do.

What else does Olga dislike, according to the songs? We learn from 'The Psychosurgery' that he's not too keen on trips to see the dentist – which he confirms, referring to a particular dentist on Stockton Road in Sunderland – though Mark Boyle, writing on a website existing prior to the official one, adds an interesting slant on the origin of the song:

> "[This song is] a passing tribute to one of The Toy Dolls' former support bands. The Psychosurgeons were a Bradford band led by The Doctor – Wild Willi Beckett. Beckett was quite a character: he helped found the famous One-In-Twelve club in Bradford that has always been a hotbed of left-wing radicalism; he helped found the Bradford Soup Run along with John Tempest – a fiercely apolitical homeless charity that has won numerous awards; and he was several times a candidate and organiser for the Official Monster Raving Loony Party in the late 1980s/early 1990s when they regularly came 4th in by-elections and were winning council seats."

There is also the suggestion in 'Poltergeist in the Pantry' that Olga is not a big fan of ghosts. True enough – who is? In fact, the song is another classic example of Olga's fertile imagination and use of poetic licence to embellish the stories he weaves in his music. He may certainly have heard the odd disturbing noise while popping downstairs to the pantry for a snack in the middle of the night, but we mustn't read too much into the apparition thing. I put it to Olga that 'it's a great song, though' and, for once, he drops his guard of humility and agrees: '*Orcastrated* was a heap of crap, but 'Poltergeist in the Pantry' was good.'

We touch on Olga's dealings with the police more fully in another section, but for the moment, let's limit ourselves to a couple of songs that seem quite generic, not referring to anyone specific. Who is the mysterious anti-hero of 'Geordie's Gone to Jail' on *Idle Gossip*? And, for that matter, who is Harry in 'Harry's Hands' on *Orcastrated*? The answer is that both of these characters are the same man, and both of them are Olga! Here's what happened:

> "Aye, it was me! But I didn't actually go to jail. I'll tell you the story. We did a gig in the Round Robin in Sunderland, and the next day we were playing somewhere else and the guy from there lent our roadie an amplifier for the sound system. I had never actually seen this amp, and on the way back from that following gig it got lost or stolen or something, and the roadie said, 'where's that amp?' and I said, 'I've never seen it!' and after all that I actually went to court and got proven guilty of stealing that amp. I've never even seen it. Anything can happen with court issues. I said, 'where is it?' and they said, 'it's in a second-hand shop in Hylton Road.' So I asked, 'which shop is it? Why don't you ask the people who sold them the amp?' And from that time I've always thought carefully about people who are proved guilty and put in prison, coz it's not always true. And anything can happen. I've never even seen the amp, and I got found guilty."

It may have come as some consolation that 'Geordie's Gone to Jail' got to Number 14 in the Indie chart in 1986. Then again, it may not.

Various things typically piss us off in life, among them queuing, taxes, June Sarpong's voice, estate agents, the price of beer, disco music and George Bush. But one early source of infuriation in Olga's life was his herculean struggle to pass his driving test. Part of the process was the time he spent being tutored by a driving school in Sunderland, an experience depicted in 'Modern Schools of Motoring', from *A Far Out Disc*. Many British fans – myself included – assumed straight away that it was a thinly-veiled reference to the British School of Motoring, the largest driving school in the UK, but the truth is that the school was actually called the Modern School of Motoring. Olga was with them as a student for a long time, and failed his test seven times in Sunderland, before buying a little orange Mini Metro, practising the manoeuvres himself, and taking his eighth test in nearby Durham, where he passed. He takes up the story:

> "We changed it to 'Modern Schools of Motoring', in the plural, because we were worried about the legal repercussions. But I went to see the Modern School of Motoring in Sunderland, and they said, 'we know it's us, and it's fine,' so we got away with it. They were really nice people but they were crap at teaching me to drive, so I just taught myself."

So there you are. He taught himself to drive, just as he taught himself to play the guitar and to speak and write Japanese. It's all about identifying a goal, then working your bollocks off to achieve it. It might be obsessiveness, or it might just be determination. Whatever it is, the next chapter will deal with how these qualities in Olga's songwriting and attention to detail produced the first – and, some would argue, best or second-best – Toy Dolls album ever. Roll on 1983...

History 1983-1984

Digging that Groove

1983 started with the classic juxtaposition of the good news and the bad news. First the good: 'Tommy Kowey's Car' and 'I've Got Asthma' made an appearance in January on a decent MFN (Music For Nations) compilation LP entitled *The Kids Are United*. Given that the lads were just about to record their first album and had another nationwide tour with The Angelic Upstarts lined up, this was a real boost. Olga recalls it less as a financial joy, but certainly as another step on the road to where they wanted to be:

> "We certainly never got any money from any of the compilations, to this day. In the case of the *Kids Are United* thing, we just thought that to be alongside Sham 69 and The Cockney Rejects would be fantastic, being a small band from the northeast. It was just doing a good, quality thing. And in fact that's exactly how it turned out. It was a good record, yeah."

The critics loved it: Jerry Harris in *Sounds* praised all the contributions – describing 'Tommy Kowey's Car' as 'great' and wishing that EMI had had the balls to bring out 'I've Got Asthma' – before quoting Garry Bushell at the end of his piece:

> "These bands proved that rock music doesn't have to be the province of snobs, trendies and high-brow virtuosos, that it could be down-to-earth and exciting, and it could challenge. Inevitably the glossy fodder that dominates today's charts will be blown away by a modern equivalent of The Sex

Pistols ... and when that happens, the years this album spans will be looked back on as a golden age for street-level rock 'n' roll."

The bad news to dampen down this enthusiasm was that, just after finishing their work on the forthcoming album and just before the start of the Upstarts tour, Flip and Happy Bob decided to quit the band. Bob – happy to have been asked to join the band originally, and prone to an occasional bout of scowling, hence his Toy Dolls name – had been the band's drummer for two important and memorable years; Flip was an original in every sense of the word. They had just reached the point where the prospect of touring the UK under such conditions – with little money coming in, and with sleeping conditions often limited to a van – had become too much. In both cases, Olga was gutted to see them go but, as tends to be the case in these matters, you have to wish people all the best and press on, otherwise things go stagnant.

The recording of *Dig That Groove, Baby* at Guardian in Pity Me was a brisk, three-day affair, to produce an album that Olga has always regarded as very special to him. Perhaps it's not the best LP in his view – although it's certainly among the best – but it does have a special aura about it, for being the first. I ask him to elaborate a bit on how they set about the recording in such a short space of time:

> "There are a few things that stand out: firstly, it's recorded completely dry, without any reverb, so it sounds like it's just in the room with you. The guitar sound is great, which is a Telecaster, through a Peavey amp – Peavey are crap in my opinion, but they make great amps for this particular guitar (I use a Marshall now, but still basically the same type of guitar – I like a 4 by 12 on the Marshall top, JCM 800). So basically the same sound. And we had 3 days to record and mix it – well, one day to record backing, one day for the vocals and one day to mix. That was all we could afford. Bob came out of his Dryburn Hospital job on his lunch

breaks, and he'd be drumming away and shouting at me, 'I've got that wrong,' and I was shouting back, 'it doesn't matter, you haven't got time to do it again.' That was it. It had to do. And there are loads of mistakes on it by Flip – obviously, bass guitarists would know that, for example just by having a close listen to 'Firey Jack' … but yeah, we all worked really hard on it and the result was an album that we were proud of, and that has sold pretty well over the years. It certainly helped to put us on the world map a bit."

Over the 21 years since the album came out, Olga reckons it's sold about 150,000 copies worldwide, which is a good tally, although not quite so impressive, he says, if you divide it by the number of years involved. Just as importantly, it climbed to Number 10 during an eight-week spell in the Indie album charts in the year of its release. On a more recent note, various impressive cover versions of the title track (including one by Lolita No. 18, about whom more later) can be heard on the band's website.

It got a good critical reception. Unsurprisingly, Garry Bushell was first in the queue to laud its greatness, offering the following challenge to record company A&R men across the country during a 5-star review:

> "… The sort of music that has made The Toy Dolls the best live band in northeast England, if not the whole of Blighty [the UK], if not the world … I can't remember a record that sounded so absolutely HAPPY … Do yourselves a favour: buy this record and give it a listen. A band this good is a rare and wonderful thing. Don't miss 'em."

I asked Olga whether the combination of songs on the album – combining personal issues, local figures, a soap opera tale, a couple of cover versions and lots of optimism – was deliberate, and was he aware then that this was likely to set the tone for the make-up of subsequent LPs?

> "It was a mixture of things. We had a lot of nice songs written for this particular album, and I suppose by the law

of Toy Dolls averages, a few were going to be in each of the categories you mentioned. But the optimism thing was certainly an important thing then. Maybe because I'm a complete pessimist, and I think about negative things all the time – that's my personality, and it gives me panic attacks, with all this negative thinking. It's just the way I am. Maybe it's just a release, and I feel I write better writing about the positive side of negative situations. So yeah, I included things like 'Stay Mellow' and 'Worse Things Happen at Sea', and I think the mix worked OK. We've more or less stuck with the same formula ever since."

I always remember the artwork on the cover of this album as being symbolic of the band's innocent, funny, slightly puerile image, with the drawings on the back and the simple block lettering on the front. I wondered whether Olga had had anything to do with it (either drawing it himself or at least designing the concept):

"The front cover wasn't my idea at all – it was something to do with Volume, and I think it's crap – but it's actually worked, because it's become part of the identity for the band. I think the back's fine, with all the little drawings – Flip did have a verruca, and Happy Bob really did go to Scarborough and have a donkey ride, that was all completely true."

Incidentally, the Herberts who feature on the cover were a group of punks who used to hang around the Old 29 in Sunderland in Olga's teens, in what he refers to as the 'time before this disco crap came in'. The term was another invention credited to Garry Bushell of *Sounds*.

Launching a first LP is a big step in anyone's life, but given the humble roots and limited budget of The Toy Dolls – and perhaps in view of Olga's obsessive, worrisome nature – it must have been a massive event for the band. Did they feel that, with the first album completed, that was the peak of all their dreams, or did they view it as a milestone on the way to big-time glory?

"I think there was a satisfaction to seeing an album in the shops, yeah, because it summed up everything. A single is just one part of what you think you can show people, but an album's much more. We were massively proud, because you can look in the shop window and see something you've created. Yeah, it felt good."

Did he worry that it wouldn't sell?

"I've always been a nervous wreck, as you know, but I didn't really think about whether it would sell. I was more concerned with whether it was good or decent – you know, the worry about whether we'd put out a good quality product that people would like and speak well of. I suppose it's the perfectionist thing."

So much for the launch of the LP, but what about personnel? One way of looking at Flip and Bob's departure was one of it being a pity that, after all their hard work and dedication to the band, they were not going to enjoy the fruits of their labour once the album took off. Another, far more pressing, viewpoint was that Olga now had precisely three days (ironically, the same time as the album had taken to record) to put a new band together so as to honour the promise to support The Angelic Upstarts on their UK tour. He remembers running frantically around the various rehearsal rooms, such as Peter Practice's Place, looking to recruit a drummer and a bassist. In the end, he found Nick Buck (his real name) and Freddie Hotrock (Frederick Robertson), who spent a frantic three days learning the set, then an equally mad month touring the UK and doing a damned good job of it.

After Freddie and Nick had moved on at the end of March, Olga spent two months auditioning replacements, and eventually came up with the pleasing combination of Bonny Baz (Barry Warne) on bass and Dirty Dicka (Alan Dixon). This trio seemed to work very well, and with the album selling in the shops and starting to attract attention abroad, the lads issued a single, 'Cheerio and Toodle Pip', in

June of 1983. Co-written by Olga and Baz, it had a catchy-as-hell melody and good backing vocals, and got to Number 10 in the UK Indie singles chart, despite Olga's reservations about the standard of the recording, which he claimed had been done too quickly. The band were chuffed at the public's response to it, and decided to push on with another single, 'Alfie From the Bronx', in September (with Peter Practice inexplicably doing the drumming on the suggestively cheeky B-side, 'Hanky Panky'). This time, the track got to Number 13 in the Indie chart, but its release coincided with yet more line-up changes. After 6 months together as a trio, Dicka left the group, proceeding to drum with other local bands (among them Red Alert) before opening the Sound World music shop in Sunderland (coincidentally very close to Marty's record shop, Hot Rats).

A replacement was quickly sought, who bore the confusingly similar nickname of Dicky (real name Malcolm Dick), and the combination of Olga, Baz and Dicky stayed together for a full year, from September 1983 to September 1984.

By this stage, the concept of fan mail had started to kick in. The *Sunderland Echo* reported as early as May 1983 that Olga was getting 'five or six fan letters a day' as the album started to sell well in Holland. This soon prompted Olga to ask his brother Ernie to step in and start answering the letters as a sort of stopgap fan club secretary, a role which actually continued for the best part of 20 years until the website, in effect, superseded him.

In the autumn of 1983, with the album out and doing well, and with their name now better known after doing so well on the tours with The Angelic Upstarts, The Toy Dolls embarked on a headlining UK tour, taking in the cities of London, Leeds, Durham, Newcastle, Sheffield, Carlisle, Brighton, Manchester, Sunderland and Birmingham. It was finally looking as if the UK was in their pocket, so the lads began to set their sights on a far more difficult market to crack: the USA.

Most UK bands at that time would make tentative inroads into the continental European market before risking their musical and financial wellbeing in the USA, but by January 1984, spurred on by the news that an American distributor had telephoned Volume and ordered no fewer than 10,000 copes of *Dig That Groove, Baby*, The Toy Dolls were ready for California, and vice versa. I ask Olga how this first 7-date tour came about:

> "Well, the very first time I got on a plane was to fly to Los Angeles – I'd never had the money to go on a plane, coming from our background. It was because of the first album, which took off only in California, not in the rest of America, and we were also getting some great radio airplay there. There seemed to be a real surge of interest in us. California was the place to be for bands like us: The Adicts, The Angelic Upstarts and Peter & The Test-tube Babies had all just been there, and we had these offers to play these huge places – huge for us, anyway – of about 3 or 4,000 people a night, and they were all sold out. Oh, it was unbelievable. You become a bit complacent with that, thinking, 'we're kind of stars here in California,' then you come back to England and you play in front of hardly anyone at Shiney Row Club."

The experience did them the power of good, and by using a fairly basic van and sleeping in humble motels, they were able to make enough money to have made the trip worthwhile – a good omen for future trips, the first of which was scheduled for later the same year: 8 nights in July. But in the meantime, after 2 months back in Britain, the lads had another first to deal with: their first foray into continental European territory: a clutch of gigs in Holland and Germany laid the foundations for a long-lasting love affair with these countries, and convinced them that the potential was there for a successful career across the world.

In June 1984, the single 'We're Mad' was launched in both 7-inch and 12-inch vinyl offerings, in a tasty package including 'Deirdre's a Slag' and 'Rupert the Bear' on the B-side. The record stayed in the higher reaches of the Indie charts throughout the summer, peaking at Number 4. The A-side track always struck me as a bit disjointed and not very Toy Dollsy, but I treasure the disc nevertheless, and 'Rupert' is an absolute dream.

By now the lads had made their mark on stage, on TV, in the print media, and on vinyl. The missing link seemed to be the glorious new medium of video (which older readers will join me in remembering from the days before CDs and DVDs, let alone MP3s and the like). To address this gap in their profile, Olga fixed up a deal with Jettisounds to bring out a video collection of sundry visual items. To many people, it's an essential document of the early Toy Dolls spirit; to others, it's a bit amateur-looking and lacking in polish. What does Olga feel about it, 20 years on?

> "Jettisounds did the best they could – they weren't the most advanced kind of outfit. They worked with a million bands, but there were problems with, for example, live gig footage having the soundtrack out of synch, even though it was the same gig. It was a long time ago, and they were nice enough. Yeah, any kind of release or exposure was welcome and exciting. Like the *Strength Thru Oi* thing: it was huge to us because it was an album – we're from Sunderland and we're all in London – look at us!"

The year's touring duties actually finished as early as September 7, when Dicky moved on to a new life drumming on cruise liners (maybe subconsciously hoping to meet and be signed up by someone like *Coronation Street*'s Alec Gilroy, who hadn't, at this point, made his first appearance in the band's lyrics), and Baz left the band to pursue his own interests (going on to form Small Town Heroes and The Sun Devils before eventually landing the job with the Stranglers). For many people at my school, Baz was right up there with Flip as the sort of bassist whose technique and stage presence you'd drool over. Quite a few girls in my class fancied him, at least one of whom said that it was clear he had a massive, muscular chest because he was getting too big for his little Toy Dolls blazer. (Maybe this was a deliberate ploy on the band's part: to use Baz to duplicate Olga's already established sex appeal – we may never know.) On a musical note Olga has, of course, kept in touch with Baz, who has provided backing vocals on a number of Toy Dolls albums since his departure 20 years ago. Dicky is now playing drums with Richie Blackmore, of Rainbow fame.

On his own again in the early autumn of 1984, Olga set about pondering his next move. As he was tugging at his chin, the opportunity arose for him to write the theme music for ITV's children's pop show *Razzmatazz* (which Toy Dolls fans would subsequently be able to hear on the 1985 album *A Far Out Disc*). As it was a project that would do him, his career and his bank balance no harm, Olga jumped at the chance, and subsequently got to appear on the show with the band.

"That was the first time I met Kim Wilde, you know? It all came about because Volume were in touch with Tyne Tees Television, who worked round the corner, and the producers and directors used to go in the shop all the time. Eventually one of the directors said, 'how about The Toy Dolls putting in an idea for the new *Razzmatazz* theme tune?' There were a few other people interested – there was a guy who almost got it, who sang 'I'm 18 with a bullet'. He'd already done a demo, but I thought I'd just go along with my acoustic guitar, so I went into the office and just sang, 'we don't say Razzmatazz,' and I got the job. I thought 'class!' It wasn't offensive in any way, and it was just for a pop programme. Plus the programme wasn't all disco stuff – there was some rock stuff on, rock bands and all that kind of thing. Gary Holton was on from *Auf Wiedersehen Pet*, doing 'Catch a Falling Star'. I didn't mind the artists who were on the programme. It was fine."

Was the money OK? How does it work for these things?

"Yeah, it all depends on how long you think it's going to last – for *Razzmatazz*, I got a couple of hundred quid every time the programme was on, and it was on every week for quite a few years, so I was thinking, 'this is unbelievable – I've just made 200 quid without doing anything.' And most importantly, it was on a programme that was a rock show, it wasn't a daft kids' thing – it was on at kids' time, but there were all sorts of bands on. I'm not saying I'm proud of that programme, but I don't mind it, and I think I did an all right job with the theme tune."

Back to the band, and Olga decided to recruit 'session musicians' – actually himself and a drummer for studio purposes – with a view to launching a serious attack on the UK singles charts. So it was that, just as the images of the Ethiopian famine were haunting the Western world and Bob Geldof's crusade to tackle the problem head-on with Band Aid's 'Do They Know It's Christmas?' was taking shape, Volume issued an updated version of 'Nellie the Elephant', and before the band could take stock of what was happening to them, their UK popularity had leapt to another level entirely. Cruising to Number 1 in the Indie chart, the song gave the band their first major entry into the main national chart, jumping gradually up and peaking at No 4. This in itself was quite a feat, and of course there would eventually be some money to come the band's way (Olga reckoned in the press at the time that it would be about a year before he saw any money from it and, logically, royalties would have to be paid to the songwriters), but the media opportunities multiplied overnight, and that was what Olga craved to push the band's profile further. What are his memories of the media circus that enveloped the band?

"It was crazy. It was great for Volume, first of all, coz it was their biggest ever hit, but yeah, we started to get a lot of coverage on TV and in the press, and I started to get recognised everywhere, in the street. People were knocking on my door, and I had to make my phone number ex-directory, because so many people were ringing up – just to congratulate me; nothing nasty. But the success of the single was also a surprise, coz the version was a bit rushed, and had the key change and everything, so I thought the 82 version would have stood a better chance. But there you go."

Tell us more about the TV shows that Christmas. For a start, there was *Top of the Pops* on December 13…

"Yeah, I remember it all. I think the record got to Number 64, then 16 or something, and we went down to London. I was only interested in getting the Marshall amplifiers on, and at the time, they had to cover them with gaffer tape, which was mad coz it didn't mean anything. It was Peter Powell and Steve Wright who introduced the show. It's mimed live, not actually played live. I hate that. I was talking to The Wildhearts' drummer, and he talks about TV things they do, where it's actually live – maybe a backing track over the top but otherwise it's properly live. But our deal was to mime live like Herman's Hermits or someone. How did it feel to have a hit? It wasn't overwhelmingly larger than life – I already thought a couple of years earlier that the song was a hit, so it was just part of the whole thing. It was the same as playing California – no big deal, just another part of what we do. OK, it was a UK TV show, but we didn't think, 'wow, England at last' – we had Germany to prepare for straight afterwards – another thing we did."

For anyone of a certain age, and to put this appearance into a kind of 80s context, the other acts on the show that day were Black Lace, Wham, Paul Young, Kool and the Gang, Madonna, Tears for Fears, Gary Glitter and, of course, Band Aid. The band, with their tongues firmly in their cheeks, had their photos taken with Black Lace, and bassist Pete Zulu, hastily re-recruited by Olga alongside drummer Little Paul essentially to cover the raft of TV appearances, had his photo taken with Paul Young. This jokey reference to the physical similarity between the two actually backfired on

Pete, as it led to his mobile fish and chip shop being mobbed by screaming female fans wherever he went to ply his trade in the northeast. The band actually issued a plea via the local press for fans to leave him alone, explaining that he was categorically not Paul Young, but rather a 30-year-old fish and chip shop owner who was standing in as a miming bassist to give The Toy Dolls a sense of plurality on the telly. In rounding off the appeal, Olga quipped:

> "Pete's fish and chip van got completely battered when 300 girls turned it upside-down in their frenzy. Do they have no sole?"

Arf, arf. There was also a delicious humble-pie-eating moment in the show itself. Peter Powell, who co-presented the programme that night, had played the 82 version of 'Nellie the Elephant' on his BBC Radio 1 show two years earlier and said, 'That definitely won't get anywhere and I'm not going to play it again.' Now he was facing The Toy Dolls having a massive hit with the song and playing it on *Top of the Tops*, but at least he was gracious enough to apologise, saying he could now see what was good about it and that he liked it second time around.

The record company used a television plugger, who got the band booked onto all the TV shows, and that proved to be a big help. Appearances on chat show *Harty*, kids' show *Saturday Superstore* and lunchtime magazine programme *Pebble Mill at One* quickly followed, and widened the band's profile further, and there was a second *Top of the Pops* booking in early January. Perhaps the most credible of all was a return to *The Tube*, two-and-a-bit years after their first performance on that show. There was also a radio plugger, who helped ensure that airplay was maximised. The only difficulty here was that it cost a fortune. I wondered idly whether, had the release of 'Nellie' not coincided with the Band Aid thing, The Toy Dolls would have sold even more records and perhaps even secured a UK No 1, with more focus on them happening naturally:

"It's difficult to say. The Band Aid thing was a big deal, and Madonna was in the charts with 'Like a Virgin', and there were other people doing really successful stuff. So maybe we'd have sold some more, but not that many more."

With a huge domestic hit under their belts and footholds already established on the European continent and in the USA, things were looking distinctly rosy for The Toy Dolls as 1984 became 1985. Grangetown was now giving way to Hollywood as a venue for Olga and his troops to show off their musical skills, wow the audience with their performance and ensure even more record sales. But before we move on and see how the lads fared as a quartet at the start of 1985, let's go back to the roots of the whole mission, and learn a little bit about the place where it all started.

Olga's Inspirations

3. Sunderland and Durham Places

It is utterly logical that Olga's initial forays into songwriting should have embraced the places where he grew up and lived and the people he knew and met along the way. This section aims to shed some light on the places in the northeast of England featuring in Toy Dolls songs. Occasionally, we step outside of what is strictly the Sunderland and Durham areas suggested in the title, but I hope this will not hinder what Californians call the 'reading experience'.

The nearest major town (now a city) to where Olga was born is Sunderland, and this is where most of the references are located. Even when we are not specifically dealing with a street, pub, launderette etc., we may still be able to sample the atmosphere or daily life of the place, which is the case in the first song to be touched upon here (as well as being the band's first song alphabetically).

'A Bunch of Fairies' takes a swipe at the police force in Sunderland, claiming that the city is an easy place to go about committing crimes, because the police presence is practically nil. The deeper meaning is that Olga used to get very pissed off with policemen concentrating on the trivial elements of wrongdoing, and leaving the more serious crimes untouched and unsolved. He recalls a clear division of the force into two categories: the older coppers, who were fine, able to see that some misdemeanours weren't worth bothering about; and the younger ones, who were out to get promotion at all costs, and perfectly willing to throw their weight about in dealing with petty criminals. Specifically, the song stemmed from a period in the early 1990s when Olga was doing some work around the area, promoting acts such as Wilko Johnson (formerly of Dr Feelgood) and the Macc Lads. He was stopped a number of times in the middle of the night while putting up posters for forthcoming gigs, and was even taken to court on 3 or 4 occasions. There's a lot of anger in the lyrics, but it's a great song.

Other songs depicting the flavour of the northeast of England include 'Kids in Tyne & Wear' (this being a county created to cover what had previously been parts of the counties of Durham and Northumberland). It's a great place to live – I was born there myself – but it is true that some parts of the county have suffered more than their fair share of social problems such as unemployment, poverty and crime. See the section on the song in the Cover Versions chapter for further comment on the area.

About 20 kilometres southwest of Sunderland we find the historic city of Durham, which is the setting for a number of Toy Dolls songs or mentions. Just outside the bounds of the city is the sprawling housing estate of Newton Hall, built gradually in the post-war years and home to Olga's brother Ernie (as anyone who ever wrote to the Fan Club address will know). It's a huge place, and Olga has, at one time or another, lived on three of its streets.

The song 'Livin' on Newton Hall' describes not so much life on the estate as the mentality of some of its inhabitants. Ernie is fine and happy living there (as are many of my friends from school), but during his time there, Olga sensed an atmosphere of 'wannabe' culture developing in certain segments of the estate. It unnerved him to see that people could not just relax and be themselves, but had to strive all the time to appear posher and more socially elevated than the neighbours.

Not far from Newton Hall, on the same side of Durham City, is the village of Pity Me, which, as eagle-eyed fans will have noticed on the various record-sleeves, is the home of Guardian Studios, where the band's first few recordings were made. Pity Me was also the home of Kendra, and it was to there that Olga made the famous bus journey described in 'I'll Get Even With Steven'. More about Kendra in the sections on Sunderland and Durham People, and Crazy Little Thing Called Love, of course.

However, you may be keen to get your teeth into some more specific details about streets and buildings in the area, so let's go there.

In the November 1983 single 'Alfie from the Bronx', it is a reasonable guess that Alfie does not come from the area of New York bearing that name. In fact, it is more than a guess: Alfie was indeed not American. Nor is the Bronx in this case the Meadow Wall estate in North Shields (another town in the northeast of England). The truth is that the song refers to the socially deprived Norman Court housing estate in Sunderland, and to a resident called Alfie Noble. The real Alfie had two friends on the Court (Robert was one; Olga can't remember the name of the other), portrayed as Johnnie and Freddie in the song because these names fitted better as lyrics. The estate was demolished, and the residents had to be rehoused elsewhere in the town, much to their desperation. A more encouraging footnote to the tale is that Alfie went on to become the concert chairman of the Ivy League Club in Hendon, Sunderland. The song, meanwhile, reached Number 13 in the UK Indie Chart.

'Fisticuffs in Frederick Street' keeps us in Sunderland, and begins a series of songs featuring street names in that city. The story with Frederick Street is that it actually contains more than one piece of Toy Dolls history. The Foster's Club where the fisticuffs in question took place was located directly opposite Peter Practice's Practice Place, where the band would rehearse in the early days. The lads recall looking out of the window of the practice rooms on numerous occasions and watching fighting going on across the road outside the club. There was no specific night that provoked the song (even though the lyrics say 'Frederick

Street was on the news tonight'); it was just composed around the ongoing theme of street and nightclub violence, generally committed by townie groovediggers.

This was to prove the most expensive Toy Dolls song to have been released, as Olga immediately found himself in deep water when the club's management brought legal action against him for tarnishing the good reputation of their nightspot and losing the club custom. Despite what looked like a solid case in their favour – Olga and the lads even installed a camera in the practice place to try and provide evidence of the sort of fights that Foster's would attract – it became clear that the band would have to pay up for libelling the club, and it cost them £10,000. Ten grand was a lot of money to a band like The Toy Dolls, especially back in the 1980s, and would have been equivalent to quite a bit more in today's terms. They also had to change a couple of things in the song – its title is deliberately misspelled on the *Bare Faced Cheek* cover as 'Fredrick' – but the club eventually closed and the matter was forgotten about, though it still rankles in Olga's memory.

In 'How Do You Deal With Neal?', we learn that the over-clingy Neal figure lives on Hereford Road. This was just round the corner from Hillview Road, where Olga lived after his family moved to Sunderland.

Park Lane – the scene of the song 'Park Lane Punch-up' from *Bare Faced Cheek* – is the area of Sunderland where the public transport network has its headquarters. It has nothing to do with the posh London street featuring on your Monopoly board. Back in the 1970s and 80s it was a very rough and desolate place to be, particularly after dark, though things have improved over the last few years since the place received some proper investment and was given a facelift. In around 1985, at the end of a night out, Olga was waiting at a taxi rank by the bus station with his girlfriend, who was going to get a taxi home while Olga (as usual) walked. Suddenly, some lads from a local band were set upon by a group of townie groovediggers and beaten up.

Olga was sickened and decided to record the incident in a song.

Another Sunderland road immortalised in a Toy Dolls song is Queen Alexandra Road, which is well up there in the top 3 all-time long titles, and featured on the band's first album. Olga was about 16 or 17, and had arranged to meet his first real girlfriend, Angela (who, as we shall see, is the unnamed heroine of many classic Toy Dolls tunes) on Queen Alexandra Road, just by the corner of Barnes Park. (Time for another uninteresting coincidence: my parents met on the very same street corner for their first date in 1950. OK, back to the interesting stuff...) Olga shudders as he remembers the night in question:

> "It got really late and it was absolutely flippin' freezing that night, and the only thing I had to look forward to on Friday nights were the late-night horror films, like the one with Vincent Price, who gets a mention in the song. That thought kept me going, but it was so late I even missed that!"

What about the title? Couldn't it just have been 'Queen Alexandra Road'?

> "I thought about it, and decided it just had to be the full thing, coz every bit was so important to the song. I've done a couple of long titles since – 'Peter Practice' and so on – but some things have to have the full name, otherwise it's just not right... I'm a bit of a perfectionist in those things."

Don't get the impression from the lyric 'I was going to land her a thump when I see her' that Olga is a man of violence. Quite the contrary. It was just a frustrating thought, which quickly evaporated, as we see in the last three lines of the song, when Angela finally turns up and asks Olga if he's been waiting long. She then 'looked into my eyes sweetly, I said "not that long".' Once a romantic fool, always a romantic fool. It's part of the guy's charm.

At this point I ask Olga about the implications of using place names from Sunderland and Durham in songs that are going to be listened to in places as far-flung as Brazil, Croatia and Japan. Does it really matter that people will not have heard of Park Lane (or Ken Dodd? Or Deirdre?)? He takes a long swig of lager, shrugs his shoulders thoughtfully and answers:

> "People often used to ask me, 'who's gonna know where Queen Alexandra Road is?', and I used to think, well, 'who knew where Penny Lane was before the Beatles sang about it?' If the song's good, properly put together and stands up to a great performance, the references matter much less, especially if the fan who's listening to it doesn't speak much English. A good song is a good song."

Hylton Road is tagged at the start of 'Tommy Kowey's Car' as being the road at the top of which Mr Kowey's motor store was located. I'll discuss the song in detail in the chapter on Sunderland and Durham People, but for the moment we just need to note that the road really exists, though the premises Tom Cowie used at the time have now changed hands a number of times, so that is one piece of Toy Dolls history that can't now be photographed for posterity.

'Blaze of the Borough' – on *Wakey Wakey* – is based on a true story, in the sense that the pub was set alight, and the landlord was indeed called Jimmy. There had been financial problems in the Borough pub on the corner of Park Lane, opposite the Odeon cinema in Sunderland, and the blaze was seen by many as an attempt to burn the place down and get hold of the insurance money. Olga can't remember now what the outcome of the whole incident was, but many readers might be worried about poor old Jimmy, who 'fried / oh yes, he fried in the Borough'. Olga smiles ruefully:

> "Ah no, he didn't actually die, no, but he might have got hurt a little bit, a few scars or whatever – a bit melodramatic again, like you have to be when you're being inventive in your songwriting."

Where in Sunderland is Elmwood Street and who was the trollop? I hear you asking. I wondered whether she isn't named in the song for legal reasons, or whether Olga didn't know her name. The truth is that we're dealing with a bit of poetic licence here:

> "No, it was nothing to do with legal reasons, but I do know the trollop in question. Elmwood Street was the next street, and actually she didn't live in Elmwood Street, she lived on Chester Road, but it fitted the song better with Elmwood Street. But there's plenty of trollops up Elmwood Street, so we don't have to pinpoint which one the song's about!"

And what was it about her character and behaviour that made her such a slag? Had Olga had an 'experience' with her, or was she well known locally as a breaker of young men's hearts? Or was there something even more sinister to be recounted?

> "I dunno. I just like the word 'trollop'. It's a good old-fashioned word that your mother might like. When you're looking through the thesaurus, which I use quite often, you come across some great words."

The area of Ashbrooke, not too far from the centre of Sunderland and known principally for housing Sunderland's cricket ground, is important in Toy Dolls history for three reasons. Perhaps the least noteworthy is that it was where Olga bought his first house – he realised early on that being in a punk band was never going to bring him great wealth, so whenever he was able to afford the deposit, he decided to invest modestly in property to provide a nest-egg for the future (and also to help finance future Toy Dolls projects and buy equipment etc.). The house was an end-terrace close to the green area of Burn Park, quite a walk from the cricket ground. The other two reasons, however, have much more relevance to our little celebration.

Ashbrooke the Jack Russell dog is recorded as having been born on 1 August 1987, and he died 6 years later on 1

June 1993 (from a heart attack while Olga was away on a world tour). He was named after Ashbrooke, where Olga was living at the time with the Japanese psychopath who went on to star in the song 'My Wife's a Psychopath' on *Absurd-Ditties*. Olga bought him from someone in the County Durham town of Crook (close to Tow Law, where the great Chris Waddle began his football career), and the two immediately became the best of buddies. Olga remembers him as the best, sweetest and cleverest dog you could ever imagine owning, and testimony to the dog's gifts can be found in the backing vocals he supplied on songs such as 'Sod the Neighbours' and 'Sabre Dance'. Was this difficult to achieve?

> "The guy in the studio said, 'how are you going to make him bark?', and I would click my fingers and he'd go, 'woof woof,' exactly the right bark at exactly the right time. The only difficulty was that flippin' daft recording studio was above a bingo hall, about 7 floors up. So every time Ashbrooke needed a piss, I had to traipse down with him."

The other Ashbrooke link is, of course, the song 'The Ashbrooke Launderette (You'll Stink ...Yer Clothes Shrink, Your Whites'll be as Black as Ink)', from *Bare Faced Cheek*. This was a real launderette where Olga used to go to do his washing, as this first house didn't have a washing machine. As far as he remembers, that was the actual name of the place, and all the problems alluded to in the bracketed part of the title really did happen. I wondered whether the owners had considered bringing legal action against the band, but Olga reckons that they're either unaware of the song, or perhaps they use it as a perverse form of publicity. Either way, he's not heard anything about being taken to court by them!

One amazing fact Olga revealed as we were chatting about the launderette is that a number of tourists – mostly Japanese – have made the pilgrimage to Sunderland to photograph the launderette, plus places like Fino's, Park Lane and Frederick Street.

Ashbrooke the dog also plays a part in the song 'Nowt Can Compare to Sunderland Fine Fare', another song from *Bare Faced Cheek*. Fine Fare is a chain of low-cost supermarkets spread across the northeast of England, and Olga and Ashbrooke were making their way to the Sunderland branch one day to do some shopping, when an incident took place that inspired the song:

> "Let me say this in the first place: that is an absolutely awful song – it's crap. I wrote that song coz I went to Fine Fare with Ashbrooke in this little Mini Metro I had, and you drive into the car park and there's a barrier, and a little guy that sits in the booth there. I said to Ashbrooke, 'there doesn't seem to be any guy sitting in that booth,' and as I was saying that I smashed BANG against the wall and the dog came flying forward and the blood came out of his nose and he fell to the floor – he was all right, though. So I wrote the Fine Fare song from that."

Perhaps the band's finest song with a title involving a Sunderland location is 'She Goes to Fino's'. We need to get to the bottom of the song: what inspired it, what sort of club it was, who the girl was.

The song dates back to the pre-Toy Dolls era, and was written by Olga in around 1977 in Hill View Community Centre in Grangetown, Sunderland. The girl, needless to say, was his girlfriend Angela, and she did sometimes go to the club, but not every night as the song suggests. Nor was she secretly meeting any other men inside, you'll be relieved to learn. Actually, the place was called Lee's Club when Olga composed the original hook and the 'lah-lah-laaah' chorus bit; it became Fino's soon afterwards.

The song was originally recorded by The Showbiz Kids, sharing a cut with a track entitled 'I Don't Want to Discuss That'. The other lads in The Showbiz Kids – Phil, Pat, Bob and Rob – had thought long and hard about which of Olga's songs ('Fino's' and 'Tommy Kowey's Car') to include, and they practised them both before eventually plumping for 'Fino's'.

Then, in due course, the historic first Toy Dolls single came out, with these two songs sitting back-to-back and blowing away the minds of all the 500 people lucky enough to get their hands on a copy of that first, limited pressing.

But what was the problem with the club depicted in the song?

> "It wasn't my kind of scene. I think I tried to get in to see Angela a couple of times, but yeah, it wasn't really my cup of tea – more of a groovediggers' thing again. They had this Members Only policy, and they wouldn't let me in. It was a bit like the scene in the video where I'm trying to get in and the bouncers aren't having any of it."

The video to the Easter 1985 single release of 'She Goes to Fino's' was the first Toy Dolls video to get a proper nationwide airing on the video-jukeboxes of the UK's pubs. I remember sitting for hours in the Nottingham House pub in Broomhill, Sheffield, watching it again and again as my student grant was gradually drunk away in a boozy haze. It's a great little video, and looks surprisingly professional given that Olga (a keen novice at film-making, to put it politely) directed it himself, as well as starring in it, of course. He recalls being quite satisfied with the product overall:

> "Peter Practice's brother made that video for us. I did watch it a few times afterwards – I thought it was all right, actually. I directed it and did everything myself. There's one point in the video when Pete Zulu's girlfriend Ali pushes me over, and I've got a jacket on, and when I land on the ground, the jacket's gone. I just didn't think about that – the whole continuity thing – when I was directing it, as I wasn't used to steering that kind of thing. So that's one for the fans to look out for now, if they hadn't spotted it before!"

After the chart success of 'Nellie the Elephant', which had

sold hundreds of thousands of copies in the UK alone just a few months previously, the band might have expected rich pickings from such a catchy song as 'Fino's', especially with a decent video to back it up and help promote it. In fact – and this is as much a comment on the state of the singles chart in 2004, as anything else – the song sold a reasonably healthy 37,000 copies, and got to Number 4 in the Independent chart, but didn't even make the Top 200 of the main UK singles chart. Nowadays, a boy band or a female soloist can get to Number 1 with sales of what 'Fino's' sold in 1985, and bands of Olga's acquaintance have got into the Top 10 with fewer than 10,000 sales.

The decline of The Toy Dolls in the eyes of the UK record-buying public had already begun, never to pick up again. We're no closer to explaining this today, nearly 20 years on, but while the band's home country seemed to be losing interest, other countries around the world were starting to catch on, thus laying the foundations for The Toy Dolls' conversion into the global favourites we know and love today. To start with, there was the pressing matter of cracking the Japanese market...

History 1985-1987

Big in Japan

Hands up anyone who's ever been the victim of a strip-o-gram. Or maybe you've ordered a gorilla-gram for one of your mates? My guess is that quite a few readers will have some sort of experience of this baffling social concept. But unless you were living in the Sunderland area in the mid-1980s, it is highly unlikely you will ever have been exposed – if that's the right word – to a Toy Dollagram. To bring in a little extra money and keep himself busy in the early months of 1985, Olga capitalised on the nationwide success of 'Nellie the Elephant' by offering his services as a Toy Dollagram. The idea arose from several charity performances of this type Olga had given, and he decided that it would be a good idea to charge members of the public £35 a time for him to come to their house and mime 'Nellie' in their front room. He would then spend about 30 minutes signing autographs and giving out pictures of the band as souvenirs.

This lucrative line of business only lasted a few weeks, however, as there were more important things for him to be getting on with in 1985. The year began with Pete Zulu (never the world's best bass-player anyway) switching to rhythm guitar to try and learn extra chords to go with the Am, G and E he could already play, Little Paul remaining on drums and Olga's brother Ernie coming in on bass. Let's not forget that Ernie had experience of playing in a club band in the 1960s, so he was quite a steady player and certainly knew his way around a bass guitar. This arrangement lasted just under 2 months, in fact the duration of a German/Swiss/Dutch tour and a dozen or so dates back in the UK, ending on 1 March. With hindsight, how does Olga view this rather strange deviation from the standard three-piece set-up?

"The four-piece thing was a mistake. It just didn't work. It seemed like a good idea at the time, because Pete wasn't a bassist but his image was good. But I never felt really comfortable with that line-up, so we changed it for the gigs later in the year."

The spring of 1985 was given over to the long awaited and keenly anticipated launch of the band's second long-player, *A Far Out Disc*. Anyone who's heard or read Olga's thoughts on this album will be clear that he's not a great fan of it, so I asked him why in particular it's among his least favourite Toy Dolls ventures:

"This happens with so many bands. The second album's usually your rejects from the first one, and you're drained with it – you're out of material and inspiration. Then it depends on what's happening with your life after that, whether you can get back the inspiration to start again. But whatever happens after a great one, to have a great one after that means you're a great band. I just think there are too many sub-standard songs on it, and the sound's not great."

But there are some songs he's happy with. 'Bless You My Son' has been a stage classic ever since, 'Florence is Deaf' he considers OK, and he's moderately pleased with 'Modern Schools of Motoring', but that's about it. Another manifestation of Olga's self-criticism – or at least his difficulty in allowing himself to feel entirely happy with his creative output – is that he never succumbed when a guy from Mute Records, who had been responsible for much of Depeche Mode's success, raved on and on about how great 'Modern Schools of Motoring' was.

I always found the 'Commercial Break', in which the

band unashamedly plug their first album, an absolute scream, and I wondered what Olga's criterion had been for including this somewhat non-standard piece of entertainment in the middle of an LP:

> "To be truthful with you, I was completely desperate. I remember doing a gig in Helsinki a few years ago, and Terrorvision and The Wildhearts were both waiting for their baggage claim, and the singer from The Wildhearts said, 'oh, you'll have to show me how to play the beginning of the *Dig That Groove, Baby* album,' and I thought, 'great, he likes the band.' Then he said, 'but your beginning to the commercial break on the second album is shite.' And he was right. I think it's absolutely crap. It's desperate."

And why that particular title? It seemed as if they were continuing a thread from the first LP of 1960s-style hippie expressions, presumably with a huge dollop of irony?

> "Yeah, it wasn't actually a conscious thing, to keep the Californian-style vocabulary going like that, but that's how it worked out. It was something Dicka the drummer used to say for a laugh – 'wow, far out, man' – so we decided we'd use that as a future album title."

If the artwork for the first album had been Volume's idea and hadn't been ideal in Olga's view, surely the jolly, colourful cover of *A Far Out Disc* must have met with his approval? Followers of the excellently puerile *Viz* comic in the early 80s will have spotted the influence straight away – you can even spot the character Roger Mellie at the front of the queue going into the record shop – but how did the artwork go down in the Toy Dolls camp?

> "I wasn't happy with that. I designed that album, then the guy from *Viz* comic, Chris Donald, did all the artwork, and I remember ringing him and saying, 'you bastard, you've put Design by Chris Donald on this.' Nowadays I would just say good luck to you, but at the time, I thought, 'I flippin' designed this – I thought of all the looking-up-here thing

and everything.' I'd designed it and told him what to draw, even though he drew it all. So yeah, it was my design and his drawings, but I don't care now. I got over it. His drawings are fantastic – and I can't draw anything."

I'm also interested in the technical aspects of comments Olga has made over the years about this album. Why, for instance, did he use a pedal for his guitar work, if he's not really comfortable with pedals?

"I think I was just experimenting by using a Stratocaster, which didn't sound right, so we had to use a pedal to make it sound better, but I would never do it again. It's interesting, the differences between the various guitars. I think a Telecaster really has to be *played* – whereas a Strat or a Les Paul (I use a Les Paul for solos and things) can be a lot easier. The Telecaster is a great big chunk of wood, like a telegraph pole. The Strat actually has the perfect shape for your body, whereas the Telecaster's less comfortable. Also, I always change the pick-up on my Telecasters, to a Seymour-Duncan, which is like a Telecaster pick-up but with a bit more balls."

Whatever Olga's reservations about the record, it climbed to No. 4 in the Indie chart, and got some good reviews. Maybe it sold a percentage of its copies on the back of the first LP, and maybe the fans just liked it and recommended it to their friends – it's hard to say. But what was clear to me in researching this book was that far more fans wrote to me mentioning *A Far Out Disc* than did to applaud *Dig That Groove, Baby*. Who knows? In my opinion, it stands as a decent album with some good tracks, and remains an important part of my vinyl and CD collections.

In between record releases and touring the new album, Olga was approached to write and perform some music to advertise the breakfast cereal Ready Brek. The premise of the product is that it makes children 'get up and glow' with health and inner warmth, so Olga's work – based loosely on a recognisable lyrical and musical rewrite of 'Nellie', which was vital as it was still in the public's mind after the song's success the previous Christmas – invited the British public to do just that. The voiceover is vintage Olga, and the commercial went down very well with the nation's young stomachs. What does Olga remember about getting the gig?

> "The Ready Brek thing was fine. I had no moral problems with it when they asked me to do it – it's Ready Brek, it's not poisonous, it's healthy for kids. It was also good money: I took an up-front payment for that one – which was still good money. And that payment, for something that wasn't dangerous or negative, pays for the backdrop for fans across the world to come and see us live, and for the website in 2004. It pays for my mortgage as well. So it was well worth doing."

The spring of 1985 saw the release of 'She Goes to Fino's' as what it was hoped would be the ideal follow-up to the success of 'Nellie'. As we saw in the chapter on Sunderland and Durham Places, 'Fino's' sold quite well in the UK, but not to the extent that would allow it to repeat the runaway success of 'Nellie'. I would much rather have seen 'Fino's' at Number 1 that Easter, rather than the Philip Bailey/Phil Collins duet 'Easy Lover', but there you go – you can't have everything. The Toy Dolls anthem, in its audio and video forms, helped me tolerate that year at college, if nothing else!

Toy Dolls records and lucratively wholesome cereals aside, 85 was a busy year for Olga. In response to Geldof's Band Aid single, the northeast as a regional musical collective decided to get together as Geordie Aid and bring out their own single, 'Try Giving Everything', to help the Ethiopian cause. The sleeve to the single – featuring a bottle of Newcastle Brown Ale with money stuffed inside – also lists the great and good of the region, not just the main musical movers such as members of Lindisfarne and AC/DC (and, of course, Olga), but also a few footballers and famous actors, all of whom gave up their time unquestioningly to take part in the recording. Listening to the recording – which

Toy Dolls website fans can now do, as it has been posted there – you can pick out Olga's unmistakable line belting out about two-thirds of the way through. The project was symbolic of the time, when the western world was horrified to see what was going on in Africa and was only too glad to rush out and help. For his part, Olga was delighted and privileged to have been a part of it.

Olga kept up the TV work with an appearance on the Tyne Tees pop show *TX45*, where he was presenter Chris Cowey's special guest, talking about the group's success in the UK and elsewhere in Europe, and watching local band Chase from nearby Middlesbrough taking the same tentative steps The Toy Dolls had taken on local telly 5 years earlier.

Another trip to the studio occurred to produce some material for County Durham band The Edge, who had supported The Toy Dolls on numerous occasions, and whose guitarist, Colin (Gem) Archer, was later to go on and play with Oasis. The Edge were an excellent live band – tight and slick, with superb melodies and a real 'edge' to their performance – and they were widely tipped for massive stardom by the Durham gig-going public. (Twenty-odd years later, check out how wrong we were! It's a great shame, though.) By this stage, Olga was starting to feel very much at home behind the controls in the studio, as well as with a guitar in his hand, and it was these early examples of production that stood him in good stead for later, more major jobs such as his work with Lolita No. 18 and, indeed, subsequent Toy Dolls albums. The work with The Edge, unfortunately, is something on which Olga looks back with red-faced bemusement, as he confesses that his mind was completely elsewhere, occupied solely with his infatuation for Kendra.

The Kendra episode – covered in more detail in the Crazy Little Thing Called Love section – did indeed occupy much of Olga's time and mindspace that year, to the extent that his songwriting was beginning to take on a solitary focus. It was a classic example of what he refers to as his obsessive nature, his refusal to leave something alone until he's achieved what he wants. On this occasion, though, Kendra's refusal to succumb to his sweeping romantic gestures and the madness of his frantic trip to Lloret de Mar eventually simmered him down, and he was finally able to move on from the experience. The legacy of Kendra is 'Olga I Cannot', the B-side of the band's September 1985 single 'James Bond Lives Down Our Street', which reached No 7 in the Indie chart and is described by Olga as 'OK'.

1985 was also the year the band finally got some proper management: Dave Chumbley, at Primary Talent International, based in London, who for the last 19 years has performed the roles of agent and manager, pulling off some great deals for the band and frequently leaving Olga awestruck at the advantages Dave has given them in their career. It was he who got in touch in the aftermath of the 'Nellie' success, asking them if they'd like to do a broader European tour, and his contacts, expertise and the clout of his agency (which also boasts Kylie Minogue, The Offspring, Oasis and a host of other top acts on its books) have served The Toy Dolls amazingly well ever since.

That same tour was scheduled by Dave for September and October, taking in Germany, Holland, Austria and Switzerland, as well as a number of UK dates. A glance down the gig list gives a clear indication that the band's European fanbase was spreading further year by year, but in order to do this tour, Olga needed some new musicians to join him, since Ernie had gone back to technical and administrative duties, and Little Paul and Pete Zulu had gone their separate ways after the Kendra debacle. Rather than risk taking a bassist and drummer from the audition process and setting off on the road with people he wouldn't necessarily be able to trust, Olga recalled Teddy Toydoll and Dean James. This line-up remained in place until the end of 1986, but we're getting ahead of ourselves again.

There was little time for the band to recover from their New Year's Eve hangovers, as 1986 dawned and Olga, Dean and Teddy jumped on a plane to Japan, to pursue the most bizarre and unforeseeable yet of their foreign success stories. The notion of three lads from Sunderland playing three nights in such a culturally alien and faraway place as Japan, then jetting straight from Tokyo to Hollywood to do what, given the time difference, was tantamount to two concerts on the same day on two different continents, is a difficult one for anyone to get their head around. They could be excused for not taking any of their first Japanese experience in properly, but if they thought that this was to be their only Japanese tour, and that they should have taken advantage of the brief trip to capture images and memories of such a distant culture, then they had another think coming. The Japanese loved them, and hence further tours would be assured.

Eight quick dates in the United States followed, the last of which constituted the band's first experience of the East Coast, at the New York Ritz. Much is made in the music industry of the difference between east and west audiences and music-buying publics in the USA, so I ask Olga what the band's experience had been of this change:

> "Aye. You've really got to work on the East Coast, and you've got to be good. On the West Coast we'd had lots of radio play and what not, and there was also the philosophy of the people – if you're crap, you're crap, but if we were all right, they would think we were doing a good job and they would give us a chance as a punk band. But the East Coast was much more like Europe – and we really had to work hard."

But by the end of January 1986, it's true to say that Olga was brimming with cautious optimism. Japan and the States were looking good, but the management had plans for further expansion. If you can make it in the Netherlands, there's no reason why you can't push further north and establish a decent presence in the Scandinavian markets, so at the end of February, the lads headed off for a nine-date Scandinavian tour, covering Norway, Sweden and Denmark. Again, this was a bit of a gamble, but the manager had done his research, and the shows went down a treat, thus ensuring that more Scandinavian gigs would be forthcoming later in the year.

February also saw the release of a mini-LP, *Singles 83/84*, containing 'Alfie from the Bronx', 'Cheerio and Toodle Pip', 'We're Mad', and the B-sides 'H.O.', 'Hanky Panky', 'Deirdre's a Slag' and 'Rupert the Bear'. It served as a useful item for anyone who hadn't managed to get hold of one or more of the earlier singles, and sold reasonably well.

Later in that year, in July, after spending much of the spring in the recording studio (but no longer at Guardian in Durham), the lads did two quick dates in Austria – when top session drummer and mate Canny Kev Scott stood in to replace Teddy, who had temporarily left, before returning amicably – and brought out the single 'Geordie's Gone to Jail' (which reached No. 14 in the Indie chart, and featured a version on the B-side sung in Japanese, despite Olga not knowing the first thing about the language in those days), followed in August by the *Idle Gossip* album. I was interested in why the band had decided to change recording studios, and put it to Olga that Hull was not everybody's cup of tea, and far from renowned as some sort of recording Mecca. The image we carry of Olga and his guitar sharing a field with a bemused cow or two is one that I'm sure would make for essential DVD material.

"Yeah, that's right – standing in a farmer's field next door and rehearsing in the sweltering heat, coz there was no air conditioning in the studio. At that particular time, the reason we went there was the producer. We decided we'd use a producer called Michael Chapman, who was used to using the Hull studio, so if he was happy there, we would give it a try. I'll tell you what, though: that album that Michael Chapman produced ... he was a great guy, but we'll never ever use him again. The fact was that he wanted things his way and I wanted them my way. If you've got a conflict of opinions with production, then it just comes out as a mish-mash. If you let either individual get on with it, it'll come out either one way or the other. But because we were both so opinionated, each wanting our way, it just came out crap. That *Idle Gossip* album was the worst album of the lot in terms of production. I can't listen to it. But what I'm saying is that if I'd left it all to him, or vice versa, it would have been better. If he'd done it alone it wouldn't have been a Michael Chapman/Michael Algar mismatch production."

That said, though, a lot of fans still like *Idle Gossip*, and it did get to Number 12 in the Indie album chart. There are plenty of excellent tracks on it: 'The Lambrusco Kid', 'Harry Cross (A Tribute to Edna)', 'Geordie's Gone to Jail' and 'Peter Practice...', to name but four. I still think Olga's being very hard on himself about the songs (he's prepared to admit that 'Peter Practice' on that album is a decent track, and that's all), but he's such a perfectionist – both in terms of striving to make his work good for his own artistic satisfaction, and so that we the listeners get the best possible deal – that you can't help but accept his views on poor production or sound quality. We chat for a few minutes about control-freakery, with my trying to persuade Olga that he is maybe just eager to make things as good as possible for the consumer, and hence takes on a lot of responsibility on his own shoulders, but he insists he's both a control freak and an obsessive. To assert my own control over the situation, I order another round of beers, and we clink glasses and press on.

The mathematicians among you will note that 1986 stands out as the band's most prolific year yet for touring, with no fewer than 70 gigs played. An extremely busy autumn saw them packing their bags for some dates across Scotland and various parts of England, before returning to Sweden and Norway, then to more familiar territory in Germany, Austria, Switzerland and Holland.

The year then finished with four dates in Japan, four in

Spain and, by way of glamorous homecoming, a solitary Christmas gig for the students of what was then Coventry Polytechinc. Olga recalls approaching the new Japanese dates with real excitement after the success of the first mini-tour earlier in the year. This time, as well as Kyoto and Tokyo, they took in Osaka, but the schedule was so tight that they had even less time to look around and find their feet than they had in January. Olga still felt good vibes, though. Little did he know that a great future lay ahead of him, not only touring there with the band, but finally working there, learning the language and immersing himself in Japanese culture. But that's a story for later.

Spain was a country that excited Olga from these very first gigs at the end of 1986 (four in four days, then back to the UK to prepare for glorious Coventry). It took a bit of work for him to get used to the Spanish way of doing things – for example, on one early trip he remembers ordering the chilled *gazpacho* soup and trying to send it back because it was cold – but once he'd chilled out himself he started to love the country, and always enjoys going back there. It's interesting – though unsurprising – to note that outside Madrid, the band is massively popular in the northern half of the country (particularly in northern Castile, the Basque Country and Catalonia) and practically unheard of in the south. But this probably reflects general trends for off-the-wall musical styles, and The Toy Dolls are perfectly well embedded in Spain without the help of Andalusia.

At the end of 1986, after the frantic schedule of live shows, the band said goodbye to Teddy, and replaced him with local drumming icon and all-round nice guy Marty Yule (a variant of the correct spelling of his genuine surname, which gave him a Christmassy feel, or something). Marty was to remain behind the drums until the dawn of the next millennium, and became the longest-serving of Olga's troops by a mile.

After the success of the first dates in Spain, the band pushed northwards into France early in 1987, starting in

March in Paris (and why not!). In terms of live gigs, 1987 stands out as the year when the band really got their feet in the French door, performing 17 gigs there, from Brest in Brittany across to Besançon and down to Lyon. A few festival dates in the summer and the by now customary dates in Holland, Germany, Austria and Switzerland were interwoven with a first gig on Belgian soil and what would prove to be – with the exception of a solitary London gig in 1993 – the last ever UK shows (until 2005 – who knows?).

A busy autumn ended with 5 dates in Japan (where the two previous tours had had 3 and 4, so they were building up gradually), and this time took in Nagoya. The importance of The Toy Dolls having played Nagoya will be revealed in the next chapter of the band's history, but for the moment, Olga remembers being delighted with the reception they got when they arrived this time. It was clear that their fanbase had gelled there and was expanding healthily, and these Japanese dates took the year's total to 52 gigs, still more than most top bands were averaging.

The solitary record release of 1987 was *Bare Faced Cheek*, which saw the band move on from the experience of the Fairview Studios near Hull, in favour of a studio much closer to home, and which was to see more Toy Dolls (and Toy Dolls-linked) action over the subsequent years: Impulse, at Wallsend (Tyne and Wear). Perhaps more significantly, this release also marked the band's latest change of record company after their split with Volume. Olga is unable to be specific about the precise reasons for leaving Volume, but admits there must have been 'various contributing factors' that led to the parting of ways. The nearest record company and recording facilities were over at Wallsend, at the headquarters of Neat Records, who were renowned locally as primarily a heavy metal sort of outfit – they had bands like Venom and Raven on their books. It didn't seem, at first glance, like the ideal spiritual home for a band like The Toy Dolls, but the relationship seemed to work initially, and Neat were happy to market Olga's material through the phonetically similar Nit records, to try and offer more of a humorous theme in keeping with the band's philosophy, as well as distancing them slightly from the metal bands around them. This arrangement remained for both *Bare Faced Cheek* and *Ten Years of Toys*, released two years later in 1989.

Bare Faced Cheek contains at least three gems in 'Fisticuffs in Frederick Street', 'The Ashbrooke Launderette' and 'Yul Brynner Was a Skinhead', but again, it's not a record of which Olga is particularly proud. I ask him firstly about the title – whether it was maybe an allusion to being ripped off, or perhaps someone's behaviour – but he assures me that the message was a lot simpler:

> "No, it was just an idea to have an arse reference linking the title and the sleeve. Quite appropriate really, coz the record was a load of crap."

We've all read about how unhappy Olga was with the guitar sound on this album, although he does admit to being satisfied with 'The Ashbrooke Launderette' and 'Yul Brynner'. It was particularly disheartening as he'd spent so long writing the album, and was gutted when his guitar broke and he had to make alternative arrangements. I ask him to run us through what exactly went wrong:

> "Yeah, that's right – I used the pedal and the guitar that belonged to the engineer, coz my guitar was out of action. I don't think there's anything wrong with using pedals, but it's not right for my kind of thing – it's very unnatural to me. On *Our Last Album?* and *Anniversary Anthems*, for example, I didn't use a pedal at all. I got all the feedback from turning the amp up full, which is unbearably loud, but it worked for me. I got a lot more satisfaction out of it that way."

The songs seemed to me to have been a solid enough set, with the highlights mentioned above, but the collection lacks the by now traditional cover version. Was there, I wonder, a particular reason for not seeking out either a rock 'n' roll or an utterly unlikely song to have a go at in Toy Dolls style this time?

"Well, I had enough crap songs with the dozen or so on the album, so I wasn't really desperate enough to go looking for another crap one."

With Neal and Neville included on this album, it's tempting to spend a bit of time getting to the bottom of exactly who all these people are. We established in the chapter on Sunderland and Durham Places that it was natural for Olga to begin his songwriting career writing about what he knew about: the people, places and events that surrounded him in his home town. It's time now for us to go through this cast of protagonists from his teenage years and later, to find out who each person was and what role they played in The Toy Dolls' history.

Olga's Inspirations

4. Sunderland and Durham People

Once you've taken the decision to write songs about the area where you've grown up, the next step is to populate them with family, friends and other people you come across in your day-to-day life. This has been one of Olga's real fortes over the years, building up a stunning portfolio of characters – goodies and baddies – many of whom have achieved cult status among the band's following.

Many songs, of course, are about Olga himself, and these can be more neatly dealt with in other sections of the book, but if we cast the net a bit wider, the first person we reach is brother Ernie. It surprises many people to learn that Ernie is around 20 years older than Olga, more of a father-figure in a lot of ways (in fact, he fulfilled just such a role after the death of their father when Olga was 11). A decorator by trade as well as sometime secretary of The Toy Dolls Fan Club, Ernie had played in a club band in the 1960s, so was well equipped to step in as The Toy Dolls' bass-player when asked to do so in 1985. He's also responsible for much of the band's record-cover artwork, as well as having worked wonders backstage with transport and technology over the years.

There are two main songs involving Ernie, of which the more popular is 'Ernie Had a Hernia', from *Absurd-Ditties*. In the Fan Club circular at the time, Ernie claimed that the song was not about him, but I'm sure most fans saw straight through the scam. The truth is that it was indeed about Ernie, but his ailment was not so serious as a hernia. I press

Olga for details, and he smirks the smirk of a man who's been rumbled:

> "Aye, it wasn't a hernia really. I had something that was called abdominal migraine, and Ernie had a nasty dose of the flu that same week – actually it was some kind of mad flippin' pneumonia or something – so I just combined the two into the lyric Ernie had a Hernia, and the song worked out fine."

I agree that it's one of my favourites from that album, but then quiz Olga about something that's been bugging me for ten years or more: what is the relationship between 'Ernie Had a Hernia' and Alvin Stardust's 1973 hit 'My Coo-ca-choo'? Readers with longer memories and sadder record collections can rummage around now for the Stardust disc, give it a spin and experience the similarity (subconscious, of course) for themselves. Olga has now been rumbled twice in a minute, the poor lad:

> "Do you know, there's only one other person has said that – there was this guy from the army, Tony Jackson, a great guy, and he came to a gig in Holland, and he said, 'do you like "My Coo-ca-choo" by Alvin Stardust?' I said, 'you bastard, you know what it is.' I suppose it was coz it was really from my era. But if you think about it and you go back far enough, everything's a copy to some extent – you could say to people, 'you've used the note E,' or 'that chord sequence is also used by some other band in their song' – but yeah, that is where it comes from."

The other Ernie-related tune is 'I Wish My Eyes Were Ernie's', from *Anniversary Anthems*. Was this a study of fraternal jealousy, self-pity or simple admiration? What was inspiring Olga to eulogise his brother to such an extent?

> "That was completely made up. I don't think it spoils a record too much if you've got occasional bits of fiction in there. But the vast majority of what I write about is real experience and real people."

Moving the focus away from the family (though, in doing so, leaving a tantalisingly oblique reference to another family member – see Famous People for scant details), we reach a series of girlfriends cropping up in songs through the quarter-century of the band's existence. Most of these songs will be dealt with in the chapter entitled Crazy Little Thing Called Love, but it would be wrong to exclude Olga's early girlfriend Angela from our section on the people of northeast England. As we have seen in earlier sections, she was the inspiration for a number of early classics, including 'She Goes to Fino's', 'Tommy Kowey's Car' and 'Queen Alexandra Road...', and she forms an important local backdrop against which Olga's initial creative output can be understood. As his first real girlfriend, she played a special part in his life for several years, although interestingly, in contrast to the early songs of most bands, she does not feature as the subject of any traditional, 'soppy' love songs (which, in any case, are not really Olga's style: romantic gestures, yes; romantic songs, no). She's more a figure in the background or, at times, someone to be complained about (e.g. 'Worky Ticket'), but nevertheless, her presence across the first few years' worth of material is tangible.

Songs about mates in Sunderland present themselves very clearly. The obvious place to begin is 'Back in 79' from *Fat Bob's Feet*, which catalogues a series of friends of the band from the early days, and outlines what disappointing fates have befallen them. We hear mentions of Nicky, Flip, Paul, Fat Bob and Ted, then, later on, Freddie and George. The song, written more than a decade after the start of the band, reveals how much Olga missed the fun and friendship of nights out with these mates, and also hints at his dissatisfaction with the dead-ends in which some of them have become stuck. As Olga has always maintained, there's absolutely nothing wrong with marriage and kids and sensible jobs, so long as these things are what you truly want and are not just a compromise into which you allow yourself to drift. It's also a song that has survived into later versions of the live set-list and, for Olga, retains its importance in its evocation of the 1979 era.

I wondered whether the changes these mates let themselves go through were really so striking:

> "When we first started out, everybody was what they were, and what they wanted to be in 79, and that was great, but then they all changed, and everyone seemed to be doing things just for girls. Most of the changes were because of the girls and the marriage thing. For example, Flip bought this red biker jacket, with all the punk zips and everything, then he sold it to get engaged. And Fat Bob was a skinhead, and he grew his hair because he met this girl called Julie, and he changed."

As discussed elsewhere in the book, this theme of getting trapped into a relationship without thinking it through first is echoed in songs like 'Up the Garden Path' from *Dig That Groove, Baby*, or the single 'Cheerio and Toodle Pip'.

Speaking of girlfriends and wives, what are we to make of 'Bored Housewife' from *One More Megabyte*? It looks as if someone was having an illicit affair with a married woman, and many of us must have wondered, when we first heard the song, what the story was behind it. Over to Olga for the low-down on his misdemeanour:

> "I think getting involved with a housewife of any nature is the most dishonourable thing you can do, because that person is married – it doesn't matter how much you don't like the husband or whatever – it's just not what you do. Once somebody is married, they're married. If you don't accept that, then what do you accept? Unfortunately, I was a lot younger, and I didn't accept that fact, and I did get involved with a housewife, which I regret. It's all based on truth, this song. I learned from the whole experience."

Olga's skill in manipulating vocabulary shines through once again in this song, as he refers to the housewife, at various points, as an adulteress, a nymphomaniac, a floozy, a jezebel, a randy swine and a whore, while the husband is dubbed a berk and a prat. Great stuff.

'When Garry Married Melanie' straddles two categorisations – love and the Sunderland area (actually South Shields) – but it seems appropriate to deal with it here. It seems reasonable to guess that this is a couple Olga knew who got married without Garry really wanting to, but why is the language so harsh (Melanie is referred to as a pain in the butt, a witch, a bitch and a bag)?

> "It's a prat I know called Garry. Melanie's all right actually – I'm being a bit melodramatic saying she's a bitch; she's quite a cutey. But I think they're still together, yeah, and they've got a kid as well."

On the *Orcastrated* album, the song 'Bowling Barmy' celebrates one man's obsession with 10 pin bowling. The man featuring in the song is a friend of Olga's named Keith who influenced Olga to get involved in bowling himself, and in fact Olga became a local champion at one stage. 'Barmy', meanwhile, is another word for 'mad', for any readers who haven't come across it before.

One of the major difficulties associated with following the ins and outs of The Toy Dolls' lyrics is keeping separate the various characters called Davy, Davey and David. To set the record straight, there are four songs, but only 2 blokes. Number One features in 'David's XR2' and 'Davey's Days', and Number Two is the star of 'Davey's Took the Plunge' and 'Poor Davey'. Both guys have, at one time or another, been guilty of falling in love too easily and/or getting trapped into relationships that were, to some extent, ill-advised.

The new album will feature 'Davey's Days' (the lyrics for which I haven't yet seen) and was scheduled to include a new version of 'David's XR2', but it was pulled at the last moment as there was not time to complete the recording satisfactorily. Anyone worrying about the fate of David, who seemingly went out in his brand new Ford Fiesta XR2 and had a gruesome accident in which the car flipped over, can rest easy, for David did not meet the sort of sticky end hinted at in the song.

> "The crash? Well, he might have just had a slight scratch on the side of the car, but you've got to accentuate the drama a bit to give the song atmosphere, haven't you?"

There are also two blokes called Dougy, alias Messrs Giro and Bell. The story behind 'Dougy Giro' (from *Dig That Groove, Baby*) is well publicised on the internet and elsewhere, but is absolutely true: he was a poor but happy bloke, who always looked forward to signing on the dole (British unemployment benefit) to get his giro cheque. All the simple things happening around him – the sunrise, flowers, kids playing football in the street – used to make him the happiest man around, and Olga was touched by how much Dougy could get out of life, despite having so little.

Dougy Bell, meanwhile, the star of 'Do You Wanna Be Like Dougy Bell?' from *Idle Gossip*, Olga describes as:

> "... a lovely guy – he's a really sweet, but very hard guy. He used to manage the Old 29 club in Sunderland, where we used to play live, and he's fine about the song. I don't know if he did all those specific things in the song, but he certainly was known as a hard man locally."

The various Keiths could also perhaps be explained, so that we're clear. It turns out that the guy in 'Keith's a Thief' (on *Idle Gossip*) is the same as the Keith who features in 'Carol Dodds is Pregnant' (*A Far Out Disc*). So was he really such a thief? Keith was in charge of a little unofficial business at Peter Practice's Practice Place, selling crisps and sandwiches and so on, while still being technically unemployed and claiming the dole. That was the extent of his felony.

The other Keith in The Toy Dolls' oeuvre is the star of 'She'll Be Back With Keith Some Day' (*One More Megabyte*). He's actually the star of 'Bowling Barmy', too.

Mentioning Carol Dodds, I can confirm that this was her real name, she was a real person from Sunderland – and

Peter Practice's sister into the bargain – and Keith was indeed the father of the resultant infant. In the interests of damage limitation, we'll leave it there.

'Dez the Demon Decorator' on *Absurd-Ditties* is an interesting one. It sounds as if this guy is the dodgiest decorator in the area, so are we dealing with a real-life tradesman here, and if so, surely Dez can't be his real name?

> "That's actually a combination of two people, merged together just for the sake of the song. It's Ernie – who's a good decorator – combined with this guy I got to do some decorating a few years ago. Most of the mishaps in the song actually happened, although there's a bit of exaggeration. I can't remember his real name now, but I think he does still work in the decorating trade occasionally. So anyway, I combined them to make this one guy Desmond, which wasn't his real name, obviously... It works OK – it's on a good album, which helps."

If the semi-fictional Dez gets a hard time in his song, there are a few other Toy Dolls songs where the subjects are slagged off in no uncertain terms. Despite being a mate from the early days (see above), and a loyal roadie, Fat Bob enjoys the dubious honour of having both an album and a constituent song named after him, and also having the personal secrets of his foot hygiene displayed publicly for the benefit of a worldwide Toy Dolls audience. His feet must have been particularly pungent for Olga to decide to devote such recording space to the issue:

> "Fat Bob was our roadie for years and years, and his feet used to stink to high heaven. I'll give you an example: we did a gig in São Paulo, at a venue that was so big, a huge place. Anyway, I broke a guitar string and thought, 'shall I shout over to the roadie?' and I decided, 'no, I'll not bother,' because the smell was overpowering. The whole crew and the television crew that were looking after us, were all asking where the smell was coming from within the group. He used to stink. I think he went for one shower on the

1985 tour after 5 weeks, then put the same clothes back on again. Having said that, Bob was a top, sincere bloke and one of the best roadies ever."

Any readers of the Scottish newspaper *The Sunday Post* who are fans of the cartoon strips Oor Wullie and The Broons, might be wondering whether the artwork for *Fat Bob's Feet* was a tribute to these cartoons, particularly as Wullie's best mate is called Fat Bob. Olga assures me that it was pure coincidence, though he has always been a fan of these Scottish characters (*The Sunday Post* has always been sold in the northeast of England, so many of us grew up enjoying the characters' adventures each weekend). Incidentally, the mention of *Look North* in the 'Fat Bob's Feet' lyrics relates to the BBC's local TV news programme serving the extreme north of England.

Also receiving a lyrical battering is the anti-hero of 'How Do You Deal With Neal?' on *Bare Faced Cheek*. Astonishingly, Olga kept the guy's real name in writing the song, although he changed the spelling from Neil to Neal to make the rhyme look neater on paper. Neil is the cousin of Pete Zulu, in fact it was through Neil that the original musical link with Pete was made. He lived on Hereford Road, just round the corner from Olga, and had the habit of turning up unexpectedly, here, there and everywhere, to spend time with Olga and his mates. Olga hasn't seen him for years now, but remembers him as a "really nice guy," and jokingly worries that Neil might turn up and ring the doorbell one of these days, demanding an explanation for the song after all these years.

One victim who cannot be named is the subject of the song 'Dorkamania' from *Anniversary Anthems*. 'Dork' is only one of a number of words used in the song to describe this obsessive kind of person, often overly keen on computers, or stamp-collecting, or trainspotting or other types of non-mainstream hobby. He obviously provoked something of a reaction in Olga, so who was he?

"Yeah, it was a specific person – I'd rather not name him – but he just fitted the kind of anorak image. It wasn't the best song in the world, that one. I think the beginning's quite good, but it goes downhill from there."

Nevertheless, it's a matter of some pride for Toy Dolls fans to note that the Australian singer Peter André's concept of 'insania' (an amalgamation of 'insane' and 'mania') which became irritatingly popular on the recent UK TV show *I'm a Celebrity: Get Me Out of Here*, was already in the public domain some 4 years before he claims to have invented it! Nice one, Olga.

Another synonym for 'dork' is 'nerd', and I wondered whether 'Neville is a Nerd', from *Bare Faced Cheek*, is about a similar character. Can the subject's name really be Neville? And did Olga get any legal comeback from this person on account of the song?

"No, his real name's not Neville, but the format of the name, with 2 syllables, is the same. It was done really to get the alliteration of the letter N. But no, there was no hassle, he's a great guy, and he's still the same as ever, aye."

'Frankie's Got the Blues', from *Fat Bob's Feet*, is about a northeastern mate of Olga's called Frankie Adams, who was also "a really nice bloke," but who had all the hallmarks of hypochondria, always complaining about this, that or the other medical problem. Olga admits that Frankie may indeed have had a few things wrong with him from time to time, but concludes that it was all "a bit excessive."

Florence, the star of the song 'Florence is Deaf (But There's no Need to Shout)' from *A Far Out Disc*, was based on a real neighbour of the Algar household, who lived round the corner in Hereford Road (near Neil/Neal). Olga recalls his mam going round to visit the lady and having all sorts of trouble getting her to hear the doorbell.

In the chapter on Cover Versions, we study 'I'll Get Even

With Steven', which is linked to 'Love me Tender'. I ask Olga for further comment on the pairing of Kendra and Steven, and whether it was painful to write the song:

> "Well, it was actually quite easy to write, coz Steven was Kendra's boyfriend and therefore he was a bit of a focus during my infatuation with her. He lived in Durham, the same as her. I never met him, though he did ring me and said he'd kick my head in and all that if I didn't stop pestering her – and I don't blame him. I don't know what he's doing now, but I'm sure he's a nice guy. I never had a problem with him. He finished with her soon afterwards, anyhow, so that put an end to that little chapter."

A surprising lyrical explanation comes in the song 'In Tommy's Head', on the *One More Megabyte* album. I was expecting it to be about a slightly dreamy twentysomething mate of Olga's, who has lost his girlfriend and is trying desperately to be philosophical about it. The truth is revealed as being somewhat different:

> "He's a friend's son, and he's actually only about 3 years old, but I did exaggerate things and make them dramatic as if he was a 23-year-old. So it was really about him and his little girlfriend around the sandpit, that kind of thing. It's greatly exaggerated, but based on a real little kid."

There are a few more, less guessable characters in the repertoire whose stories could do with being explained. What about 'Fred Olivier', for example, from *One More Megabyte*? Was he a real-life budding actor?

> "Yeah, he was a mate, and he thought he was going to be a professional actor. I think he went for some auditions and that kind of thing, but he was just absolutely diabolical, which is funny in itself."

'Pot Belly Bill' from *Wakey Wakey* is quite a sinister song (with a gruesome ending), and the main character seems to have a lot of problems with violence, alcohol and so on. I asked Olga how much of the song is true, and to what extent:

> "Pot Belly Bill is my sister-in-law's sister's husband. He's not such a bad guy after all, but he has got a pot belly and he is called Bill. There was a car crash, which I actually exaggerated. He did have a low-point at one time, when he was going through a nervous breakdown, and I exaggerated all that, but he was called Bill, and he was pot-bellied. I based it on a song by a band called Cruella de Vil."

On a lighter note, Olga cracks me up with his rationale for 'Pot Luck Percy', the eighth song on *Orcastrated*. I wondered who this was based on, and why he should have proved to be lucky in both love and gambling, when the society norm is that we are only fortunate in one or the other:

> "That was a fictional thing. It was a bit desperate, because it was from the *Orcastrated* album, which was quite a desperate album. I did know one person called Percy, who wasn't lucky, and it wasn't about him."

We order another round of beers, and move on to the last batch of characters from the northeast who feature in Olga's songs. 'Terry Talking' had always bamboozled me, as I hadn't been able to piece together where anyone called Terry could have fitted into the Toy Dolls story. Was I missing someone obvious? It turns out I hadn't been paying as much attention to the small print on my record sleeves as I should have done:

> "Yeah, Terry Gavighan's the guy who ran the Guardian recording studio in Pity Me. I lost contact with him and he became a complete recluse from 1986. I'd really love to get in contact with him coz he's from that era. But the only voice we heard used to be his answer-phone."

'Silly Billy' (*Idle Gossip*) seems a little risqué in its portrayal of a man whose partner doesn't seem as keen on him as he is on her. The Babs figure is given quite a pasting in the lyrics, so I wondered whether there had been any legal repercussions:

> "Yeah, Billy wasn't very happy about that, but he didn't take me to court. I can't remember his second name. Yeah, Billy and Barbara, I'm not sure whether they actually got married. I actually went out with Barbara's sister a couple of times – I've forgotten her name. They might be married now; he lived somewhere outside of Newcastle. But yeah, it's a true story. He was a really tall, lank guy with long features and all that, and she wasn't really interested in him."

'Rodney's Memory', from *Fat Bob's Feet*, is a song that has always rung some sort of bell in the musical brain, but I couldn't quite place it. The lyrics didn't suggest that it had anything to do with the characters Rodney and Sheila from *Brookside* (see TV and Soap Operas), so I was stumped as to where it came from. Olga enlightened me:

> "Again, that was another fictional thing – from time to time, out of desperation really, I do some completely fictional things. I can't find factual stuff 100% of the time. The characters in this song are based on real people in terms of their names, but no, it's fictional. It's not a very good song, but it does always remind me of that 'Johnny remember me' thing – do you remember that? – which I thought was a great song."

There's an interesting story attached to the song 'Melancholy Margaret' (*Absurd-Ditties*). At face value, it looks like the journal of an extremely unlucky woman, who keeps on losing man after man, and can't seem to hold on to any of her lovers. The number of minor characters contained in the song, and the ease with which their names fall into convenient rhyming groups, would lead us to suspect that they're invented for the purpose, but otherwise the song seems to be a plausible description of loves gained and lost in an unfortunate woman's life. Olga?

> "Well, it is about a specific person – a real person – but it's actually about a guy losing girls all the time, rather than the other way round. He was a guitar pupil of mine from Southwick in Sunderland. Actually he was the guy who worked on the buses (who ended up being Tommy in the song), but I changed it around so that he was the girl losing guys all the time. Yeah, the rhymes were nice, but it is a good example of how you can reach a kind of writer's block when you're trying to think of names. If you find yourself writing Joseph and all these kinds of less resonant names, and you're sitting for 6 weeks trying to find a rhyme, and your girlfriend says, 'what's wrong? Do you want something to eat?' and you say, 'fuck off,' then you know it's starting to get to you. Then you carry on, thinking 'John, Robert...,' and then you come across Ronnie Timmy Micky Jimmy and you think, 'there, that wasn't so hard after all.' But it can happen both ways."

Equally depressed due to lovesickness, but under very different circumstances, was the heroine of 'What She Had with Huey', from *Anniversary Anthems*. This is a very sad story, and is based on a married couple from a village near Durham, whom Olga and I both knew at different times. The character who became Huey in the song was well known locally as the man who came round with the ice-cream van, and at one time he was also involved with renting wedding cars out. This is how Olga met him, when Olga was setting up his own company – Durham Wedding Cars – which he subsequently sold (to one of the mob vocalists from *Our Last Album?*, incidentally). After Olga had known the couple for a while, the Huey figure became very ill, went into hospital and then died. The song is a study of the emptiness in his wife's life without her husband around her to keep her on an even keel.

Time for a quick foray into the new album, where I reckon there are at least four songs involving local characters we've not yet touched upon (See above for 'Davey's Days', and in the section on Famous People for comment on 'Caught it off Camilla'.) Obviously we can't have access to the lyrics yet, but Olga was good enough to give me some background on the people involved.

'Tony Talks Tripe' began life as 'Tycoon Tony', and describes the personality of a bloke from the northeast of England who always wanted to be a business tycoon. Instead of getting on and trying to achieve anything, he apparently spent all his time talking crap about how big he was going to be in the future. He was what we might refer to as a 'wannabe local businessman'. The title change, incidentally, was not effected due to pressure – Olga just felt it would fit better that way.

'Chenky is a Puff' springs from an idea that started out as the quite different song 'Jenky is a Puff', in reference to a well known local figure in Sunderland, who threatened to sue Olga if the band brought the song out. The good news is that the new song is to be included on the new album, so its flavour will finally reach the audience it deserves. The song itself in its new form and with its new subject matter, of course, is not about Jenky; it's about Chenky, which is a different matter altogether.

> "I remember Jenky – I knew him personally – he's a nice guy, again, and I remember him calling me because he had my ex-girlfriend's number, and he said, 'put that single out and I'll sue you.' And I thought, 'well, how do you know it's you?' And he said, 'well, the little drawings of this fat guy with glasses, with an arrow saying JENKY next to it.' That might have been a hint, I guess. But no, the song on *Our Last Album?* is a completely different thing. It's about Chenky, who is a skinny guy with perfect eyesight."

'I Gave My Heart to a Slag Called Sharon From Whitley Bay' – which is likely to be played on Our Last Tour? – reassures us that Olga has lost none of his skill with the manipulation of long titles, and it seems to me to be one of those songs where the title tells you pretty much all you need to know about which way the song is going to go. Whitley Bay, for anyone not familiar with the northeast of England, is the local seaside resort, perhaps equating to Blackpool in the northwest, though with less of the worldwide fame or infamy. It has an amusement/funfair area called the Spanish City (which will bring back memories to anyone old enough or brave enough to admit to having been a Dire Straits fan in the 1980s). It remains to be seen to what extent Sharon proves, in the song, to be a slag, but the story behind it is that she was going out with a friend of Olga's, and she had previously been out with the guy who ran the dodgem cars in the Spanish City. Olga sounded quite pleased with how the song had turned out, and thought – at the time of completing the songs, though they had not yet been recorded – that this, plus 'Davey's Days' and 'Barry the Roofer', were looking like they might be the best of the bunch.

'Barry the Roofer'? As yes, 'The Death of Barry the Roofer with Vertigo'. A great title, but shouldn't we be worried about the consequences of the story, and should we be approaching our first listen to the album this autumn wearing a black armband and a solemn expression as a mark of respect to the hapless roofing technician?

> "No, he didn't die. He's still alive, but he did actually fall off the roof. Yeah, he's fine – a bit of poetic licence on my part again! I can't say his second name, but I've used him loads of times when I've needed roofing jobs doing on any of the houses I've owned over the years. It's a really good song, that one. It's a kind of 'long agoooo, in a bungaloooow' sort of thing."

Can we have a bigger snatch of the lyrics, please? I'll get some crisps in with the next round of beers. Go on, please...

'Long agooo
With vertigo –oh –oh
He had a fa –tal
Acci –dent

The balance of Barry's had went
And nothing could pre –vent
Him falling off
The bu– bu– bu– bungalow.'

Ah, yes. The hallmark of brilliance. Watch out for that song on the tour, too. Finally from the *Our Last Album?* opus, there's quite a straightforward song, 'Jean's Been'. Jean is a woman who lives on the Newton Hall estate near Durham, and her notable characteristic is one-upmanship – wherever you say you've been on holiday, she's been there, or somewhere better. Whatever gadget you've bought for the house, Jean has bought the next model up or the next generation. She's one of those people who will always try to outdo you. Perhaps unconsciously, Olga is harking back to the song 'Livin' on Newton Hall' (see the chapter on Sunderland and Durham Places), where just such a philosophy was aired and given a good old kicking.

Of all the local characters who might have had a good reason to threaten Olga with legal action (but didn't), Peter Practice stands out as one who might have had a half-decent chance of succeeding. As we know, he's in not one but two songs: 'If you're in a Pop Group You'll end up Paying a Fortune Practising at Peter Practice's Practice Place' on *Idle Gossip*, and 'Poverty Pleadin' Peter' (*Wakey Wakey*), neither of which leaves anything to the imagination about what sort of person the band perceived Peter to be. Yet there are all sorts of positive links between Mr Practice and the band (his brother made the Fino's video for them; he allowed them to put cameras on his premises to try and provide evidence in the 'Fisticuffs' case; he played the drums on 'Hanky Panky'). So how did he take it? Peter Dodds (his real name) was apparently fine about the whole thing – a bit pissed off initially, maybe, but he eventually saw the funny side. What are Olga's memories of the early rehearsal sessions that led to the song?

"I haven't heard from Peter for a while. He finished doing

the practices about 10 years ago. I really miss him, because he's part of that era, you know, recording in the basement and that kind of thing. When we first started, we used to practise on a Friday night, then for tours, we never used to practise apart from 3 months before a tour we used to practise 4 nights a week – that's the way it used to be. But yeah, I keep in touch with him from time to time."

And, with regard to the stinginess implied in both songs, what sort of a hard-nosed businessman was Peter, and did he really rip off the cream of Sunderland's up-and-coming bands?

"Well, he'd agree to being called stingy, it's OK, you've got no complaints on that score. He used to charge – I can't really remember how much it was per practice – but he really used to capitalise, and there's nothing out of the ordinary about that, coz the country's run on capitalism, in my opinion. He used to charge for sandwiches, electricity and everything on top of that. He used to have a little tuck shop – that sounds really 1950s, doesn't it, when it was actually written in about 1984 – and he'd come round (or Keith from 'Keith's a Thief' would come round) with this little sandwich tray and sell marshmallows and all that kind of thing – at an unbelievable profit. But he's a great guy."

OK, you've waited long enough. Here comes 'Tommy Kowey's Car'. It's many people's favourite Toy Dolls song, and, of course, it's one of the first songs Olga ever wrote. Here's the story:

Tom Cowie had started his motor trade in Sunderland shortly after World War 2 – my father recalls being charged an extortionate amount of money by him for a motorbike gearbox cog in 1948 – and before long, he had opened his first proper car showroom. If we flick the story forward nearly 30 years, we reach the late 1970s and discover Tom's son Andrew Cowie (middle name Thomas, apparently) now working at his father's car showroom at the top of Hylton Road. Also working there was Olga's girlfriend Angela, who had long blonde hair and was a secretary. The crucial bit is to make it clear that the song is written about Mr Cowie junior, and that no affair between him and Olga's girlfriend ever took place. I press Olga further for details:

> "It's about 90% true, but of course it's about Tommy Cowie's son. We took legal advice straight away, and changed the C in his surname to a K, and little touches like that. There were rumours that Tommy senior was going mad about it, but there was nothing he could do legally at the time (not that it was about him, anyway). So no, there wasn't an affair as such. I think he did ask her out, and she got a lift, and it was on a Tuesday night, but they weren't 'having dinner out' or anything."

'Tommy Kowey's Car' was the band's first single and part of the classic *Toy Dolls EP*, and has since featured on various compilation albums at home and abroad. Although Olga says that there were no concrete legal problems, the band did tread warily for a time: several press articles from the weeks preceding the launch of the subsequent EP talk of the inclusion of 'a song we're not allowed to name at the moment for legal reasons'. Back to 2004, and the song is expected to be included in the set for the forthcoming world tour – Our Last Tour? If it is, it'll help to provide a very tidy resolution, proving that early songs from the late 70s can sound just as fresh on stage, and be just as valid in the minds of the fans, as they were when they were first performed 25 years ago.

A footnote to the Tom Cowie/Tommy Kowey saga is that the band planned a follow-up song on a related theme entitled 'Rock on Tommy', but sadly the project never made it to a vinyl pressing. Shame.

So there you have it: a run-through of the main dramatis personae from the northeast of England whose names and/or character traits are immortalised in Toy Dolls songs. You can judge for yourselves how many of these people will have been pleased to have found fame in such a manner, and how many utterly pissed off. But whatever they think, they have served a most worthwhile purpose: adding to the madcap flavour and ever-present realism of 25 years of superb Toy Dolls music.

History 1988-1990

Psychopaths and Brazil Nuts

As 1988 dawned, Olga found himself living in his little house in Ashbrooke, Sunderland, with his current girlfriend and his new dog, Ashbrooke. All seemed well: the band now had over eight years of life, plus a string of albums, singles, impressive tours and media coverage behind them, and Olga's girlfriend – a Japanese fan whom he'd met when the band played in Nagoya – had moved over to be with him in Sunderland. After the split from his long-term girlfriend Angela a few years earlier, and with the Kendra business now firmly in the past, his life seemed to be on an even keel. However, the demons returned: this domestic bliss, plus Olga's delight at discovering his new canine friend, was increasingly tempered by a growing feeling that all was not well with the band. He couldn't put his finger on exactly what was wrong, but a bad vibe was definitely being given off. For the moment, he decided to push the thought to the back of his mind and press on.

1988 was a quiet year on the recording front, so quiet, in fact, that for the first time in the band's history (excluding the tail-end of 1979), a calendar year elapsed without a vinyl release from The Toy Dolls. Fans began to worry: coupled with the lack of new material emerging, British followers were gutted to see that, for the first time ever, they would have no opportunity to see their idols play live, and the same was true for most of continental Europe. The lucky few were the Swedes, with 9 shows in March, the Spanish (5 concerts in May) and the French (3 gigs in the early summer). But another surprise was round the corner at the end of April: just when we thought Japan and North America were the only non-European territories the band would get to conquer, they baffled us all by heading off to play to packed houses in São Paulo, Brazil. Again, it was something of a gamble, as is the case with the first trip to any new country, and particularly one so far away and for such a short tour, but Dave Chumbley had looked carefully at record sales – *Bare Faced Cheek* was doing very well out there – and had correctly judged that it would be worth the band's while to get out there sharpish. The sell-out for 4 nights at the Projeto venue was something they wouldn't have dreamed of just a short time earlier, but it was reality – it happened, and it augured well for the future, a future that would see the lads head back there in 1995 and, we hope and pray, as part of the Our Last Tour? mission coming up in 2005.

Brazil has, since then, been a special memory for Olga, and the bond between band and country has always been strong, even if the local press in São Paulo didn't seem quite sure what to make of the band initially, with their jokey answers to interview questions. It's a shame that Brazil and Argentina are so far away and involve so much expense for the band to reach, but with a bit of luck, the forthcoming tour will put things right. An indication of the esteem in which The Toy Dolls are held in Brazil is that The Lambrusco Kids recently offered Olga the change to travel over and conduct a series of guitar workshops. The offer was to include free flights for him and his girlfriend, hotels, everything. He was sorely tempted, but there were so many other things going on that he reluctantly had to turn them down. But the Brazilian link remains strong, which is more than can be said for the tooth Olga lost when a São Paulo skinhead jumped onto the stage during a gig and awarded Olga a celebratory smack in the mouth, before coming up to him afterwards to compliment him on a great show!

Also ticking along nicely in the band's absence was the Japanese market. On the strength of their gigs in Japan at the end of 1987, the April 1988 edition of the Japanese *Doll* magazine voted The Toy Dolls the second best live band in the world, beaten only by Elvis Costello, and ahead of such luminaries as Iggy Pop, PIL, The Beastie Boys, The Damned and Ian Dury.

So what was going on in 1989 if there was no recording and only 21 gigs? The answer is that this was the year Olga got heavily into promoting other acts, principally Wilko Johnson, the Guana Batz and The Macc Lads. (For anyone prepared to believe the press stories that The Macc Lads are off their heads, Olga has a stern denial: "they're the nicest, hardest-working, most professional group of guys I've ever come across.") For the first time in nearly a decade, he was able to devote time to something other than The Toy Dolls, even though the experience eventually brought him some unwelcome legal hassle (detailed in our chapter on Sunderland and Durham Places). Promoting was something in which he was very interested, but it also meant that he wasn't either out on the road touring or locked away in his bedroom writing new material. Perhaps because the traditional Toy Dolls focus was not present in his life and he was not immersed so deeply in his accustomed forms of work, he began to note little niggles creeping into his relationship at home. These minor disagreements gradually became more serious, and in time the girlfriend started to display a darker side to her character, later to be enshrined in 'My Wife's a Psychopath'. With a certain amount of sadness, but probably a greater dollop of relief (at least on Olga's part), the decision was taken for her to move out about 8 months into the relationship, and she went back to Japan. Olga says quietly that the whole relationship, and particularly how it ended, "knocked my entire thinking process for six," and it took him a while to get his life back into shape. It's always sad when a relationship turns sour in this way, but you'd think it would serve at least for Olga to observe the 'once bitten, twice shy' maxim, taking extra care not to get involved with anyone like this again in the future.

Wrong again – fast forward a year and he's back to his old tricks. But let's leave that episode for later.

After an open-air show in Toulouse, in the south of France on 9 July, Dean decided to leave the band, citing the relentless touring obligations as his reason, and went on to play with other bands in the northeast, among them the Evil Mothers. He wasn't the first band member to leave on account of the – often brutal – touring schedules, but it just shows what sort of commitment is required by someone intending to put their heart and soul into a band like The Toy Dolls. It can take a vast amount of single-mindedness and determination to make such a project work, as we have seen over the years with Olga himself. He is the only 1979 member left, and someone who frequently puts all aspects of his life on hold, and discharges all his powers of obsessiveness and control freakery, to ensure that the show – a quality show, otherwise it wouldn't be worth doing – goes on.

At the start of this chapter, I mentioned a dip in Olga's enthusiasm for how things were going in the band. What was probably needed was a change of circumstances, and as 1988 became 1989, with the 'psychopath' period now behind him, Olga was pleased to do some spring cleaning, welcoming in John Casey (K'Cee) as the new bassist alongside Marty, who was still there on drums, and negotiating a change of record company, from Nit to Receiver.

Before moving over to Receiver, however, there was one further bit of business to be done with Nit: the issuing of 1989's *Ten Years of Toys* compilation LP. I remember being thrilled at the choice of songs when I got hold of my copy back then, but I wanted to be sure that Olga was also happy with the combination that was finally agreed on:

"The combination of songs was all right, yeah. The big mistake with that album was the re-recording. That was a bad decision. Or rather, it was a good choice to take the opportunity to re-record the songs for freshness, but the bad

Flip, Olga & Happy Bob, early 1980's

Olga, 1985

From Olga's private collection

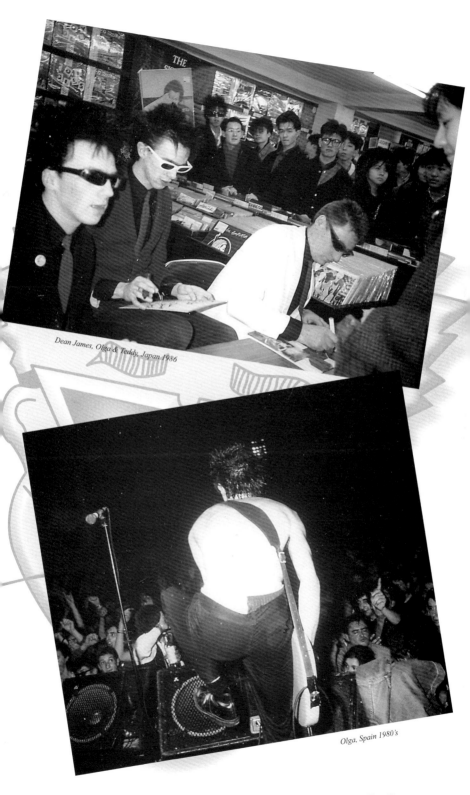

Dean James, Olga & Teddy, Japan 1986

Olga, Spain 1980's

Dean James, Marty & Olga
Japan 1980's

Olga, Holland 1993

From Olga's private collection

Olga and the tour bus, Los Angeles

On tour again! Marty, K'Cee and Olga

Prague 1991

Kawasaki 1991

From Olga's private collection

K'Cee & Olga, Holland early 90's

Olga & K'Cee, Germany 1995

From Olga's private collection

Olga, Tommy Goober & Dave The Nut, April 2004
Photos by Ciaron Lee Marlow
Olga & the author 2004
From author's private collection

idea was to use the drum machine. But we admitted that. What's the point in pretending, or lying about these things? 'We used a drummer!' – no we didn't, we used a flippin' daft computerised drum machine, which was crap. To do one drum roll – 'duh-duh-duh-duh-duh-duh-duh' – we recorded 'duh', then had to confirm 'yes' to 'duh', and that's one sound recorded. We did 20 of them on one song. It took so flippin' long to record one album with the drum machine, which we wanted to try, but it turned out really poor and computerised in the end. We made a mistake, and we'll never do it again. But that's a big part of the Toy Dolls thing, or even my life: you make mistakes and learn from them."

I wondered whether, alongside the album released to mark the tenth anniversary, there was a particular mindset, or maybe a feeling – be it satisfaction, pride, relief, or whatever – to go with it as the band celebrated 10 years of The Toy Dolls. Olga was quite sanguine in his reply:

"I know what you mean, but no, there was no real feeling like that. It was just another year, really. The chart success hadn't really meant that much, it was just one of the things that happened in the UK – there are so many more countries in the world. People in the UK might think that was the time, the 'Nellie' period, but it's different for other countries: France, Holland, Austria, Germany, Switzerland, even Russia. It's nothing to do with 'Nellie the Elephant', really. 'Nellie' was a good point, sure, but it's only a small part of the whole thing. If only the UK had existed, then maybe it would have been a bigger deal. The whole thing had been a ten-year journey up to that point, with so many factors making it up."

And so to Receiver, a company with which – either as Secret or Receiver – the band has stayed ever since. Such a long-term relationship must inevitably suggest that they're a good outfit to work with?

"Yeah, they're a great record company, which is why we've

been with them for so many years. It's a bit complicated: they're Secret Records; they were Receiver, then they sold that on, and now they're Secret again. The main thing is that they let me do exactly what I want, and that's the only way it can be. I've done various stints at producing over the years – the Japanese group and so on – and I've learned that to be a producer is to let people play exactly what they want, and never cramp their style. You'll remember that we recorded with EMI once, and it was the worst thing in the world. I had this young kid telling me how to sing and how to play the guitar, saying, 'it sounds fine in the control room,' but if it sounds crap where you are, you're just gonna play crap. If it's cramping your style, then it's no good. You should be able to play at what volume, what tone you like."

So how did the first experience of working with Receiver work out? It happened in the summer of 1989, with the recording of the new album *Wakey Wakey* – the title makes reference to re-awakening the public after a fair period of silence on the band's part, similarly to the Boomtown Rats' album *In the Long Grass*, before which they had been lying low and keeping quiet – which again took place at Impulse in Wallsend, and which was released in September. For the first time in a while, we're able to get Olga to make positive noises about one of his albums:

> "It was all right. The production was a bit weak, but overall it was all right. There were some good songs on: I like 'Sabre Dance', for instance."

The conversation actually sounds a lot more positive than that short quotation looks, and we talk about the album and 1989 at some length. It strikes me that Olga immediately felt much happier once *Wakey Wakey* was out, both with the new record company and, principally, with the new line-up. The addition of K'Cee on bass seems to be at the root of this:

> "Yeah, that's true. As soon as K'Cee started, I could see that he was the best bass-player we'd had. This may sound

ridiculous, but I think he's actually the best bassist in the world. He's the best I've ever heard. Having said that, Tommy Goober, the new guy, is proving to be unbelievable as well, although at the moment [March 2004] we're still at the early rehearsal stage."

1989's touring was restricted to the last three months, beginning in Holland in early October, carrying on through Germany, Austria, Switzerland (the beloved Albani in Winterthur), France, Belgium and Spain, and ending on New Year's Eve in Tokyo, and these three months served to prove to Olga that K'Cee was indeed an asset to the band, in his bass-playing, his singing, his on-stage presence, and how well he got on with the rest of the band and crew. Japan was continuing to expand in Toy Dolls terms: this time they played eight shows there in a week, including a gruelling 2 each on 24, 26 and 28 December. It was a useful tour for another reason, too: it provided the footage for the following year's live album, *Twenty-two Tunes Live From Tokyo*. I put it to Olga that the business of ending the year in Japan was becoming something of a habit, but at least they got Christmas Day off, in case they fancied simulating their home festivities. Wasn't he bothered about missing the whole yuletide experience back from in the UK?

"Christmas itself doesn't mean much in Japan, so they were glad of the chance to see us at that time of the year. New Year's quite a big thing there, though. No, I didn't mind a bit. I still thought it was like a different planet, but there was certainly an exciting thing there, as I thought it should have been in England, maybe ten years earlier. It was a great time to be in Japan, and we couldn't have been happier with the way things were going there. K'Cee was getting into it, as well. He ended up marrying a Japanese girl, and they lived out in Japan for a few years, but they're back in Sunderland now, I think."

Meanwhile, back in England, Olga had got himself involved with a Chinese girlfriend from Hong Kong, a relationship which was destined to end in more heartbreak. It's difficult to tease the details out of him, but there was a certain amount of cuckolding foul play on the part of the girl, and she chose to inflict her treatment on him while he was trying to juggle a house move and the elaboration of new material for the band. As mentioned in an earlier chapter, this led to the first of his nervous breakdowns, and constituted a very low moment in his life, to add yet another counterpoint to a better period with the band. But, as he always does, he bounced back eventually with a musical vengeance.

That said, 1990 involved even less touring: two summer festivals – one each in Austria and Germany – then a nine-date tour of Sweden and Norway in October, on which Richard 'Dicky' Hammond took the place of K'Cee on bass, while the latter had a rest. The year also saw minimal record company releases: only the live album, *Twenty-two Tunes Live From Tokyo* in October and the single 'Turtle Crazy' a month later, both described as "crap" by Olga. I wondered why the band had chosen Japan, in particular, as the setting for their first live album:

> "It was just by chance that it worked out that way. Well, being Japan, where we were very popular, there was an audience there, which was a big, big thing with our group. That was guaranteed. And sometimes when there's a proper audience there you do actually play a bit better. Anyway, an English guy was there with a walkman in the audience – crazy really, but that's the reason. It wasn't a mobile recording studio, and it wasn't planned, it was just a guy came in with a walkman and recorded it. The fact that it was on the other side of the world didn't mean anything, not to me anyway. As long as the band's good, I don't really mind where a recording takes place."

Olga has admitted, since the record was brought out, that they tinkered with the sound, overdubbing various bits and pieces, and has apologised on the website. But Olga shouldn't worry, as nobody minds: we have a document that shows our heroes playing live somewhere on the other side of the world (depending on where you're listening, of course), and we're not fussed about a bit of dubbing. We can still sit down in our favourite armchair, close our eyes and sing along. Just out of interest, did it sell well in Japan?

> "Not necessarily. I think the sales were normal – no more and no less than if it had been recorded in London. Bands record live albums out in Japan all the time, so it wasn't really a special concept. I can't really remember the figures. It can't have been spectacular, otherwise I'd have remembered."

We deal with 'Turtle Crazy' in the Cover Versions section, so let's not dwell on it here, except to use the television profile of the ninja turtles themselves to provide a link to the next chapter, in which we look at the characters from TV programmes and soap operas who have found parallel stardom as the subjects of Toy Dolls songs.

Olga's Inspirations

5. TV and Soap Operas

Every country has its long-running TV dramas, and every nationality identifies characters from these and holds them up as strong figures to be loved or admired, or as oily miscreants whom the nation loves to hate. Venezuela has some crackers. In Britain, the genre is perhaps longer-established than it is in many other countries, and it has given the public – and, more importantly, The Toy Dolls – a whole range of characters to talk about, argue about, bitch about and, crucially, sing about. This chapter leaves aside the more mainstream figures of TV such as the film star figure of James Bond, and looks specifically at Toy Dolls songs involving characters from UK soap operas.

Channel 4 has, since its inception in 1982, been responsible for a shed-load of award-winning drama, and right from the start it set about creating a gritty northern drama that would run twice a week and deal with issues no other broadcaster had dared to tackle. *Brookside*, set in a small housing estate just outside Liverpool city centre, started off flying, but audiences fell and it has now been relegated to a single spot on Saturday evenings. It's not Olga's favourite soap opera, and never was (as we'll see in a moment), but he did watch it religiously for a few years – as most of the UK did – and it did provide him with two great songs.

The Dixon family moved onto Brookside Close to provide characters to match the success of the original Grant family. The father, Ron, had a mobile shop (a huge van called Moby, from which he sold groceries direct to the public in their streets), and was considered to be a solid, dependable, working-class bloke. Unfortunately, he was married to a horse. Not a real one, you understand. But what a face she had. D-D Dixon was an interesting character, and well acted, but she had a whining way of going on that soon got Ron pissed off. Right on time, a character called Bev came on the scene and stole Ron away from D-D. Bev and Ron then moved in together and lived happily until I got pissed off with the programme, so anything could have happened since.

The song 'Ron Dixon Dumped D-D', from *Orcastrated*, stands out mostly for its equine imagery to describe the horsiness of D-D's face, and for the excellence of its rhymes: 'Too ugly to discuss ... a bird so hid-e-ous' and 'he gave D-D the push ... Ronny saw D-D's monstrous mush'. I am not aware of any other song to have given an honourable mention to Red Rum, who won 3 UK Grand National races in the 1970s. Does Olga agree that it's a great song? "The words are good, but I think the song's crap," he says, frank as ever. So there we go.

The other *Brookside*-inspired tune is 'Harry Cross (a Tribute to Edna)' from *Idle Gossip*. The eponymous Harry Cross (played by actor Bill Dean) was a resident of the Close, who made it his business to complain about everyone and everything in his sight. He was the most miserable old bastard ever to grace the screens of a British soap opera (with the possible exception of Percy Sugden from *Coronation Street*), and was a lazybones too, relying on his wife Edna to do everything. Then his world fell apart when Edna had a stroke and died, leaving him to fend for himself. This event made Harry even more cantankerous than ever, and when his friend Ralph took pity on him and started to come round more frequently to help Harry out, he was met by a barrage of abuse or, at best, indifference.

I remember sitting opposite Bill Dean on a train near Manchester once, in about 1989. I was intrigued and delighted to be sitting opposite someone famous, and noted with satisfaction that he took out 4 cans of beer and opened 2 of them: one for his agent who was sitting next to him, one for himself, and none for me. Would he turn out to be a really likeable bloke, the epitome of graciousness and humour? No chance. He proceeded to swear his way through the beer, tearing a strip out of his agent and generally making fellow passengers feel uncomfortable about travelling in his company.

A friend of mine who used to work editing the scripts for *Brookside* confirmed that he could be quite funny, particularly when he'd had a drink, but was nonetheless a grumpy old bugger both on-set and in real life.

We'll come to *Coronation Street* in a moment, but first, let us look at the other soap operas to have provided inspiration for Toy Dolls songs.

Crossroads has recently been reinstated a couple of times on British television after a long gap, but it now seems to have died for good. It was set in a motel in the West Midlands (close to Birmingham, UK) and revolved around the lives of the motel workers and their families, friends and work. In the original format, there was a character in the early 1980s called Glenda Banks, who desperately wanted a baby with her husband Kevin, but he didn't seem quite so keen. Maybe this was because Glenda was rather podgy and a bit dull-looking – who knows? Gradually Kevin began to sow his wild oats elsewhere, going out with Carol Sands and sending Glenda into deep depression. She seemed to be losing her husband, and if that were to happen, there would be even less chance of conceiving a baby.

A couple of years earlier, the world had witnessed the birth of the first ever test-tube baby, Louise Brown, so spurred on by this, Glenda decided that this could be the way forward, so she went to see the doctor to discuss the matter. Olga picked up on the issue and crafted what is, in many people's opinion, one of the finest Toy Dolls ditties ever, 'Glenda and the Test-tube Baby'. It certainly gets things bouncing at gigs, and even lends itself, when the mood takes Olga, to a slower introduction before kicking off at the regulation, breakneck pace.

Many Toy Dolls fans, particularly in Britain, wonder why more exposure is not given in the songs to characters from the BBC1 soap *EastEnders*, set in the fictitious borough of Walford in the East End of London. The truth is that, whilst he has watched it and even had a drink with members of the cast, it is far from Olga's favourite soap. He feels – like many other people – that the programme lacks humour, and that all the characters are too depressing. The only one of these to have featured in a song by the band is Dot Cotton (an obsessive, zealously religious grandmother). Dot is now married to Jim Branning, but her husband of many years before that was called Charlie, an idle, good-for-nothing oaf who left her and ran off with a younger woman and eventually died. For years, Dot would refuse to do anything in society because her precious Charlie might have been 'watching' her, and her beliefs and misguided loyalty (to say nothing of her ugliness and irritation factor) forbade her from getting romantically involved with another man.

But the song 'Charlie's Watching' is not purely about Dot Cotton: it is actually an odd amalgamation of her and UK Subs singer Charlie Harper.

A passing mention is due here for the Australian soap *Neighbours*, whose theme tune is wailed by the mob in the introduction to 'Sod the Neighbours' on *Absurd-Ditties*. Speaking of 'Sod the Neighbours', if there are any Anthrax fans reading this, have a rummage through your CD collection and rake out 'Got the Time', and check out the bass introduction for an example of subconscious similarity.

Of the *Coronation Street*-inspired tracks, perhaps the best loved – and certainly the oldest – is 'Deirdre's a Slag'. The actress Anne Kirkbride joined the show – set in the fictitious, working-class Manchester suburb of Weatherfield – in the early 1970s as Deirdre Hunt, and is still there, though her surname has changed a few times over the years, as the song lyrics suggest. Her first husband was Ray Langton, who was a long-haired, David Cassidy-style wide-boy and completely swept the young Deirdre off her feet, before running off and leaving her a few years later. (One of the early versions of 'Deirdre' has Olga rasping 'Deirdre Langton' during the introduction.) Thus began a catalogue of desperate attempts on Deirdre's part to find true love with a dependable bloke who would stay around for her. She turned next to Cockney business tycoon Mike Baldwin (the actor Johnny Briggs, also still in the show, all these years later), who was able to show Deirdre a new world of money, flashy cars ('he had a Jag-u-ar and cash', let's remember) and a short period of living life dangerously in the fast lane.

When that relationship fell through, Deirdre moved on to the solid-but-boring character of Ken Barlow (William Roache), a local teacher and sometime journalist. His first mention in the song is when he goes to the cinema and spots Deirdre (whom he has always fancied) canoodling with Mike in the dark, and is seized by jealousy and rage. The song then goes on to hint at Ken's obsessive, envious manner, when in the third verse he asks Deirdre about all the other men she's been with, and she gives him short shrift: 'what's it got to do with you? / It's up to me what I do.'

One of the all-time classic periods of *Coronation Street* was when, during her subsequent marriage to Ken, Deirdre felt pangs of lust for Mike, and a love triangle was established, keeping the nation enthralled in a number of cliff-hanging episodes, one of which – when the situation came to a violent head – broke British audience viewing records.

Incidentally, Mike Baldwin is Olga's all-time favourite *Coronation Street* character.

It struck me that Deirdre's aggregate number of men – particularly when averaged out over all the years she's been on the show – is not really so high as for her to merit the term 'slag'. OK, she's been married a few times (most recently to a young North African bloke called Samir

Rachid, whose surname she now bears, despite being shacked up once again with Ken) and has had a few short-lived affairs, but she's hardly in the league of, say, the Fat Slags from *Viz*. I asked Olga whether it might be a good idea to update the song, adding an extra 17 verses or so to keep up-to-date with the full gamut of Deirdre's conquests, but we were interrupted by the arrival of 2 more pints, and the conversation veered off onto the pressing topic of which of the show's actresses over the years have been the best looking. Olga professed a weakness for the early Rita Sullivan (about whom, more later), and suggested that Deirdre in her younger days wasn't bad looking, and nor is her daughter Tracy in her present-day incarnation. We agreed that the current crown sits on the pretty head of Maria, on-and-off girlfriend of Nick Tilsley.

A few songs date back a few years. Nick Tilsley's grandmother Ivy, played by Lyn Perrie, was a key member of the cast in the 1970s and 80s, but then the actress decided to have collagen implants in her lips, and ruined her face for life. The song 'Ivy's Lurid Lips' (from *Orcastrated*) takes an amusing look at the issue, feeding Ivy a number of lines of thought regarding how her second husband Don – a one-legged taxi-driver, would you believe? – would 'want to snog' her once her lips were fuller. Her lips are described as 'a bleedin' disgrace' and like a 'chipmunk's face', which is appropriate, as her on-screen daughter-in-law, Gail Platt, is variously likened to a hamster, a gerbil, a frog and other members of the Weatherfield wildlife community.

The upshot of the sorry tale was that Lyn Perrie was sacked from *Coronation Street*, and her alcoholism then spiralled out of control and she became a public laughing-stock, appearing pissed on various TV quiz shows and doing nothing to salvage her reputation.

Audrey Roberts is the star of 'Audrey's Alone at Last', from the *Anniversary Anthems* album. In the show, she is the mother of Gail Platt and maternal grandmother of Nick Tilsley (see above), and was married most recently to local councillor and corner-shop-owner Alf Roberts. It was clear to everyone that she didn't really love him, being far more interested in his money to fund her extravagant lifestyle. The final irony was that Alf – who had a reputation as being extremely careful with his money – died a few minutes past midnight on New Year's Day, and had not renewed his life assurance policy due to start that day, thus leaving Audrey penniless. As her then son-in-law Martin Platt (Sean Wilson) says to Audrey in the song: 'Audrey, Oi! Yer get nowt.'

The only *Coronation Street* character – indeed the only soap opera character – to be the subject of two Toy Dolls songs is Alec Gilroy, played by Roy Barrowclough. He and the character Reg Holdsworth are up there in the élite of the show's actors, alongside Mike Baldwin. Alec appears first in 'Alec's Gone' on *Absurd-Ditties*, where his wife Bet is grieving at the loss of Alec, who has left the street and the Rovers Return pub they jointly run, to return to his previous occupation, running the cabaret entertainment on cruise ships. Olga was such a fan of Alec's character that he simply had to write a song (or two) about him, although he admits that the story he wove in 'Alec's Gone' was not really based on the truth of the episode: Bet was not really bothered about Alec's departure, as their marriage had been simply a means of getting a marriage certificate to keep the Newton and Ridley brewery company (the owners of the pub) happy. Check out the influence of the James hit 'Sit Down' on 'Alec's Gone', incidentally.

The other Alec song – 'Alec's Back' on *Anniversary Anthems* – was a fine reply to the earlier ditty. The story is that Alec returns from the cruise ships, expecting to find Bet still behind the bar of the Rovers Return, and hoping to rekindle their relationship. To his shock, he discovers that Bet has left the pub, and a new couple (actually a long-standing pair of residents from the Street, Vera and Jack Duckworth) have taken over. More recently, ITV ran a kind of update drama featuring Alec and Bet up in Blackpool (for anyone not familiar with the geography of northern

England, this is more famous nowadays as the scene of the Holidays in the Sun punk festival). There were moments of tenderness, but the romance was destined not to resume, so I think we may have seen the last of Alec Gilroy in The Toy Dolls' oeuvre.

When Alec Gilroy was a regular on *Coronation Street*, we learned that when he was a young man he had been the manager of a promising club singer, who went on to become the character Rita Fairclough (now called Rita Sullivan, and played by the actress Barbara Knox – no relation, as far as I'm aware, to The Vibrators' singer). As mentioned above, Olga had something of a soft spot for Rita in her earlier years, so it is perhaps fitting that one of the songs on the new Toy Dolls opus *Our Last Album?* – 'Rita is Innocent' – should be dedicated to her. Time has moved on, and Rita now runs the post office on the street, where, earlier this year, she got into trouble for giving an old-fashioned clip around the ear to a young ginger shoplifting scamp called Chesney. Chesney's mam immediately saw the prospect of compensation, and reported Rita to the police, and she was arrested. Rita stuck to her principles, pleaded guilty to assault and spent some time in custody, before the issue was resolved after the police and the legal team got to the bottom of the matter. Absurdly, Rita and Chesney are now the best of friends, and she gives him chocolate and moral guidance whenever the need arises. Olga suggests that hardcore fans of *Coronation Street* listen carefully in the song for a solitary mention of Rita's post office employee and all-round pain in the arse, Norris Cole.

So there we are. A short stroll through the streets of British soap operas and their relevance to The Toy Dolls' lyrics. Olga remains a fan of *Coronation Street*, so who knows whether in the future we will see further adventures of the soap's characters in his songs, or whether, now that we've proved Rita's innocence, she, together with a slag, a test-tube baby, an alcoholic chipmunk and a horse, will be consigned to the graveyard of Toy Dolls history.

History 1991-1993

Things Get Absurd

The hard work of sitting down again and writing new material for the band's next album saw its fruits reaped in 1991 with the release of *Fat Bob's Feet*. A straightforward tribute to the band's faithful, long-serving roadie, this LP is widely loved by the fans and tolerated by Olga. After a troublesome couple of years in matters of the heart, Olga was by now pulling his life back together, but there are still hints of a darker mood on the album, with the gloomy intro and outro. 'Bitten by a Bedbug' and 'The Sphinx Stinks' are the only two tracks he's really keen on, though he does admit that he would have been much prouder of the album overall if the vocals and guitar hadn't been so quiet. Again, it's a shame, as a different style and focus in the production could have yielded an entirely different product and a much higher degree of satisfaction on his part:

> "In retrospect, I could have done things differently, yeah, but it's already gone now, it's released. It's my fault. It's a bit like doing a jigsaw puzzle and you're so closely involved, doing all these different things, and you step back and you don't know whether it's finished, or whether it's good, or what. There may be mistakes, but you're so closely involved you might not even notice. And you get tired, so it's always best to do a mix. We usually take one day per song for a mix, and spend all day doing it, then leave it, then check it the next morning and only *then* master it. I even do that with my little Pro Tools thing – listen the next morning, coz if you listen the same night, you think it's good, then you

listen the next morning and think, 'Jesus, what was I thinking about?' Even though it doesn't really matter, coz it's only really for reference, that. But still..."

What stands out for me about the *Fat Bob's Feet* album is the quality of the lyrics. If you glance at the Top Rhymes section later in this book, you'll see that over a quarter of my chosen rhymes come from this album, so Olga must have been doing something right. Maybe it has something to do with the bad times he'd gone through: having his back against the wall, and a lot of time to sit gloomily in his room and ponder, may have deepened his thought process and sharpened his lyrical focus. Whatever it was that spurred him on, I found the lyrics instantly memorable and the album itself hugely enjoyable.

This album also consolidated the quality of the trio of Olga, K'Cee and Marty (or quartet, if we include backing vocalist Ashbrooke) and, with hindsight, Olga feels that this period constituted the rise towards a definite peak around 1993, when K'Cee was playing out of his skin and *Absurd-Ditties* came out to such a good reception and did so well. But more of that later.

The early 1990s also saw Olga branching out in different areas of life, musical and otherwise. His promotion work continued – as did the consequent brushes with the law – and he also began to think about investing what money he'd managed to make from the band. Durham Wedding Cars was set up as a reaction to spotting a gap in the market for quality wedding experiences: there were various car-hire firms around – among them Red Rose Wedding Cars, run by the subject of 'What She Had With Huey' – and plenty of companies who would plan your wedding day for you, but at the time nobody was really getting it right in the Durham area and offering the perfect package. Olga recalls his involvement in that area of business with fondness:

"I'd like to think my wedding company – Durham Wedding Cars – we were the best of the lot, and we used to give a spot-on service, with champagne and all the trimmings. We learned all the bad points from the other companies, and made it a really special experience for the customers, but then I sold the company on to somebody else and moved on."

Having moved from Sunderland to Durham by this point, Olga also began to dabble in the property market. His philosophy was – and is – that even if the market suffers a minor setback and prices are inflated then drop a little, overall the trend will always be upwards. With this in mind, he bought a series of cheap houses in villages outside Durham – some of them to do up and sell quickly, perhaps living there himself while he was getting the work done, and others to rent out to families in search of a home. He still retains a small number of these properties to this day: a nice investment for any rainy days in the future.

The band did 69 gigs in 1991, a healthy number, embracing Holland, Germany, Czechoslovakia, Austria, Switzerland, France, Spain and a show in Sweden in the spring and summer, before heading to Japan again – this time in September – for 6 shows there. This trip to Japan was significant in that it supplied the footage for what became the *Live in Japan* video that Receiver brought out the next year. Whilst noting that the audio track to this video is not ideal, and that the lighting is rather dark, Olga still says that it's a worthwhile document capturing a trio that was, by this stage, rocking effortlessly on stage.

1992 provided time and space for a bit of a rest from touring, couched as it was between two very busy years on the road. The band did only 5 shows that year: one in France and four in California. But the main focus that year was getting material together for another new album. Olga knew that he had it within him to write a blockbuster and make sure it was properly produced, but the previous few recordings had all suffered in some way, whether through lack of time, weakness of certain songs or deficiencies in the production arrangements (again, often linked to time, as well as the inevitable evil of money). As such, Olga spent a good part of the year thinking about and bringing together the album that would become *Absurd-Ditties*, delving deep into his reservoir of ideas and fishing out themes involving what we identified elsewhere in this book as the classic mix of soap operas, TV celebrities, trouble with women and colourful characters from the northeast.

Whilst he was locked away in his bedroom in Durham plotting his masterpiece, Olga watched the release in March 1992 of *The Collection*, an album with which he's utterly nonplussed. Whilst it offers the fan looking for an overview of the band a decent range of songs, Olga had nothing to do with the choice of songs and the artwork and so on, so it's a release about which he couldn't get particularly excited.

On to 1993 and, as alluded to earlier, this was the year when, in Olga's opinion, the band were really on a roll. The Absurd World tour took up the period between March and July, and took in most of continental Europe and a short Japanese leg in April. I was curious why the USA hadn't been included this time:

> "America's a bit different from other countries in this respect. Europe is normally scheduled to coincide with a release, more or less the same time as the release; it's the same with Japan, although Japan's usually a month or so *after* the release. We didn't have an American record deal, so it's usually just at whatever time suits. That year there was no obvious slot really."

This tour also provided what was to be the band's last UK show (ever?), at New Cross in south London on 8 May. I don't want to harp on about the not-playing-in-the-UK thing, but ask Olga nevertheless how the gig came about after their absence from the British stage for six years:

> "I remember that well. It was a really good gig – we played well. There were 2 reasons why we did it: firstly, the record company were begging us to do an English gig – actually, they were saying, 'why not do an English gig?' rather than

trying to force us – and we also thought we were ready. We had the bassist K'Cee in the group, we'd just completed half a huge European tour, which was about 7 weeks or something, and we were going to do another huge half, with Big Boy Tomato supporting, who were an excellent band. So we were on the ball and playing well, so we thought, 'why not?' We did the gig, then set off the following day to central Europe somewhere. It was just a kind of in-the-middle thing. We might do it again, you never know."

How tantalising is that? Meanwhile, *Absurd-Ditties* was released, and even after waiting his customary month or two and *then* looking back at the record and judging objectively whether it was any good, Olga remained thrilled. It's such a landmark in the band's recording history that I ask Olga to think back to that period and put us in the picture as to what exactly went right with that album:

"Well firstly, the production on that album is fantastic, compared with the crap I'd done on the other ones, but there were a few different things. I used a Les Paul for left and right speaker whereas I used to use a Telecaster and a Les Paul, one for each, and that worked really well. We used a few sample drums, although it actually was the drummer playing. It all worked really well, but I wasn't really aware of that until maybe 2 or 3 months later – it just sounded like any other album to me. I didn't realise that the 'Toccata' thing, and 'Drooling Banjos', and 'My Wife's a Psychopath' and 'Sod the Neighbours' had turned out to be really good. I remember Danny from The Wildhearts wearing a t-shirt from that time on their 'Superpunch' video, which I was really proud about. But because I was so closely involved, I couldn't tell initially whether it was going to be good or bad."

I sense Olga is on a roll with this one, so I sit back, swig my beer (not sure how many pints we've had by this stage) and lap up his proud memories:

"I like 'Alec's Gone' too, and that became a stage favourite after a while. 'Sod the Neighbours' we might be doing on the next tour. We'll definitely be doing 'Alec's Gone'. But, as I say, we still didn't know, at the time of recording, whether they were going to be good, bad or average. I mean 'Sod the Neighbours' I wrote in one afternoon, because I was stuck for one more song for the album. There you go. I liked Alec's character, but a song is a song – it's just the way it goes. Fortunately for Alec [Olga laughs] it's worked out best for him that he went."

I mentioned above Olga's habit of waiting a couple of months after the release of an album and only then sitting down to decide whether it's any good. But can he tell us a bit about the emotion of finishing an album for which he has high hopes. What does he feel when he's leaving the studio once it's all over? Excitement? Sadness? Expectation?

"Do you know what? In 1993 after we finished *Absurd-Ditties* – which we thought was mega – there was nobody left in the studio apart from me and the engineer doing the mixing (of course the drums and the bass and backing vocals had all been done earlier). We finished quite late, then I drove back from Hull through the countryside, and I was bawling with tears, because that was the end of it, and I thought there was nobody there to tell me that it was great or bad – I just didn't know. But I've thought every album had been either great or all right, until 6 or 7 weeks later, when you realise 'that's crap', or 'that's really good'. I did think *Absurd-Ditties* and the first album were really good – unfortunately, all the others were either average or crap."

On the website, Olga mentions that *Absurd-Ditties* is one of the few Toy Dolls albums he's happy to listen to with any frequency. It occurs to me to ask what he thinks generally about the concept of an artist listening to his or her own music:

"Generally, it's not very healthy, but it can be OK. Do you

know, I listened to that guy Prince, and a lot of his ideas – things he deals with – seem to be a little bit like mine. But he's a million times better than I could ever be, but still comparatively the same kind of things. And I thought, 'wow.' And I'm not really a fan of the guy at all, but everything he was saying I could relate to. Yeah, I can listen to my stuff – if you listen to it loud enough you can convince yourself it's good, but if the volume is just average, you realize that some of it is good, but some of it is crap. It's best not to listen to too many poor albums, otherwise when you're writing, you start being influenced by your poor albums. Sometimes you can think up an idea or a rhythm for a new song, and think, 'wow, that's really good,' then you realise it's actually the second chorus from the third song on the previous album. So it's best to listen to other bands' albums, though there's nothing wrong with listening to your own stuff as well, if it's a decent one, and you can see what the good points and bad points are on that album. If I have to choose a good album of ours to listen to, the choice is narrowed down to one, or maybe 2."

While we're on the subject of favourite music, with his vision of the whole songwriting process, and his intimate knowledge of the songs as they're being crafted and as they reach completion, is it possible to predict which of them will turn out to be stage favourites, or is that something that just happens against all logic?

"No way in a million years. You occasionally get a little bit of an idea, maybe with something like 'Alec's Gone' – I kind of guessed there – and I guessed and hoped that 'Dougy Giro' might be, and 'Fisticuffs'. But guessing and hoping is different from actually knowing. I was surprised that 'Glenda' turned out to be a stage favourite, but happy – we really like it, and we'll be doing it on the next tour. But whichever songs the audience might like, there's also the flip side of songs that we really like doing on stage. Playing live is hard work – especially the fast guitar songs – so anything that sounds fast as hell but is easier to play is great for the stage. 'Yul Brynner', for example, is nothing for me, and the drummer's doing all the work."

Yul Brynner? How fortuitous that Olga should mention him now! Here comes a chapter devoted to the line-up of famous people sprinkled across 25 years of The Toy Dolls' songs, covering sports stars, TV presenters, all sorts of people, and we'll maybe even make reference to a member of the British royal family. We'll just have to wait and see.

Olga's Inspirations

6. Famous People

Whether we like it or not, the concept of celebrity is with us to stay. Our TV screens and newspapers are filled with idle gossip involving footballers, actors, singers and women whose contribution to popular culture is to boast an impressive pair of breasts. Many ordinary people strive to achieve fame – often via wanky TV programmes such as *Pop Idol*, *Big Brother*, *Fame Academy* and *Stars in Their Eyes* – and others have become famous or notorious through no fault of their own, perhaps by being in the wrong place at the wrong time.

As social commentators and observers of life *par excellence*, The Toy Dolls have felt it their duty to write songs about – or, in some cases, merely mentioning – a wide range of the A-list, B-list, Z-list and indeed listless celebrities who have made the headlines over the last 25 years. This section discusses a dozen or more such songs and offers Olga's thoughts on each.

We've all had a day off work or school and found ourselves mesmerised by the phenomenon of breakfast TV. We may switch it on to get the morning news, or to check the weather for the rest of the day, but we invariably find that if we persist for more than 7 minutes, we're hooked. It's a dangerous time of the day. So long as there's a kettle within each reach, we can easily fill four hours being educated about a broad gamut of issues whose common denominator is the term 'banal shite'.

What we forget is that this branch of TV is not much

more than 20 years old. Before it was invented, we must have been far less irritable – though perhaps also less educated – individuals. Maybe we listened to the radio in the mornings. I can't remember. But I do remember the first real attempt on British television to bring breakfast TV, and its colourful presenters, into our homes. One of the first batch to emerge was Anne Diamond, whose lurid woolly jumpers and perma-smile on the show *TV-AM* aimed to charm us and set us up for a happy day ahead.

Anne Diamond was harmless enough, and her career progressed fluently as she won the hearts of the British public with her 'girl next door' image. But up in Sunderland, anger was bubbling. "I didn't like her then, and I cannot stand her now," says Olga. "She just wasn't TV material." But it would have been a bit unfair just to write a song about simply not liking her – what he needed was some incident: some bit of scandal he could get his teeth into. He bided his time, and before long, the UK tabloid press had given him all the ammunition he needed: 'Nobody can believe what the Sun's gone and written,' screams the first line of the song 'A Diamond' from the *Bare Faced Cheek* album.

Nowadays, celebrities have babies all the time, especially female celebrities. A good percentage of these infants are born out of wedlock, and often to parents whose marital circumstances are complicated, to put it mildly. But to get pregnant by a man who was married to someone else, after cultivating a wholesome, goody-goody image on TV, was not something you would dare to attempt in the 1980s in the UK ... unless you were Anne Diamond, that is. Anne had the baby, was vilified by the British press and public, lost her job, then tragically lost the baby to sudden infant death syndrome soon after its birth.

There's a chance that the song title 'A Diamond' might have been deliberately formatted in the hope that any *TV-AM* lackey who happened to be scanning the back of the CD cover may have assumed it to be about a precious mineral. At the very least, we would imagine the band to have been a bit nervous about claiming in the song that Ms Diamond had 'been putting herself about,' and referring to her as a 'scrubber ... dodgy boiler ... dirty Jezebel.' Olga recalls no such concerns:

> "No, we're lucky because it's so underground, on such a small scale, at such a low level, that you can get away with lots of things. But also, the thing is I'm so stubborn. If somebody says, 'you're gonna get sued,' I think, 'tough, let me get on with it,' you know? I could have changed her name to Vanessa Diamond, or whatever, but if you're singing about the real people, you just sing so much better."

As always in The Toy Dolls' philosophy, it's all about being true to yourself and doing exactly what you want.

Other celebrities mentioned in the song are the presenter Nick Kelly and newsreader Gordon Honeycombe (who had, for many years, anchored the British ITV evening news with such an unsmiling, austere face, that many observers doubted he would have the charisma to form part of the happy-clappy, cardigans-and-coffee-mugs breakfast TV team. Russell Grant was (and, unfortunately, still is) a grossly overweight and irksome 'expert' in the field of horoscopes, and his job was to talk twaddle to the British public about what fate was likely to befall them later that day. The one time he got anything correct was when he accurate predicted I would put my boot through the TV screen into his face. Jimmy Greaves was one of English football's finest centre-forwards, who was left out of the team to face West Germany in the 1966 World Cup Final because his recent form had not been great and he'd picked up an injury. His replacement, Geoff Hurst, scored three goals in England's 4-2 victory, history was made, and a dejected Greaves spiralled into alcoholism and football punditry – the two often performed simultaneously.

Another famous footballing legend who was known to like a drink was Brian Clough, hero of the bouncy live standard 'Cloughy is a Boot Boy!' from the *Wakey Wakey* album. Just before this book went to print in September 2004, the football world was shocked to learn of Cloughy's death from stomach cancer at the age of 69. After a promising few years as a free-scoring centre-forward for Middlesbrough, Sunderland and England, Clough's career was cruelly cut short by injury. What people had not realised was that he had taken the unprecedented (in those days) step of insuring himself against such a disaster, so he emerged from his playing days financially healthy and ready to embark on a career in club management. Having succeeded at Hartlepool, Derby and Brighton (and stayed at Leeds United for an eventful six weeks), he landed the job at Nottingham Forest and set about building a squad which, as it turned out, would win him 2 European Cups within the next five years.

So all seemed well with Cloughy. We both loved and hated him because he was always rude to TV interviewers, but the frequent, frank exchanges of opinions on our TV screens also revealed another, darker secret: Cloughy was developing a strawberry-red nose, so it was clear to the British public that Cloughy was drinking heavily to cope with the pressures of the job. We were aware that he was a great manager, and we knew that his outspokenness was an essential part of his personality, but we feared that his volatility – especially if fuelled by booze – might lead to an unsavoury incident.

This arrived in 1988 when, after an important Cup game, 2 spectators ran onto the pitch and Cloughy restrained them for fear of his club being disciplined by the Football Association. His 'restraint' was perhaps a little more forceful than was strictly necessary, and the next thing we knew there was national uproar and threats of assault charges. Although Cloughy was confident that he had the moral high ground, he made a comic incident out of the matter by apologising to the fans – once they had apologised to him – and giving them each a kiss to show that there were no hard feelings.

In the song itself, the action is far more dramatic. The

atmosphere in the dressing-room is accurate enough, as the manager 'screams and yells and just because / Cloughy knows that he's the boss / Cloughy's rough and Cloughy's tough / Cloughy's barmy.' But the incident that spawned the song begins with a simple request for an autograph, and Cloughy 'nuts ... smacks ... kicks ... slaps ... thumps and cracks' the victims. Furthermore, he is 'a football hooligan,' who is 'only at his prime with his fist in yer nose.' Even for someone as volatile as Brian Clough, this is heavy going, but the language rounds off the song into something quite forceful as well as hilarious.

Although in real life there were no criminal proceedings, the latter half of the song fictionalises a courtroom scene, in which 'the judge tells Cloughy to keep calm / he's up for grievous bodily harm,' to which Cloughy replies that 'he's gonna cruc / -ify the cops when he gets out the cell.' Another classic line-split, and plenty more material to convince listeners of how batty this semi-fictional Cloughy is.

There aren't too many football references in the band's lyrics, so I asked Olga about the reason for immortalising the Brian Clough incident in a song:

> "I'm not really a football fan as such – I've got nothing against it, but I think I just saw that incident on the news and heard that Cloughy had got involved in some aggro with the 2 fans. At the time, I already had the 'Brian-Brian' thing written as part of a song, but I didn't have a reason to put it in. It's not a bad song, that one. It goes down well at gigs, as well."

The other obvious footballing focus in the band's songwriting history is 'The Memory of Nobby', from *One More Megabyte*. Nobby Stiles was a young Manchester United midfielder who had broken into the same England national team as Jimmy Greaves (see 'A Diamond', above) in time for the 1966 World Cup finals, held in England. In the final itself, Nobby is famous for three things: running and working throughout the 120 minutes of the game until his legs turned to jelly; dancing a happy but inelegant jig for the TV cameras during the post-match celebrations; and the fact that he always removed his false teeth for games, so his smile was as toothless as it was broad.

Whilst we're on the subject of sports-related mentions in Toy Dolls songs, the list is completed by four more famous figures. 'There's a Trollop up Elmwood Street' contains a catalogue of things Olga would rather do than walk up Elmwood Street and face meeting up with the trollop again, among them 'box with Frankie Bruno' and 'hitch a lift from James Hunt'. Frank Bruno (born 1961) strove for years to become world heavyweight boxing champion, a feat he eventually achieved, beating Oliver McCall on points, before losing the title to Mike Tyson. He has suffered from mental illness recently, but is still adored by the British public. James Hunt takes us further back in time. He was born in 1947, and became world Formula 1 champion in 1976, as well as appearing on the BBC's *Superstars* series and enjoying something of a playboy lifestyle. The British public loved him, despite his posh accent, until his premature death in 1993.

'Yul Brynner was a Skinhead' has a nifty comparison in the first verse, where Mr Brynner – famed across the world for his parts in a string of films, most notably *The King and I* – is compared to one Duncan Goodhew. Sports fans with long memories will recall Goodhew as being a champion British swimmer, possibly more famous for his bald head – the result of a childhood illness – than for his feats in the pool. He won an Olympic gold medal at his peak, and nowadays works full-time raising money for charity. Just as worthy an achievement was his surname providing the perfect rhyme for 'tattoo' in the song. Watch out for 'Yul' featuring in the set for the forthcoming world tour.

The song – from the *Bare Faced Cheek* album – is widely regarded as a stage favourite, although the band only played it live for a short time after its release in 1987, then abandoned it for some 15 years. The good news is that it is hoped to resurrect the song for the forthcoming 2004-05 world tour. It is not that Olga is a particular fan of the actor – he only recalls seeing *The King and I* – but he was tickled by the comic possibilities of a skinhead not qualifying to be a skinhead because he was already a skinhead, and because he didn't wear Doctor Marten shoes or sport a tattoo. Incidentally, for the benefit of non-UK fans, *The Krypton Factor* was a 1980s British TV quiz show for the highly intellectual, Silvikrin was a brand of shampoo and Mr Sheen was a furniture polish spray which claimed to 'shine umpteen things clean' (though Yul Brynner's head was not used in the original product trials).

The final sportsman to feature in Olga's lyrics is a retired horse-racing jockey by the name of Lester Piggott. A champion jockey on the British racing scene for what seemed like 200 years, and the possessor of one of the strangest voices known to mankind (and often imitated to widespread hilarity on the satirical TV programme *Spitting Image*), Piggott got himself into something of a tangle with his income tax, and was found guilty of avoidance in the late 1980s and sent to prison. Olga is not a racing fan, but again, the song 'Lester Fiddled the Tax Man' (on *Wakey Wakey*) needed to be written because it was in the news at the time and offered plenty of comic potential, to say nothing of some fabulous rhymes. There were no legal implications for The Toy Dolls, firstly because the song did not stray too far from the truth, and secondly because, once again, it is unlikely that Lester Piggott would be so cultured and discerning as to listen to a Toy Dolls album. References of note in this song include two British racecourses (Ascot and Aintree), two TV sports programmes (*World of Sport* and *Grandstand* – the former now defunct but the latter still going strong on BBC1), and Dartmoor, the high-security prison hidden away in the wilds of Devon, in southwest England.

Also in court shortly after Lester Piggott was Liverpool entertainer Ken Dodd. In a career spanning several decades, he has had a Number 1 hit (with 'Tears', in 1965) plus nearly

20 other UK hits, a string of TV shows and almost constant sell-out tours around the world. All this has brought him considerable wealth, and closer than average scrutiny by the Inland Revenue. When the case came to court, it seemed that Ken was doomed to follow Lester to jail, but bafflingly, he was found not guilty. His career has since gone from strength to strength, and he was most recently in the news for winning a stalking case against a fan. The song 'The Coppers Copt Ken's Cash', from *Fat Bob's Feet*, is quite risky in comparison to 'Lester Fiddled the Tax Man', in that Ken was proved innocent and yet is still referred to as an 'Income Tax thief … greedy pig' and the references to his avoidance of Income Tax and stashing away half a million pounds under his bed run thick and fast. Olga professes to "quite like" Ken Dodd, so again there is no personal grudge – rather, the story was making the headlines and Olga thought it would make a good song. Anyone who was not brought up on 1970s British TV will need to know that a tickling stick was Ken's trademark dusting stick with a feathery end, which he waved about for no reason; and the Diddymen were his posse of puppets, who looked a bit like Irish leprechauns and lived fictitiously in the real Liverpool suburb of Knotty Ash. I tried to contact one of the Diddymen for an interview for this book, but his mobile was switched off. For legal reasons I am unable to name him, but suffice it to say that he lives in tax exile on the Isle of Man with wads of diddymoney under his bed.

If we are suggesting that Ken Dodd was a successful singer, then we must also make fleeting reference to Simon Le Bon, lead singer of 1980s Birmingham popsters Duran Duran. Simon features briefly in 'Neville is a Nerd', as someone that Neville bullshits that he knows. I put it to Olga that it must have been irritating to have had a tribe of New Romantics weakening The Toy Dolls' monopoly on pin-up glamour in the 1980s UK music scene, but Olga was gracious in defeat: "No, to be fair, I don't remember anyone ever preferring me to Simon Le Bon, like."

In the classic 'James Bond Lives Down Our Street' – which fictionalises a version of James Bond living in Sunderland and doing everyday things like catching the number 32 bus, as well as carrying a gun, using a helicopter and getting involved in espionage – we'd expect to see reference to various real James Bonds, and these are present in the shape of Sean Connery and Roger Moore. But a few lines from the end, we hear it said that the Bond figure 'went to school with Russell Harty'. This was used just to create a decent rhyme, but Russell Harty did exist. He was a British cultural commentator and TV presenter, famous for his nasal voice and the banality of his jackets. He died in the 1980s.

Another celebrity to have died, and to feature on a Toy Dolls track – though this time in a far more major, and very sad, fashion – is Rod Hull. Rod became popular in the late 1970s (and then massive in the 1980s) as a TV ventriloquist whose arm was up the arse of the self-explanatory puppet Emu, who caused chaos wherever the pair went. After the duo's popularity had peaked, they went into rapid decline, to the extent that, by the mid-1990s, Rod had lost most of his assets and was living in a modest house and struggling to pay the bills. On the night of Manchester United's Champions League triumph in Barcelona in 1999, Rod had climbed up onto his house roof to adjust the TV aerial so that he could watch the match, and he lost his footing and fell to his death.

'No-one Knew the Real Emu', from *Our Last Album?*, looks at how Emu's downfall from popularity – a form of 'death' in one sense – led to an unhappy life for Rod. Rod's death then deprived the nation of one of its best-loved characters, and meant that the true story behind the real Emu, the driving force of the pair, would go with him to the grave.

The final celebrity worthy of mention in this section is Jimmy Saville, star of the tune 'When You're Jimmy Saville' from *Absurd-Ditties*. Saville began his working life as a professional wrestler (in the old-fashioned British sense – none of your WWF stuff that you get nowadays) and a radio

DJ, forming part of the founding team of BBC Radio 1 and spinning the station's first ever disc – 'Flowers in the Rain' by The Move – in 1967. He then went on to star on a TV programme called *Jim'll Fix It*, where, despite his legendary hatred of children, he made children's dreams come true. He is perhaps most famous for having bleached hair – he decided on white after trying all sorts of colours and styles in his younger years, including tartan – and for running marathons and undertaking all sorts of other sponsored events in aid of charity. Recently, however, some alleged darker sides of his character have emerged in the UK media, regarding his supposed involvement with teenage girls and his worship of his dead mother and her untouched bedroom and wardrobe. Olga quite likes Jimmy Saville, and it was precisely Saville's excessive willingness to get involved in so many marathons that brought on the fictional idea of getting pissed off with being so available and charitable.

Anyone turning to this section in the hope of finding sexual scandal involving members of the British royal family (or, more specifically, Prince Charles's girlfriend) will, alas, be unlucky. 'Caught it off Camilla', also from 2004's *Our Last Album?*, and introduced by a brilliant bit of 'Jaws' music, does not refer to Camilla Parker-Bowles – that would have been an epic adventure for Olga to write a song about! If you're wondering about the 'it', then yes, it does refer to a sexually transmitted decease, but if you had in mind that the song was the story of Olga's fling with that Camilla, then you're wrong. It was a different Camilla – that's all I'm at liberty to say about her – and the recipient of the genital upset was not Olga, but it was a member of his family. I push him further. No, it wasn't Ernie either. It was a more distant relative, but one who'll be perfectly aware of his immortalisation as soon as he hears the lyrics. Enough said.

History 1994-1996

Making History

After the euphoria of 1993 – with the triple delights of the Absurd World tour, the commercial, critical and creative success of *Absurd-Ditties*, and the gelling of the trio into a tight, powerful music unit – 1994 provided time for a break from touring and recording. The lads went about their business, and enjoyed spending time with family and friends, without having to jump on a plane or into a van and head off into the sunset. Following the physical and mental exertions of such a punishing live schedule, K'Cee began to withdraw a bit from the band, and revealed that, although he was happy to do all the recording required of him and a certain amount of touring, he was unable to commit to the band full-time in the longer term. This came as a blow to Olga, but it was also an inevitable reminder that touring the world and putting other aspects of your life on hold is a big ask, a major commitment.

Still based in Durham, Olga realised shortly into 1994 that we would need to start thinking about another album, so he decided to use the whole calendar year to try and prepare material that could match or improve on the standard set with *Absurd-Ditties*. Ideas were slow to emerge initially, but by setting out a structure that would take in the traditional components of soap opera, local people, love-torn angst and a couple of unpredictable cover versions, Olga soon found that the album was beginning to take shape. Without a tour to distract his attention, he found this one of the most intense periods of songwriting he had experienced. Ideas would come to him at the weirdest times, and in the interests of capitalising on his moments of clarity and insight, he had to act quickly to make sure the ideas weren't lost:

> "Yeah, I could never tell when an idea was going to occur to me. That album was typical of the process, really. I usually write best in the spare bedroom, not because it's necessarily an ideal place, but it's where the tape-recorder and other equipment is. I can sit in the bedroom all day long and think of nothing, then go in the bath because I'm so sick of not thinking of anything, and I instantly think of something. I get out of the bath, switch the recorder on... Aye, it happens all the time, and it's so frightening, that sometimes when I go in the bath, I deliberately, consciously try not to think about thinking about anything to do with the album, because I know I'm going to think of something and I'll have to get out of the bath. It happens every time. And I have to react, because I know that if I don't, I'll forget about it. I've got no flippin' choice."

He also remembers doing very little drinking during that year. For many songwriters, alcohol can be just the stimulant they need, and can even help to dredge up melancholy, depressive feelings or, conversely, evoke massive highs to write about. But for Olga, mental sharpness is key:

> "This idea of getting pissed and relaxing and that kind of thing, I cannot write like that, or perform, or rehearse. I love getting pissed, it's what I want to do, but *after* the job's done. I have to be completely alert, and I can't be that way if I've had any kind of drink – that's just me, personally. And I like to be in England to write my kind of music, rather than being in some sort of hot place. Then if you think about drinking before a gig, it's different for everyone. If I were only singing with a band, I'd have 20 pints, because I just wouldn't care – you can do what you like, and there's not so much tension, or anxious nerves. But with this band, playing guitar as well as singing, I'll maybe have a quarter

of a pint. I'm so anxious. I need to be so sharp, doing all the downstrokes and that kind of thing. But out of preference I'd have 6 pints, and have loads of pints on the stage – that would be fantastic, if it was just singing, with no precise musical playing to be concerned about. You still have to get it right, of course."

The mention of preferring to write songs in England leads me to ask about the notion of writing songs on the road. You also read of songwriters who'll use experiences gained around the world as the basis for future songs, and some even take a guitar, notebook and tape-recorder with them on the tour bus, to make sure no ideas are missed. It strikes me that there's also the danger, for Olga, that if he listens to too much material of other bands to relax, he'll end up being overly influenced by what he's heard and what's remained lodged in his subconscious:

"I set out not to think about writing a song when I'm on tour, but if one comes to me, that's fine. That's a fair point about getting influenced, but I don't really have time to listen to music anyway. Touring is really a case of soundcheck, gig, sleep; soundcheck, gig, sleep. So there's not much time for anything else, though of course being in the band is an activity in itself. It's hard. But I don't think I've ever written anything on the road. But there again, that's just me. If I was playing with a different band, doing nothing else but playing my little part, and not having to sort out the hotels and petrol and the t-shirts and so on, I might think differently."

As the months went by, the album was gradually completed and given the title of *Orcastrated*, another decent punning title, this time on the orchestration of pieces of music, but perhaps one that holds hidden depths?

"I should have been castrated for producing the album – that's the only hidden secret. My brother Ernie thought of that album title, and the *Absurd-Ditties* one, which was a good title. We got the intro music from the band Cruella de Vil. We had really high hopes for that album, because of the *Absurd-Ditties* thing doing so well, but apart from 'Poltergeist in the Pantry', it was crap."

Its release in early 1995 saw brisk sales, as many people had been so impressed with the previous album that they bought this one expecting more of the same. Generally, fans weren't disappointed, though of course it proved far harder to tease anything positive out of Olga. He is slightly more positive, however, about the band's single released at the same time, 'Lazy Sunday Afternoon', sung excellently by Marty both on the record and many times on stage. His only reservation is that it sounds a little too much like the original, Small Faces version. How did it come about? I know that Olga was a big fan of both The Small Faces and The Kinks, so was the song a straightforward tribute?

"I love The Small Faces – unbelievable – Steve Marriott and all that kind of thing. I love it. We were doing that live, just as a filler, something for the drummer to sing, and then we decided to put it on the album, coz he was singing it quite well really. That was it. The Kinks were also a great band, in my opinion. We supported them in about 1990 in Zurich, and it was a weird gig, coz there were 14,000 or 15,000 people all there to see them, and 3,000 to see us, but they were so boisterous, shouting for us all the way through The Kinks' set, which was enough to spoil it. I wish they hadn't, but it was weird. I never actually got to talk to Ray Davies – he was doing interviews and so on. But we played a good gig, and it went down really well. They were fantastic of course, but we supported them well. They did a medley of 'You've Really Got Me' and so on, and when you do medleys it makes it look as if the songs are not worthy of being sung by themselves, you know? That spoiled it a bit for me, but I still love them."

With high hopes for *Orcastrated* and refreshed after a year without taking to the road, the band plotted their touring schedule for 1995, the bulk of which was to be made up of a European leg from March to June, then a first experience of Argentina and a welcome return to Brazil for four nights. The touring seemed to have settled down now into something of a rhythm. Was Olga happy with this?

> "Yeah, I think so. It was starting to become once every 2 years. Lots of bands tour every year, and we were doing major tours every 2 years. I'm comfortable with that. I discipline myself. If you're going to work, then you've just got to get on with it. If you're in a 9-5 job, you work from 9 to 5. I get physically tired touring, but not so much mentally, and by the time the tour comes around, I've done my training and I'm ready. You can always relax afterwards."

The tour went very well – with the Argentine audience particularly happy to have been included on the schedule for the first time – and the lads were able to pick up a couple of extra shows in Switzerland later in the year. Marty was still happy to remain behind the drums, but K'Cee still had reservations about continuing long-term. He thought long and hard about what to do, and ultimately decided that the 1996 tour – in effect only seven nights in Japan in January – would be his last, and he left the band amicably at that point.

Despite K'Cee's predicament, the Japanese dates went well, and consolidated the band's presence in that country. Olga noted that, by now, the audience was changing from almost exclusively female to nearly half male, which was probably a good situation to be in, in the greater scheme of things. His popularity as charismatic front man remained strong, and it was clear that Japanese bands were starting to become influenced by The Toy Dolls – an example being Lolita No. 18, who were destined to have a close working relationship with the band a couple of years later.

Into February, Olga sat down to rake over initial ideas he'd been having for some new songs for the planned 1997 album. One day, he got a phone call from the record company, who suggested it might be about time the band put out an official 'best of' album, one that had full input from Olga and involved comprehensive sleeve notes, photos and other information. Olga immediately thought this was a great idea, and set about picking out which songs he thought should be included. But across the world of Toy Dolls fandom, there was widespread unease. Many of us had already been through the nerves in 1983 of learning that Stiff Little Fingers were releasing a 'best of' album – *All the Best* – amid rumours of an impending split, which indeed proved to be the case. Surely this couldn't now happen to our beloved Toy Dolls? Were there any thoughts at that point of splitting up?

> "No. We never thought about splitting up, certainly not at that stage, anyway. No, there was nothing to be read into bringing the *History* out in that sense. The record company suggested it and we thought, 'why not?' It was a good idea and a decent package."

The relief was palpable when Olga confirmed that the band were to carry on business as usual. Why, he argued, would he be spending so much of the current year writing new material if the band were about to fold? No, we could all relax and look forward to a new album and a massive world tour in 1997. We took a collective deep breath and looked forward with our fingers and all other crossable parts crossed.

The release of this ultimate compilation was never intended to be the first of two such packages, which was why it was simply entitled *The History 1979-96*, rather than *History Part 1*, which fans habitually call it to distinguish it from the later *Part 2*. All very confusing. What is certain is that *The History* is a superb document, beautifully packaged and with pretty much all the top tunes you could have hoped for at that stage of the band's career. Covering seventeen years of releases – singles and favourite album tracks alike – it pushes all the right buttons for most fans. It's inevitable on an album of this type that some people's favourites will have been missed off, but I think Olga correctly read the minds of the majority of fans (which may have overlapped in no small measure with his own predilections) in pinpointing the final choices.

These choices contrasted dramatically with the ones Olga had to make two years later when the *History Part 2* was launched. This was a far more mercenary – though not entirely cynical – venture, and was aimed principally at diehard fans who would buy pretty much anything. As Olga puts it:

> "All the best songs had been used up in the first *History*, so *Part 2* was really just everything that was left. It had a few nice tunes on it, but basically it was crap. If I'd known there were going to be 2 albums in the first place, I would have arranged them completely differently. If you're told it's just going to be one, you choose everything that represents the best of you. Then if a second one emerges, then obviously it's a case of what's left."

Whatever his opinions in retrospect, Olga finished 1996 with two missions in mind: to find a new bassist to replace K'Cee, and to ensure that 1997's album, *One More Megabyte*, became a success. He could also take a certain satisfaction (though whether he allowed himself to do so is a different matter altogether) in the presence on the market of a full history of his songwriting gems accumulated over 17 years of The Toy Dolls. It must be one of the biggest highs achievable by a songwriter: to see their work compiled in such a lavish, comprehensive fashion, and to learn that fans are going out and buying this compilation – and all his other work, for that matter – by the shed-load.

Eagle-eyed fans will have noted that not many of Olga's pining 'infatuation' – I hesitate to say 'love' – songs are included on the *History* album. It's tempting to suspect that an artist wouldn't want to lay his soul bare for a second time if such a song had already been released, but in fact, Olga simply thinks that his songs of an emotional persuasion don't rank among his better tunes. Either way, there's no escape: here comes a chapter looking at our main man's tangles and escapades with the female of the species.

Olga's Inspirations

7. Crazy Little Thing Called Love

"Love's a big thing. People get mixed up between being in love – infatuated if you want to call it that – and loving someone, which is more of the whole package. I mean, you can fall in love with someone, just like that, but obviously you don't love them coz you don't know them. You can't love someone you don't know. So I will call the 'in love' thing 'infatuation' – same kind of thing. I've been infatuated numerous times, and confused it with loving someone, or trying to convince myself that I love that person. So yeah, it plays a big part in a lot of my songs, the love theme."

Olga's words set the tone for a whole chapter about the role his relationships (and 'nearly relationships') with women have played in The Toy Dolls' songs, from 'She Goes to Fino's' right through to the present day. They also suggest to us that, with the benefit of hindsight, he's quite well clued up on what it was he was experiencing each time he met a female who took his fancy. 'Infatuation' is a word he uses quite a lot as we chat about this aspect of his music, but does he believe in true love or, at least, in its inclusion in Toy Dolls songs? It's noticeable that the word 'love' doesn't feature in many songs; certainly not to suggest that Olga 'loves' anyone in his music.

"I do pine for women in the songs, but I don't like soppy songs as such, and it would never occur to me to write 'I love you, baby' in a song – maybe 'darling, I loathe you', yes! I'm not a big fan of soppy lyrics. For example, take the song 'Unbreak My Heart' – that makes me want to puke."

That's nice and clear, then. So how does he stand on the falling-in-love-and-getting-married issue? There seems to be overwhelming evidence, in songs like 'Up the Garden Path' and 'Cheerio and Toddle Pip', that he might not be entirely comfortable with what happens to blokes who get trapped into a relationship that's not working, or that changes them beyond recognition. I ask him about this issue that seems to have affected so many of his mates from the punk scene in Sunderland, and his reply is quite striking in its clarity:

"Surely the punk thing is about doing exactly what you want to do, regardless. These people who get married and have kids … having kids is something I would never do, because I don't want to do it. People who have kids and don't want them, they're massive idiots. If they want them, that's fine; it's the same as me not wanting them and not having them. Most of these people we sing about, they're getting married and having kids and they never wanted this in the first place. This business of getting trapped, it's absolutely ridiculous."

Against this backdrop, we proceed through the catalogue of songs involving girls, relationships or both. The songs seem to divide into two sub-categories: firstly, there are those about girls slightly out of Olga's reach, or who aren't interested in him, despite the infatuation he's experiencing. Then there are songs about how a relationship has got started but has then turned sour or, at least, started to create problems. In either scenario, Olga produces some of his finest lyrical output, and brings to mind the atmosphere of some of the early Buzzcocks songs.

As mentioned earlier, Olga's first real girlfriend, Angela, provided the inspiration for several of the initial Toy Dolls songs. As well as 'Tommy Kowey's Car' and 'She Goes to Fino's', which are analysed elsewhere in the book, she's also the star of 'She's a Worky Ticket'. For background, a 'worky ticket' is someone who winds you up, pushing your powers of tolerance to the limit. Olga says it never occurred to him at the time that anyone could possibly have a problem understanding such vocabulary (but perhaps he never imagined the band would ever get such a global fanbase!). He just wrote the song and they got on with it. So did the incidents in the song really take place?

> "Aye, we were in the cinema in Sunderland, down High Street – not the Odeon, somewhere else, I think – and I went over to the usherette (ha! That's something you don't see nowadays!) and got the only type of King Cone [ice cream] they had left, which wasn't a chocolate one, obviously. Then I went to the shops for the Lambert & Butler, and she shouted at me when I got back, that was true. Also, I was really depressed at the time, so I saved up loads of money and got her a watch, but it was too big, so I took it down the washhouse to try and alter the size, and got a flippin' mallet and smashed it to bits, and I was trying to fix it so that it would fit her!"

The line in the chorus, that she 'leaves me standing in the rain and freezing in the snow', ties in nicely with the image created in 'Queen Alexandra Road...', another Angela song discussed in the Sunderland and Durham Places chapter.

'My Girlfriend's Dad's a Vicar' and 'Bless You My Son' combine on *A Far Out Disc* (and on the *Tokyo* live album) to cover an improbable theme for a punk band to be singing about. It was tempting, when these songs were released, to think that this was just a flight of fancy, but in fact the girlfriend was once again Angela, and her father was involved with religious work. He wasn't strictly a vicar (he was a pastor at Burn Park Church in Sunderland), and the cath-e-dral mentioned is not the monumental Norman edifice in Durham, but Olga thought that the songs would benefit from being made a lot more melodramatic. The lines in 'Bless You My Son', that Olga should 'get out of her life', and 'there'll be another girl', are not verbatim statements made by the pastor, but they are certainly believable sentiments, as it must be any parent's nightmare to see their well-brought-up daughter associating with the singer in a local punk band (even one as pleasant and sincere as Olga).

'My Girlfriend's Dad's a Vicar' immediately became a singalong anthem, worthy of inclusion on the *Tokyo* disc, and benefits from nifty guitar octaves at the end, representing church bells ringing out. But 'Bless You My Son' is probably more popular with fans, possibly because of the change in tempo between the almost spoken verses and the bouncy chorus, and possibly also on account of the superb lyrics. The song wins the Toy Dolls prize as the song with the most (and the best) rhyming syllable splits – there are no fewer than five classics for us to feast our ears on: (1) You tell me I'm not good e- / nough for you, what can I do?; (2) I got so sick I told a vic- / ar her dad, I must be mad; (3) You always said you wanted a stead- / y boyfriend, now don't pretend; (4) I took the path up to the cath- / edral where he stood there; (5) I never thought, that I would be court- / ing with you, but it's true.

Also worth a mention here is the wordplay following the sneeze to introduce 'Bless You My Son', where 'Bless you' is both something said by a vicar in giving someone a blessing, and also a reaction to a sneeze. The sneeze itself is the theme of the previous song on *A Far Out Disc*, 'You and a Box of Handkerchiefs', where much is made of the pun of 'atishyoo' / 'it's you' / 'a tissue' in the middle of what comes dangerously close to being a love song. It's all very clever lyrically.

The 1983 single 'Cheerio and Toodle Pip' is a song that crystallises Olga's disregard for mates getting trapped into relationships or marriages which really won't suit them. The song is pretty well unique in The Toy Dolls' back catalogue, in that it is co-written (by Olga and Bonny Baz). Baz had just joined the band, and had some great ideas for songs, so they sat down and wrote the song together in an attempt to make

Baz feel welcome and a real part of the group. Lyrically, it deals partly with Olga and partly with Bonny Baz's then girlfriend (whom Olga saw recently at one of Baz's gigs with The Stranglers, with whom he now plays). The misdemeanours mentioned – which were "sort of true" – range in seriousness from the fairly innocuous dressing up of the boyfriend in a tie, through the medium-sized sin of talking about weddings and babies' things, to the unforgivable transgression of sending him out for fish and chips during *Coronation Street*. The B-side, 'H.O.', with its nifty bass riff and tight harmonies, tells the story of a girl called Helen (her initials form the title, but we're not in the habit of giving out surnames unless we have to!) from the dim, distant, murky folds of Olga's past. She was clearly fiery stuff, but it's anyone's guess whether she's aware of her immortality on the back of a Toy Dolls single.

There's a fairly light-hearted study of holiday jealousy running through the track 'I've Had Enough o' Magaluf' from *Anniversary Anthems*. Olga recalls arriving there for a holiday with his girlfriend of the time, Joanne, and whilst the up-side was that the title and lyrics came to him very quickly, the negative side was that they were inspired by his girlfriend playing up to the attentions of Spanish waiters and tourists round the hotel. For someone as focused and – as he admits himself – obsessed and obsessive as Olga, there is bound to be room for some envy and possessiveness in his character make-up. To counter any negative vibes we may encounter in listening to the song, all we need to do is concentrate on the alpha quality of the lyrics, especially the rhymes and the slang. Several mates of mine have commented that they consider Olga to be at his best lyrically when the theme he's dealing with is a negative one, and there may just be an element of truth in this.

Considerably darker in tone are a series of songs over the years in which we see Olga reaching the depths of despair. These range from the very blue 'Griefsville', which was the B-side of 1985's 'James Bond Lives Down Our Street' single, through the slightly angrier title track of 1987's *Bare Faced Cheek* album, 'Do You Want to Finish...Or What?!' (which was about a mixture of various women) from *A Far Out Disc*, and 'She's a Leech' from *One More Megabyte*, to the classically unambiguous 'My Baby is a Battleaxe' on *Anniversary Anthems* and 'My Wife's a Psychopath' from *Absurd-Ditties*. The last three of these all deal with the same person. Let's look at one of them for context.

'My Wife's a Psychopath' is typical of the branch of Toy Dolls relationship songs in which things start off okay then degenerate into hell. In this case, in the 1987-88 period, Olga was living in Ashbrooke, Sunderland, with a Japanese girlfriend (not a wife, as suggested in the title – he's never been married) whom he had met as she was a fan of the band. The relationship began well, but soon the girl became clingy (to put it mildly), and began to show signs of being insecure, psychotic and generally unstable. Olga appreciates how hard it must have been to leave Nagoya for England – not even for London, where at least there is a sizeable Japanese community, but for Sunderland, where, at the time, there was next to none. The relationship fell apart after about 8 months, and she went back to Japan, where she's since become happily married and has children, and where Olga has seen her since. On a lighter note, Olga was very happy with the song that came out of the whole episode, although a night out on the beer with members of The Vibrators revealed their feeling that it was "the craziest song in the world."

Not dissimilarly, there's a song on the new album called 'Cheatin' Chick from China'. Again, it has not been possible to get hold of the full lyrics, but I can confirm that the song refers to Olga's 1989 relationship with the Chinese girl from Hong Kong, who was one of the factors behind his nervous breakdown that year. I did get hold of a tiny snippet of the lyrics, with which we can whet our appetites: Olga reveals that he is actually a bit out of order stating that she swindled him out of ten thousand pounds. If his memory serves him correctly (and it usually does), the sum involved was ten pounds. But where would we be in life without a bit of melodrama and timely exaggeration?

On the subject of feeling frustrated or depressed after a relationship has turned sour or has not started in the first place, is there someone nameless in Sunderland who drowns his lovesickness with the cheap, fizzy wine known as Lambrusco? It probably surprises nobody to learn that the object of the track 'The Lambrusco Kid' (on *Idle Gossip*) was Olga himself, but it might come as a shock to us to realise that Olga was well into his 20s before he started drinking alcohol "properly". During his teens he hadn't bothered, instead concentrating his time, his energy and what little money he had on making progress with his bands. However, he did eventually succumb, and the song is a memorable paean to the state we've all been in at one time or another, when our love lives aren't going well and we reach for a bottle to make the problems disappear.

Incidentally, the South American band The Lambrusco Kids are indeed named after this song. Olga met them after the Dickies gig at Morecambe, and describes them as "lovely guys". A big hello if any of them are reading this...

The chief reason for much of Olga's early forays into drinking was the famous Kendra – "a sweet, pretty teenager" – from Durham. This was a relationship that never happened, but which would surely have had a profound effect on the band's music if it had. As we learn in the song 'Olga I Cannot' – which has one of the finest spoken intros of the entire Toy Dolls oeuvre, and where the role of Kendra's mam on the phone is played by the wife of Guardian Studios guru Terry Gavighan – he met her early in 1985 at the Ramside Hall, at a hairdressing demonstration organised by the Raffles Hair Design Centre in Durham (she was a hairdresser, and Olga was booked to do a turn with 'Nellie' as the event's cabaret). Rather than a pub, the Ramside Hall is actually a kind of country house-cum-restaurant-cum-bar, situated just off the main road between Durham and Sunderland, but it was indeed the backdrop for the beginning of possibly the biggest unfulfilled infatuation of Olga's adult life.

Unable to take the hint that she was flattered but fundamentally uninterested, Olga persisted with his quest, getting Kendra's phone number and subjecting her and her family (including a member who has two Toy Dolls songs written about him – see the chapter on Cover Versions for details) to a barrage of calls. The song catalogues not only the fact that Kendra had a boyfriend (later immortalised in 'I'll Get Even With Steven (Steve is Tender)' on *Idle Gossip*), but also the fact that Olga was driving around in those days in a Rolls-Royce. This is absolutely true – the car belonged to Olga's wedding hire business. Even faced with such opulence, Kendra was still unwilling to be swayed, so Olga moved on to higher-level tactics to win her affections, which are not recorded in the song.

One of the most famous stories is that Olga heard Kendra had a cold, so he sent a taxi full of medicine round to her house to make her feel better. We laugh briefly about this, and I persuade Olga to delve deep and pull out a catalogue of other Kendra-inspired, crazily romantic episodes:

"Ah, I've done some mad things. The craziest thing I ever did was arranging a tank to go around, from the flippin' Territorial Army, to impress her. Then I went to Spain to try and find her on her holidays in Lloret, and I went round every single hotel, before I found her in the end. She knew I was just a flippin' obsessive crazy stalker really. I was always getting infatuated by girls like that."

We want more.

"Ah, the whole thing just got ridiculous. I organized Securicor, or Group 4 Security – one of those companies, anyway – to deliver a rose inside a case, which she had to cut and open, at this hairdresser's salon where she worked. I don't know whether that's being a romantic or an absolute flippin' idiot or what. I'm really sorry, Kendra, if you're reading this. We'll have a pint sometime."

There were a few interesting articles in the local press at the time about Olga and Kendra. The *Sunday Sun* reported in September 1985 that Pete Zulu and Little Paul had 'packed their trunks and said goodbye to the band' because of Olga's obsession with Kendra and his intention to bring out an album entirely devoted to her. Seemingly the last straw for drummer Paul was when Olga asked them to wear t-shirts with Kendra's name on them.

There are two footnotes to the Kendra episode. One is that Olga had to battle with the record company to keep the name Kendra in the song. True to form, the record company thought it knew best – suggesting that Olga should change the name to Sharon or something better known – but Olga held firm, and the song was completed just as we know it today. The second relates to the scratching of the message 'Meet me at the Redhills' into the vinyl of the 12-inch version of the 'James Bond Lives Down Our Street' single. The official story here is that the Redhills referred to is the pub behind the Johnston School in the Crossgate Moor area of Durham City, and the message was a plea from Olga to Kendra to meet up with him. He told me that's the sort of thing you do "when you're besotted." Quite right, too.

Life has moved on for us all since then, not least for Olga, who's now very happy with his girlfriend Mihoko in London. It's sad in a way that he should have to have undergone so much heartache and unrequited infatuation during his 25 years in The Toy Dolls, but the flip-side is that his misfortunes have enriched the band's repertoire beyond measure. The ups and downs of Olga's adult life have left us, the fans, with a rollercoaster of material, ranging from the blues of despair to the inexplicable high of unfettered optimism. And if Olga ever feels down and unloved, all he has to do is think of his hundreds of thousands of devoted fans across the globe, and all will be well with his world.

History 1997-1999
Production and Seduction

The loss of K'Cee – as a superb bassist, lively harmonist and bundle of on-stage energy – was a harsh blow for Olga and Marty, but life had to go on, and the lads recruited local bass-player Gary Dunn (altering his surname to Fun – sometimes spelt Funn – for Toy Dolls purposes) to fill the gap. Gary – like drummer Little Paul back in the mid-80s – had previously worked with northeast band Martin Stephenson and the Daintees, and joined The Toy Dolls in time to embark on a busy year of touring, a jaunt that lasted from Sweden in April through to Japan just before Christmas. The business of touring Japan just before Christmas therefore happened once again. Olga reassures me that it's nothing to do with festivities – rather, after a full year of touring Europe (and, on occasions, the USA and South America) through into November, then December is the only slot left, and Japan has always served as a rousing place to finish off the year.

As well as being the last time The Toy Dolls went to Japan as a band (until 2005?), 1997 was the year when they played for the first time in Italy, Finland and Russia. I chat to Olga for a while about each of these countries – where, once again, he had a great time and carries happy memories in his head – and we move on to discuss the expansion into the East Coast of America, where they did shows in Philadelphia and New York before moving west to the more established circuit of California. We laugh at the irony of a band from Sunderland playing a venue called Hollywood Palace, but

Olga confirms that there was no time during that tour for hobnobbing with the richer-than-rich and hanging out in dingy bars with Kirk or Michael Douglas:

> "No, there was no time for any celebrity stuff. Days off are so costly on tour, because you're paying the crew and everything, so a day off is almost non-existent. That's especially the case on a short tour of America or somewhere. If you imagine something like fifty quid a night, and there's always going to be 8 people – including the t-shirt guy, the sound guy and all the rest of them. Then you've got to hire the van, including for your day off. So it all mounts up, and you've got to play the following night to actually get your money back for the previous night. So you think, 'what's the point?' To a certain extent it is about money, but obviously there are a lot of other factors as well."

Marty now had a decade of solid Toy Dolls service under his belt, and was drumming and singing better than ever, but from the very beginning of the 1997 tour, there was a question mark in Olga's mind about Gary's capabilities as a bass-player. His presence and image on stage were fine, and he was a nice bloke, but there was just a hovering niggle that his style of bass-playing wasn't quite right for The Toy Dolls.

Whatever the internal misgivings about musicianship, the new album *One More Megabyte* came out in April 1997 and left Olga uneasy about the guitar sound it contained. It was all do to with an amplification problem, but again, such are the time demands on the band in the weeks they spend in the studio, that often they are forced to accept these disappointments in the interests of getting the recording done on schedule. It's devilishly difficult to handle for someone as devoted to quality as Olga is. He shrugs his shoulders and accepts that, while the cover of The Proclaimers' '500 Miles' and 'The Devil Went Down to Scunthorpe' are for him the lowest points on the album, *One More Megabyte* as a whole is simply "nondescript."

There was no particular reason for this album's technology theme, incidentally: it was just another idea for just another album. It did offer the opportunity for a great cover design, however, with the lads' faces crammed into a computer monitor trying desperately to escape. Given Olga's feelings for the record, this might be seen as a thinly-veiled reference to wanting to get the hell out of the album and have nothing more to do with it but, as we've seen, he has no regrets about any of his musical projects. If something doesn't work out the way he'd intended, he shrugs, gets back into his spare bedroom and makes sure that the next piece of writing turns out better. The fans still love his work whatever he thinks of it, on or off the record.

As mentioned earlier, 1998 was the year in which *History Part 2* was released. It has a similar packaging to the 1979-96 compilation, with some newer photos, an interview and sections on the lads' biographies, but Olga has always thought of this as more of a money-making venture, and something to interest only the purists among the band's fans. Nevertheless, proof of its worth is the fact that it continued to sell well across the world into the new millennium.

The early spring saw The Toy Dolls heading off for an extensive American tour. This time, with a USA record deal in the bag, the tour was able to embrace more American dates than ever before, taking in cities as widely separated as Chicago, Detroit, Pittsburgh, Salt Lake City and New York, as well as the more familiar territory of San Francisco and Las Vegas. Olga remembers the two-and-a-half-week tour as being a hell of a slog, with what seemed like months spent in the van, but as usual, it was well worth it to keep themselves live and visible, and to see the fans.

The remainder of the year saw the lads perform only 5 more times, in festivals taking place in Switzerland, Hungary, Spain, Holland and Croatia (this last one, in Zagreb, being the band's first foray into Croatia, a country with a strong tradition for punk and new wave music). All of these went well, but we find ourselves chatting again about Olga's feelings for festivals:

"Yeah, I'm not so keen on festivals as a fan. The band you've come to see will generally do a shorter spot, and outside sound can't be up to the usual standard. But as for doing festivals ourselves – brilliant! Firstly, you have to cut your set short to include just your best songs, which is good for the group and the fans. Also it's usually in the afternoon or early evening, which is good because you're more alert. And it's more money. But as a fan, no, I don't like them – you're too far away from the band, whereas I like to be close up."

There was no Japanese tour for the English lads in 1998, but that did not mean to say things were not happening musically and otherwise between the two countries. Completely out of the blue, Olga got an e-mail from the management of a Japanese all-girl band called Lolita No. 18, who had been fans of The Toy Dolls for a long time and whose music bore an unmistakable influence of Olga and the lads. The link was that their management had been a branch of the promotions company that had looked after The Toy Dolls in the early years. The e-mail asked whether Olga would be interested in producing an album for the girls, and he quickly decided this would be worth investigating further:

"The singer – seemingly I was her guitar-hero, in fact her all-time hero full-stop – she used to come to our gigs in Japan, but I'd never actually met her. I was quite flattered by that, and by the offer of the production work in general. So I asked them to send a tape so I could have a listen and see what I reckoned, and I thought, 'oh, I might be able to do something with this.' So they asked me formally to do an album and we ended up doing it in Hull, which was a bit surreal, but it did really well…"

So began a musical relationship that would last over the next couple of years, in the UK, across Europe and in Japan. The decision to record in Hull was taken for two reasons, really, one dependent on the other. The girls were keen to come to Britain to record, rather than do it in Japan, largely because of the Sex Pistols link. But their obvious choice of London as a recording base was a non-starter for financial reasons. Olga remembered the Fairview studio up in Hull where he'd recorded several times with The Toy Dolls, and figured it would be fine for Lolita No. 18 – and so it proved.

The production work led to a brief closeness between Olga and the band's drummer, Aya, but later, in Japan, this fizzled out. As luck would have it, whilst out in Japan at the turn of the millennium, Olga answered an advertisement in the newspaper looking for an English-Japanese language exchange, and he ended up meeting his girlfriend Mihoko, with whom he's shared a great relationship ever since. Particularly against the backdrop of his earlier experiences of Japanese relationships, this cemented his attachment to Japanese language and culture, as well as giving him personal happiness and a balanced lifestyle.

Working with the Japanese band on their albums – *Toy Doll* (in honour of you-know-who) and *Angel of the North* (a nod to the now famous sculpture on the A1 road outside Gateshead, just south of Newcastle) – gave Olga perhaps his best experience yet of production. Applying his usual, highly regimented sense of discipline to the task, he quickly had a strict agenda for the girls to follow, which came as something of a surprise to them after the laid-back experience of being produced by Joey Ramone on their previous cut. With hindsight, how does he feel he did, working with someone else's material (although including a version of 'Dig That Groove, Baby')? Could he now consider himself a competent producer, one who could go on and make a subsequent living in that side of the music business?

> "I like to think I did a good job, aye. But like I said before, it's hit and miss. I'd love to make it as a producer. I really

need an engineer there, but I like to think I can do a good job, yeah. I may never get any more producing work, but so what? I'm happy to have done what I've done. I'd also like to write theme tunes and so on. The problem there is that you get a bit typecast, you know, him from The Toy Dolls with the squeaky voice – it's an automatic thought."

And what about the results of Lolita No. 18's albums, specifically?

"They were all very nice people, for a start. The first album I did with them, I think the songs are really good and I did a good job. The second album, the songs weren't so good and I did an OK job, but not as good as the first one. But the previous album, before I got involved, had been produced by Joey Ramone, which was all right as well, probably with better songs, so I had a hard act to follow. But yeah, it was as enjoyable as hell – unbelievable. Fantastic, a lovely time."

But the involvement entailed more than mere record production. Olga joined the girls as their tour manager on two European tours, one after each of the 2 albums, then in effect that was the end of his dealings with them, though they are good friends and keep in touch.

Back to Toy Dolls duties, and October 1999 heralded the release of the *Live in Stuttgart* album. I wondered why Olga had chosen that particular venue (Die Rohre in Stuttgart, recorded on 2 November 1998) for the recording of a live show:

"Stuttgart has always been a good audience, always nice. And the venue is a decent size, not too big, not too small. It holds about 600 or 700 – we did that with The Dickies as well. We knew in advance it was going to be more or less right – it's a good place for recording. We took a mobile recording studio, so we could make a better job of it than the Tokyo one a few years earlier."

And, knowing they were going to be filmed, did they think

about altering the set, or choosing the songs carefully with any particular reason in mind?

> "No, we just did the usual set. I'm not saying that we do the same set every single tour – what we do is the same set *within* every tour. That gig was in the middle of a tour, so by that time we were playing quite well, so it was a good snapshot of what we were doing at the time. I'm OK with that album – I think it's passable."

The year of 1999 also marked the band's twentieth anniversary, but any thoughts of a celebratory tour were scuppered with the news that there would only be three gigs that year. The last of these, in Barcelona on 18 December, proved to be the last Toy Dolls show until further notice – in effect, until the new tour we're looking forward to now. The reason – as I've alluded to elsewhere in the book – was that Olga no longer believed in the live product they were offering the fans, and let's remember that the live performance is the crucial factor in the band's relationship with the public. Gary's style wasn't gelling well; the lustre and dynamism had gone from their live work, and frankly it was time for a break for The Toy Dolls as a band and as a concept to recharge their collective batteries and see whether there was a future worth reaching out to. Olga remembers his thought process from that time:

> "I just thought we weren't performing as well as we should be, and I knew then that that was the last gig for the time being. You've got all these coaches pulling up outside with the logo on and all that – they're diehard fans, but if they were new fans, that's what you have to think of. You can't become complacent at any time – if you do, then you start going downhill, in my opinion. Anyway, they were all there, and we couldn't do a thing wrong, but I think if we'd kept that up for a few more gigs, it would have spiralled, and so when we came off, I thought that was the last gig, but I didn't know how long for. I didn't want any of this big-last-tour thing, like Status Quo might do, and whatever offers

came in I'd just reject – no festivals, nothing. And I thought that the next time we toured would be when we got a proper line-up and we really wanted to do it."

A new album with a celebratory air was promised for 2000, but we were still left a little bit rudderless, wondering whether we'd see Olga and the lads back on a stage after the release of *Anniversary Anthems*. He did his best to reassure us, but as the world prepared for the dawn of a new millennium, the worldwide Toy Dolls fraternity sat down to endure the tantalising wait for news of their heroes' future plans.

Olga's Inspirations

8. The Cover Versions

It's part of the joy of being a Toy Dolls fan: spending months predicting what will be the cover version(s) on the next album to be released. You hear a bit of a rumour, or pick something up from a website. Sometimes it turns out to be true; sometimes not.

Football fans spend hours watching Teletext, checking out which players are being transferred to which clubs, and even if a particular transfer turns out not to happen, there's still some kind of logic attached to the possibility. The Argentine defender Gabriel Heinze is a great player; Manchester United is a club he wants to play for; the club can afford to buy him; the transfer happens; the fans are happy.

If you're a Toy Dolls fan, however, things aren't so straightforward. You can be fairly sure there's going to be a cover version on the album, by the law of averages (though *Bare Faced Cheek* is a notable exception), but what sort of song is it going to be? Punk bands in the late 70s used to do versions of other punk bands' songs, or sometimes speeded-up versions of slower songs, usually rock 'n' roll classics. The Toy Dolls aren't that predictable. Just when we think it's time for another Carl Perkins-style punky updating, Olga surprises us with a Latino beat; we hear rumours of a Boomtown Rats number, and the official news comes through as a double whammy featuring a glammy 80s stadium opus from Sweden; a classical piece is as likely as a children's nursery rhyme or an Andrew Lloyd Webber composition.

There is, however, a common denominator. In each of the following tunes, there's a clearly stamped Toy Dolls identity. It will not necessarily be a punked-up, breakneck version of something traditionally slow, but it will inevitably feature skilful guitar, a large dose of humour or irony, and that intangible quality that Olga is referring to when he says that the band's music is not punk, or oi, or new wave, or whatever: it's Toy Dolls Music.

I asked Olga a bit about each of the choices, and was also interested to know how he approached the business of 'borrowing' someone else's song. He was far more laid-back about it than I was expecting. So long as you keep the lyrics the same as the original, and pay whatever royalty is required to the publisher of the original, there's no need to acquire permission as such. In reality, Olga maintains that The Toy Dolls are such a low-key, underground kind of enterprise that he could probably get away with a lot more, legally speaking, than he tries to, as it's unlikely that anyone important would notice.

The list below includes the two songs to be included on *Our Last Album?*: 'She's so Modern' and 'The Final Countdown'. What can't be known at the time of writing is what sort of treatment they'll be given, but I'm sure we're unanimous in hoping for kazoos on the latter. Not on the list are some of the short-listed songs that didn't make it to the final cut. We're left to wonder just what The Toy Dolls would have done with The Bay City Rollers' 1975 No 1 smash 'Bye Bye Baby' or, from the same year, Jonathan King's reworking of the Spanish folk classic 'Una Paloma Blanca'.

'Anniversary Waltz'

This piece, credited as a Franklin/Dubin composition, served, alongside 'We're 21 Today', to add a celebratory tone to the 2000 album *Anniversary Anthems*. It was maybe a bit of a predictable inclusion, but what we were served up with (twice!) was a 'sensible' version that had me, the first time I listened to it, wondering at what point the drums were going to come thundering in so that the band could personalise it as only they can. But no, there is no such half-way point: instead, the song in its two outings segues effortlessly into 'My Baby is a Battleaxe' and 'We're 21 Today' respectively. Perhaps that's part of The Toy Dolls' charm and appeal: we never know what they're going to come up with next. Characteristically, Olga thinks the song is 'crap'.

'Any Dream Will Do'

Andrew Lloyd Webber (music) and Tim Rice (lyrics) wrote this song at a prodigiously young age for inclusion in the musical *Joseph and the Amazing Technicolor Dreamcoat* in 1969, which has been phenomenally successful ever since. During one particularly long run in a theatre in London's West End, Australian pop idol Jason Donovan was chosen to play the lead role, and this led to him having a Number 1 UK hit with 'Any Dream Will Do' in 1991. (Not quite so successful the following year was children's TV entertainer Phillip Schofield, by now in the title role of the show, who got to Number 27 with another of the musical's songs – 'Close Every Door'.) Olga talks us through the story behind the decision to tackle the song for inclusion on the *Orcastrated* album:

> "I really like that song. I saw it done at the school production and various other places in the northeast of England. It's a great musical and that's a fantastic song. Then Jason Donovan did it, and his manager is also our manager, so we fixed it up. It's a great song and we did it worse. But I wouldn't mind doing that song again sometime, actually. Maybe with the same arrangement, but in a better environment."

The bit at the end with a spoof of Andrew Lloyd Webber knocking on Olga's door to threaten legal action is brilliant, but of course, in real life he was paid some money as the songwriter because the lyrics were unaltered in The Toy Dolls' version, and there was no trouble. We order another round of beers and ponder for a moment the issue of Andrew Lloyd Webber's physical appearance, and possible reasons why much of his subsequent material is not quite up to the standard of *Joseph*. For legal reasons, very little of this section of the conversation can be reproduced here. Sorry. It was very funny, though.

'Bachelor Boy'

Anyone watching the Wimbledon tennis championships each June/July and scanning the audience just as the inevitable rain is starting, will spot British rock 'n' roll singing 'legend' Sir Cliff Richard, looking far younger than his 64 years. It was Cliff, with his original band The Shadows, who hit the top of the charts with this song at the beginning of January 1963 – Cliff's only Number 1 as a songwriter – when Olga was just a wee slip of a lad. All say "ahhhh."

Olga wanted to use an appropriate song on *One More Megabyte* to set the tone for 'When Garry Married Melanie', and 'Bachelor Boy' seemed to fit the bill. After a rasping throat-clearance, the song offers a passable impersonation of Cliff Richard's voice, then gives way to the discussion of Garry and Melanie's nuptials.

'Blue Suede Shoes'

As mentioned in an earlier chapter, the presence of so many rock 'n' roll standards among The Toy Dolls' initial repertoire was due in great measure to Ernie leaving his 50s and 60s records for Olga when he left home. 'Blue Suede Shoes' stands out not only for the amusement value of the speed Olga's arrangement gave it, but also for the humour of the two 'aborted' attempts deemed 'too slow, man'. But what is just as impressive is the dexterity of the guitar work: it's as fast as hell and incorporates a number of key-changes and an ascending number of bars played before the vocal comes back in each time. The track featured on the *Dig That Groove, Baby* LP in 1983. Carl Perkins and Elvis Presley both had UK Top 10 hits with the song in 1956, but played it so slowly that their versions took way over 3 minutes to complete. Shame on them!

'California Man'

Written by Roy Wood and originally a UK hit for The Move in 1972, it's tempting to think that this live favourite from the early Toy Dolls stage shows was another remnant of the piles of vinyl Ernie left behind. In fact, the version the band adopted owed more to the song's treatment by US band Cheap Trick (best known commercially for their 1979 hit 'I Want You to Want Me'). Flip was a real fan of Cheap Trick's version, and perfected the harmonies in their style. Olga recalls that they used to "love playing that song – Cheap Trick's version was magnificent," although it was gradually dropped from the set-list as personnel changed. I remember considering 'California Man' to be among the highlights of the early gigs, and somewhere in my mate's attic there is a bootleg tape to vouch for the quality of Flip's harmonies. Happy days.

'Eine Kleine Nacht Muzik'

It may surprise a lot of people to learn that Olga is quite a fan of classical music to relax him in quieter moments. This in turn may not fit with everyone's image of the stereotypical punk singer/songwriter, but let us remember that Olga is anything but typical. He's an eclectic dude who appreciates a wide range of musical styles and can turn his hand, guitar-wise, to pretty much whatever he fancies.

This version of Mozart's well-known piece (track 7 on *Anniversary Anthems*), complete with tuneful flatulence and outrageous vibratos, evolves into a fluent piece of guitar work, worthy of inclusion simply because we all like to hear Olga getting stuck into something complicated in which he can show his talents as the king of the fretboard.T

'I'm Gonna Be 500 Miles'

This song reached Number 11 in the UK charts in 1988 for its composers, Scottish twins and harmony duo Charlie and Craig Reid, otherwise known as The Proclaimers. Critics at the time lauded it as a classic modern love song. Olga fancied a stab at it for the *One More Megabyte* album – sitting just before 'Bachelor Boy' – and found that the requirements of the studio served only to spoil the song's possibilities in comparison with the experience of performing it on stage. Basically he hates this recorded version, and here's why:

> "What happened was we did the recording in the studio and I think we doubled up the choruses to twice the speed of the verse, whereas live we just did the chorus as fast as we could, without it being necessarily double. It worked much better that way, whereas on the record it's crap."

'Kids in Tyne & Wear'

One of only 3 Toy Dolls cover versions to have been written since the band got together (the others being 'Livin' la Vida Loca' and 'I'm Gonna Be 500 Miles'), this was originally a 1981 Kim Wilde hit bearing the slightly different – and some would say more romantically evocative – title 'Kids in America'. To keep things in the family, it was written by her famous father and her unfamous brother.

The new lyrics provided by Olga for 'Kids in Tyne & Wear' on the *Fat Bob's Feet* LP focus on the grimness and poverty of living in the northeast of England, and make reference to Tyne and Wear towns and cities such as Newcastle (beautifully rhymed with 'hassle'), Sunderland, Gateshead (plus its Metro Centre shopping complex), South Shields and Whitley Bay. The county in the extreme northwest corner of England, Cumbria, makes a guest appearance in the penultimate line, purely to provide a rhyme for 'come 'ere'. Great stuff.

More importantly, did Olga fancy Kim Wilde? And what about nowadays, now that she's given up music and retrained as a horticulturist, and makes a living doing gardening programmes on TV and writing a gardening column for the *Guardian* newspaper?

> "Well, I think everybody fancied her a bit in those days. The original 'Kids in America' I love. I saw Kim Wilde and I thought she was this cute little girl – I didn't realize the rest of her band were on platforms and she was a tall girl. I mean I don't fancy her now, coz she looks completely different with the gardening thing and all that. I met her and shook her hand at the TV pop show *Razzmatazz* coz I'd done the theme tune."

There's also an amusing incident relating to the fickle nature of fame. Olga fills us in with the delights and horrors of being recognised in public:

> "I used to go out with a girl at the time with blonde hair, and she used to dress the same as Kim Wilde. And we played near Scarborough one night, and we were in Scarborough walking down the beach and some guys came over, and I was saying, 'look, they're recognizing me!' and one of them came over and said, 'excuse me, is your girlfriend Kim Wilde?' I was gutted."

'Lazy Sunday Afternoon'
Before its release on *Orcastrated* in 1995, the band had been doing this 1968 Small Faces classic as a filler in live performances, giving drummer Marty something to sing for variety (and giving Olga's voice a rest). Marty's faux-Cockney twang was proving very successful, and Olga rated it highly, so the decision was taken to include the song on the album.

Like most of The Small Faces' hits, this song was a Steve Marriott/Ronnie Lane composition, a songwriting partnership whose work Olga has always loved, (he describes them as "unbelievable").

'Livin' la Vida Loca'

Olga is often asked questions along the lines of, "it's such a shit song – why did you cover it?" The answer is simple:

> "I think it's an excellent song – I love Ricky Martin's version of it, I thought it was fantastic, and I thought our version was really good. I don't think it was any better; it was different. There was a chance of it getting released as a single, and we thought it was going to be unbelievable, but it just didn't happen, because it was going to cost too much money. I still think it could have been a Top 10 in the UK. It's a great song, and I think we did a really good version, with the kazoos and stuff."

Feedback via the website and word of mouth has been generally very positive, but what many people don't realise is that it nearly didn't happen. The Toy Dolls were all set up to do The Mavericks' 1998 worldwide smash 'Dance the Night Away' on the *Anniversary Anthems* album, but Olga changed his mind at the last moment in favour of 'Livin' la Vida Loca'. Olga explained that it was just one of those last-minute things that happen in life, but which can often reap good results.

I put it to Olga that it was an interesting idea for the band to try out some Latino material, developing what we agreed was best described as Fulwell Latin, and to use the kazoos. He chuckles as he remembers the kazoos, and sings me the first line of the second verse: "The bit where it goes 'Woke up in New York City' – it's straight in your face – brilliant!"

The only downside of the song is that it's nearly impossible to play live, as the guitar has to be tuned down a tone from E to D, so we mustn't expect to see the band play it on the forthcoming world tour – even in Latin America, where it would perhaps find its spiritual home.

'Love Me Tender'

We're way back nearly 50 years for this one, made famous by Elvis Presley in December 1956. It was also the song that nearly cost The Beatles dearly, when they were trying to convey a rocking image to potentially interested record company executives in the early days in Hamburg.

There are obvious similarities with The Toy Dolls' version of '(Please) Release Me', in that both songs act as introductions to quite caustic tunes about difficult times in Olga's love life. 'Love Me Tender' lasts just one verse, and makes a bitter attack on Steven, who was Kendra's boyfriend at the time – and hence Olga's rival for her affections – before giving way uncompromisingly to 'I'll Get Even With Steven'. Olga sums up the reason for beginning with such a heartstring-plucker of a love song:

> "The Elvis intro thing was just because I felt so much about her – or thought I did. That's what happens when you're infatuated with someone."

'Nellie the Elephant'

If you ask anyone over the age of 30 in the UK whether they've heard of The Toy Dolls, the overwhelming answer will be 'no'. If, however, you ask if they remember a band doing a fast version of 'Nellie the Elephant' on *Top of the Pops* in 1984, then their faces light up with recognition and they ask you to repeat the name of the band. This is the problem: for far too many people, Olga and his fellow musicians are not themselves as individuals and a group – they're the Nellie People. Olga remembers an incident in the late 1980s, when he was recognised in a way that was not entirely to his satisfaction:

> "I remember waiting in Newcastle Airport, and this lad said, 'Dad, dad, is that the Nellie man?' And I thought, 'you little swine – we're The Toy Dolls, man. We're a band.' But that was it – Nellie rather than the band as such. But over in Germany it got to Number 30-something in the charts, which is class, because it kept us away from that kind of sell-out thing, and it's kept going for so many years. So that's great."

The song – credited to Butler and Hart – is one of a small number of children's songs given the Toy Dolls treatment by the band and, as is well known, there are two main versions for us to compare, plus more recent updates. But why choose such a song in the first place? Olga takes up the story:

> "I already had the idea about the 'whooooah' thing, which I thought might work, and I saw that programme *A Handful of Songs* on the telly [an educational music show from the 1970s and 80s, in which characters called Rod, Jane and Freddie wore dungarees and sang songs], and they played 'Nellie the Elephant' there. I thought the idea would work well with that, so we started to do it live, and it worked well, and that was it, really."

I push the matter of the 'whooooah' crescendo further, as I'm keen to trace its origins, and Olga reveals that it goes back to The Scaffold's UK Number 1 hit from 1968, 'Lily the Pink'. The similarity is, of course, purely subconscious. I take a sip of beer and scan my mental database, and suddenly it all makes sense.

After playing the song live for some time, the band decided to record a version, which came out as their first Volume release in November 1982. This first take jumped to Number 11 in the UK Independent Chart, and meant that all the early classics – 'She Goes to Fino's', 'Tommy Kowey's Car', 'I've got Asthma', 'She's a Worky Ticket', 'Deirdre's a Slag', 'Everybody Jitterbug' and 'Nellie' – were now available on vinyl for the band's growing legions of fans to collect. The song was later to feature on the *Dig That Groove, Baby* album before being re-recorded for another assault on the UK Singles Chart late in 1984. The versions are very different musically, so I asked Olga if it is possible for him to state a preference:

> "I think they're both wrong. I preferred the speed of the 82 version, because the later one was a little bit rushed, a bit hectic. I don't mind the thing about changing the key, that's all right, it makes it commercial, I think that's fine, because

I still like it – it's not sell-out commercial, it's nice – but I think it's just a little bit too fast. In those days we didn't use any click, tick-tock kind of thing, which we use all the time now. I preferred the early version because I think it had more of that ploddy thing, but I like the key-change of the later one, so combining the two would have made the ideal combination."

Did the popularity of 'Nellie' in the UK in December 1984 and the subsequent months make much difference to Olga's life, I wondered? He recalls finishing with his current girlfriend – not because of the newly-acquired fame; it just happened that way – and being recognised in the street, particularly in the UK, and people knocking on his door for a time. Then he disappeared from public view for a while, and re-emerged in Japan a couple of years later, when the whole fame thing started up again. But one of the funniest stories associated with 'Nellie' was an incident backstage after a gig, when an elderly gentleman – probably around 85 years old – wandered across and engaged Olga furtively in conversation. After a shifty greeting, he asked if The Toy Dolls would be interested in playing a song he'd written many years earlier for ancient British variety singer Max Bygraves, called 'Pink Toothbrush'. Olga was intrigued, but tried to worm his way out of the situation by stating that they'd have to think carefully about the musical arrangement for a new version. No, the songwriter enthused, there'd be no need – he'd already done the arrangement: 'whooooah ... [exactly the same as 'Nellie'] ... I'm a pink toothbrush...' Olga pissed himself laughing, thought the idea was fantastic, but unfortunately nothing ever came of it.

Let's keep this matter in perspective, though: 'Nellie' is a great Toy Dolls song, and the band played it before and after it was a hit, with a lot of pride and no hint of shame. But it would be wrong to assume that it's their be-all and end-all. It's just one song of well over 100 The Toy Dolls have included in their repertoire. Sure, it was a massive hit in one particular country in one particular year – which was great, of course – but as this book sets out to celebrate, The Toy Dolls are a 25-year-old, worldwide phenomenon, with far more to be proud of than just one hit single.

'No Particular Place to Go'
Yet another song to feature on an album left for Olga by Ernie, this was a hit for Chuck Berry back in 1964. Whilst the lyrics are largely the same as in the original version, The Toy Dolls' arrangement – performed by the classic line-up of Olga, K'Cee and Marty, and coming in at Track 10 on *Wakey Wakey* – benefits from much more pace and a liberal sprinkling of 'Cockney-style' mob vocals. Great drumming too, by the way.

'Olga Crack Corn'
The American folk tune 'Jimmy Crack Corn' was given a personalised twist in this version, which appeared on *Fat Bob's Feet*. It's made all the better by the inclusion of impeccably harmonised kazoos.

'(Please) Release Me'
Written way back in 1950 by a snappy combination of Miller/Yount/Williams/Harris, this was a Number 1 smash for perma-tanned English singer Engelbert Humperdinck in 1967, and was actually his first chart entry, a full seven years after he had made his first recording! The Toy Dolls did far better than that, as we know. Wilson Phillips then had a less impressive hit with it 23 years later. But the most meaningful version of all is to be found on The Toy Dolls' album *Orcastrated*, where it serves to introduce 'Darling I Loathe You' (a song that harks back to the difficulties Olga experienced with an earlier girlfriend). There's nothing noteworthy about it otherwise.

'Popeye Medley'
A bit of fun based around the music to the popular TV cartoon *Popeye the Sailor Man*, the star of which ate spinach

to make him strong and win the never-ending affections of Olive Oil. Again, this was a one-time stage favourite, and was an excuse for Olga to climb up on top of the speakers and show off his guitar skills. There's a very atmospheric version on the *Twenty-two Tunes Live From Tokyo* album, containing other stuff in the medley such as the maritime quandary 'What shall we do with the drunken sailor?'

'Rupert the Bear'

Yet another children's song, this time depicting the adventures of a cartoon/comic book bear called Rupert, who knocked about with other animals and had a very safe and innocent time in the middle of the English countryside. (This was in the days before paedophilia and bear-tampering became big in the UK.) Olga was inspired to take the song on as he could see straight away that it had potential as a speeded-up punky classic. The main version features on the B-side of the 'We're Mad' single from July 1984, but the song can be found on various other cuts across the band's discography.

Surprisingly, Olga recalls that the band only ever played the song about 4 times on stage, and that was during a South American tour. The same applies to 'Queen Alexandra Road...', incidentally. It just didn't feel right, so they dropped it for future dates. Don't be surprised if 'Rupert' re-emerges on the 2004-05 world tour, though: at the time of writing, there's a strong rumour it'll be included in the set.

I'd always thought that it is Olga's voice we can hear doing the third harmony on top of his own melody in the chorus. In fact, it's Bonny Baz, whom Olga reckons to be a much better singer and guitarist than he himself is. Other touches of note in the song are the amusing comment half way through, that 'All these verses are exactly the same' (the TV cartoon's version was always very short, with just one verse and a chorus), and the beautifully harmonised 'Ruuuuuu-peeeeeert' at the end.

'Sabre Dance'

We seem to be in the habit of going back to the late 1960s, so let's journey back in time once more, this time to 1968, when Love Sculpture, a UK band featuring the yet-to-be-famous singer, songwriter, instrumentalist and producer Dave Edmunds, brought out 'Sabre Dance' and thus achieved their only UK hit. Within two years, Mr Edmunds had moved on to record 'I hear you knocking', in hindsight a far more lucrative course of action.

The Toy Dolls' version on *Wakey Wakey* – pencilled in as a possible for the forthcoming Our Last Tour? extravaganza – is a feast of steady, fast drumming and Olga at his finest on guitar. Put it on, sit down, close your eyes and drift off into the realms of guitar heaven.

'She's so Modern'

One of the two cover versions scheduled for the new LP *Our Last Album?*, this was originally a UK Number 12 hit for The Boomtown Rats in 1978, their third single. It is widely thought that the song was written about the late Paula Yates, the journalist and TV presenter who was Bob Geldof's partner for over 15 years (and who introduced The Toy Dolls when the band played on *The Tube*), but in fact Geldof and Johnnie Fingers deleted the verse about Yates before the recording took place, so the lyrics are actually about an amalgamation of 1970s 'hip girls'.

In March 2004 Olga bought the classic Boomtown Rats album *Tonic for the Troops*, and immediately started thinking back to what fabulous material the band had brought out in the late 1970s. Without further ado, he determined that 'She's so Modern' would be a definite for the new Toy Dolls album. Again, there's no way of hearing it at the time of writing, but my hopes are high.

'Teenager in Love'

It was a delight recently to rediscover this track on the band's official website, complete with vinyl crackles. Written by

Marty Wilde (father of Kim, who had the original hit with the song that became The Toy Dolls' 'Kids in Tyne and Wear' – see, there are links everywhere: you just have to look for them) and a hit for him, plus Dion, plus Craig Douglas, all in 1959, it was a song Olga and the boys desperately wanted to do in their early shows, but one whose structure worried them.

> "We thought about a few things, but realised we couldn't do anything special with the song, and we didn't want to just carry on and do a slightly faster version of the same song. The 'too slow, man' thing, we'd already done with our 'Blue Suede Shoes' version. We wanted something different and striking."

The solution was a novel stroke of genius. Similarly to 'Blue Suede Shoes', the initial attempt is aborted, then Olga's voice comes storming in and spits out the first 2 lines up to the syllable 'teen-', where he stops abruptly and thanks us. Brilliant.

'The Devil Went Down to Georgia/Scunthorpe'

I'd like to start a rumour here: that The Charlie Daniels Band released this song – their only UK hit – as 'The Devil Went Down to Georgia' in late September 1979 purely to celebrate Olga's birthday and to herald the start of The Toy Dolls as we know them a month later. It's a theory that may not hold water, but I'm sticking to it.

The song was intended originally to be a soulful kind of Country & Western ballad, describing a guitar-playing competition between the hero Johnny and the devil down in the US state of Georgia (or, in The Toy Dolls' version, the northern English town of Scunthorpe), which Johnny eventually wins. It's easy to see why Olga fancied the challenge on *One More Megabyte*: there's plenty of great guitar work in there, which he executes very competently. But why Scunthorpe?

Scunthorpe is one of a handful of northern English

towns whose names evoke a sensation of grim ugliness in the ears of the listener. Others include Rotherham, Doncaster, Grimsby, Rochdale, Barnsley and Huddersfield. It's as simple as that: choosing somewhere closer to home than Georgia, somewhere that sounds a bit grimy, as well as amusingly unlikely, is just right for entertainment value.

I bet you're thinking Olga was extremely satisfied with the version, aren't you? Judge for yourselves, and keep an eye out for a neat pun towards the end of his answer: "That 'Devil Went Down to Scunthorpe' thing is flippin' diabolical, too, in my opinion."

'The Final Countdown'
Swede Joey Tempest and his band Europe released this Europop-electro-glam anthem – if that's the term – in 1986, accepting from the start that it would take the best part of 20 years for someone else to come up with a decent version involving (we hope) multiple kazoos. I'm hamstrung as I write this by not having heard the lads' version yet, but I'm sure it'll be a belter: 80% skill, 20% irony, and 100% blissful class. Bring it on...

'Toccata in Dm'
Olga's arrangement of this classical piece for the *Absurd-Ditties* LP was little short of superb. Check out not only the breadth and excellence of guitar skill, but also the precision and speed of Marty's drumming. What's more, the quality of the version is confirmed in a rare display of satisfaction on Olga's part: on that album, he particularly likes 'Toccata in Dm', along with 'Drooling Banjos', 'My Wife's a Psychopath' and 'Sod the Neighbours'.

'Turtle Crazy'
At the beginning of the 1990s, an otherwise civilised world went mad for a series of cartoon turtles whose adventures were followed by children across the globe in books,

cartoons, films and TV programmes, to say nothing of the toy and clothing merchandise possibilities.

There are times in our lives when we do something for a particular reason, without really being enthused by it. Maybe it's a favour, or something that will create the right impression in the eyes of someone else, but our heart's not really in the project. This was the case with this song, which the record company pleaded with Olga to write and bring out to capitalise on the turtle fad at the time. He was far from keen, but went along with it just to satisfy the record bosses, which is something that he would never do again.

The tune is a traditional British folk song that describes the football craziness of a cousin of the singer, called Paul, and the chorus refers to Paul as being 'football crazy', and 'football mad'. It also served as the inspiration for the theme tune of the BBC football programme *Match of the Day*. All Olga had to do was make up some lyrics and focus his attention on the young people around him and their complete immersion in all things turtle-related. The figure of Sid – vaguely based on a relative of Olga – represents any kid's infatuation with the turtle trend.

'We're 21 Today'

This traditional track, credited to Kendal and used at 21st birthday celebrations across the English-speaking world, joins forces with the 'Anniversary Waltz' to finish off the *Anniversary Anthems* album. Its inclusion is self-explanatory, but it's up to us, the listeners and fans, to figure out what we make of it. I think it's 18 seconds of pure class. Olga thinks it's "okay."

'Wipe Out'

This instrumental song – originally a hit for The Surfaris with a considerably slower version in 1963 – was reworked by the band in the early days and quickly became a live standard, as well as appearing on *A Far Out Disc*. It owes its Toy Dolls life to having featured in Ernie's record collection.

It shows plenty of tight, fast musical discipline, and I suggest to Olga that I've heard various versions, some even faster than others, so it must be difficult to play live on account of the speed. He concedes that the guitar is "a piece of piss," but takes me through the difficulties associated with getting the drumming right, using his knuckles and the bar-room table as makeshift props. A couple of yuppies glance over and wonder what we're up to. I mouth the explanation "genius at work" and they go back to their pints, unaware that this is Olga and he, unlike them, has been on *Top of the Pops*.

> "The speed was sometimes a problem. We did a fast version with Dicky. We fixed it so he could use the floor tom and the snare drum, but he needed a small tom, so he used to click the snare off the snare-drum to use it as a tom-tom, then click it back on for when the guitar comes back in. That made it easier for him."

'Yellow Burt'

This is another traditional tune, originally a Caribbean calypso ditty bearing various titles, including 'Mocking Bird' and 'Yellow Bird'. This last title brought Olga the title of his own song, where Burt is the guy's name and yellow refers to his supposed cowardice.

Anyone wondering who Burt was will be delighted to learn that Burt is one and the same as PC Stoker, who features in his own Toy Dolls song. While 'PC Stoker' concentrates on the harder side of the policeman's character, 'Yellow Burt' portrays him as a softy, even going so far as to call him a 'puff' (only as a loose rhyme for 'off', of course; there's no question of calling into question Burt's sexuality here). Do you want to know who the copper really was? Kendra's stepfather. There you go.

History 2000-2003

Bassist for Hire

After the disappointment of feeling that the band's live shows were no longer cutting the mustard, and deciding to take a period of time to reassess the future of The Toy Dolls, Olga embraced the new millennium knowing that there would at least be an album to release in 2000. *Anniversary Anthems* constituted an opportunity for the fans to commemorate the band's longevity, and it was thought by Olga and the record company that 21 years, rather than 20, would be a better landmark to celebrate (two decades of anything is a big deal but, at least in the UK, 21 is a far more important birthday than 20 – a historical concept to do with coming of age).

Released in October 2000, the album itself was well received by the fans (who, as we have already noted, remained anxious as to the band's future). The impression we got at the time was that Olga was far happier with the finished product than he had been with previous albums since *Absurd-Ditties*: the website quotes him as being satisfied with 'Charlie's Watching', 'Livin' la Vida Loca' and 'I've Had Enough o' Magaluf'. I ask him to pin-point what he thinks were the good and bad points of that album:

> "Apart from those three songs – which are quite good – it's OK, though there is some crap on there was well. That 'Anniversary Waltz' introduction thing is dire, for instance. But generally speaking, I'm quite happy with how that album turned out – the production's OK and the guitar sounds all right. There's also an interesting technical story

about that album: we used a piccolo snare drum this time, which is higher-pitched than the usual type. I'd heard an album by Therapy? and they'd used a really high-tuned snare drum, which I liked, but the piccolo turned out to be too high for us, and it didn't sound snarey enough, if you get what I mean. But other than that, it was quite a nice album, yeah."

With the album written and recorded by the end of the spring, and the certainty of no Toy Dolls gigs that year, Olga threw himself deeply into the remaining production work with Lolita No. 18 we described in the previous History section. The 2000 stage of his dealings with the band saw him going out to Tokyo, this time to live for around nine months.

Having met Mihoko there through the language exchange, Olga set about learning the language a lot more. His abiding memory of this linguistic learning curve is of sitting at weekends in the little flat he'd rented, trying desperately to get his head around the symbols used in the Japanese writing system. As usual, his perfectionism came back to haunt him:

"Well, my Japanese language is all right now, I can get by OK. It was a struggle initially to get past the basics, but it started to click into place eventually. At school, I didn't really learn much French or anything, so I wasn't really prepared for language learning, but in Japan I just wanted to prove myself really, a bit like the guitar thing. There's loads more to learn with Japanese, but I was keen to be able to write it – the symbols and everything. You can imagine how obsessive I became with it all. I made myself ill sitting there at weekends in my flat – I was throwing up with it."

But it was important for him to get properly immersed in the local culture as a welcome break from the work schedule, so life with Mihoko and the improvement of his language skills came as a pleasant surprise to him. The stay in Japan was prolonged until the middle of 2001, when Olga (and

Mihoko, once the visa paperwork had been sorted out) decided to come back to the UK to live.

However, while Olga was still in Tokyo, a bizarre contact came through from The Dickies, who wanted to know if he'd be interested in standing in as their bass-player for two tours they had coming up: one in November and December 2001 covering the USA and Europe, and a second from March to July the following year, this time doing roughly the same countries plus Japan, and finishing up at the Holidays in the Sun punk festival in Blackpool, England. To say that Olga didn't have to think twice about accepting their offer is to win the Understatement of the Decade prize. With characteristic zeal, he sat down in his bedroom with a tape – sent to him by guitarist Stan – of the songs The Dickies would be doing, and tried to pick out the bass-lines as best he could. With quite a few of the songs, it proved impossible, so Olga did his own thing and worked out what he thought would sound good, whether it matched the original or not. (As it was to turn out, The Dickies were thrilled with both his company on tour and his bass-playing.) What he didn't know at the time was that he was the only Dickie putting anything like that amount of effort into preparing for the tour. Did he find the band's tour preparation markedly different from what he'd experienced with The Toy Dolls?

"Let me give you a comparison. On a Toy Dolls tour, you'll see me coming out of the hotel room in the morning way ahead of schedule – I have to be first, coz I'm responsible for making sure everything goes smoothly. We're leaving at 9 o'clock, and I can't abide anybody arriving later than five past nine. Everybody has to be spot-on-time. If anybody's later than 9.10 we'll have to think about deducting money or at least getting an explanation. People wonder why it's so strict, but if you really care about your fans 700 miles away, you'll be there on time for them. It's not really about being in charge or anything – I just think that somebody has to be responsible for getting the job done properly. But with The

Dickies, you're leaving at 12.00, so I think I'll go down at 12, and I know I'm going to be the first there, as usual. But I'm not going to wait in the foyer, I'll go for a pint in the bar, or a coffee, and I know they'll find me there, coz they're not going to leave until 1.00 or even 2.00, and sure enough, come 1.30, they start to turn up. It's so relaxed and laid-back for The Dickies, and that really helped me to chill out. But I still think if it were my band we'd be leaving spot-on-time. The latest I'll ever be for The Dickies is actually the time they say, so I'll always be the first there. Not even the tour manager's there."

So anyway, Olga left Japan briefly and flew over to California to get some initial rehearsals done with Leonard and the lads. Might we have expected that The Dickies would have been lined up waiting for him in the rehearsal room, with his bass already plugged in for him?

"Well, I flew from Tokyo to Los Angeles to do these rehearsals, maybe 25 or 30 rehearsals, I thought. No way, they were planning 3 rehearsals. I got there, met the guitar-player, and asked him where the itinerary was, like I would have had if it had been my band – and he said, 'what do you mean?' I said, 'when are we rehearsing?' He said, 'when do you want to rehearse?' I said, 'well, I've left Japan and come here expecting to rehearse for 6 weeks.' He said, 'what about 3 rehearsals?' I said, 'what about 30?' He said, 'what about 4?' The singer came to none, except the last one for an hour. The guitar-player came to 2, and they had a new drummer, who was also having to learn new stuff. It was ridiculous. But that's the thing with The Dickies – they're so Californian and laid-back about everything, that it becomes infectious and you realise that it's actually a much nicer way to go about things. Having said that, The Dickies were one of the tightest, most well-oiled bands I've ever played with."

Not for the first time in our conversation, Olga contrasts the approaches to performing of The Toy Dolls and The Dickies. We talk about the full-time job and constant worry of being singer, guitarist, songwriter and all-round organiser, versus being bass-player full stop. As we sip our pints, Olga returns to the theme of drinking before gigs. With The Toy Dolls it's pretty much a no-no, as there is so much pressure on him to get everything right. With The Dickies, on the other hand, he could have as much or as little alcohol as he wanted before each show, as he was hardly nervous at all – no puking, no inhaler, no hassle. His mind could be exclusively focused on the music and his own enjoyment of the gig. I remember seeing him and Leonard sloping off through a side door at the Bradford Rio in November 2001 while the support band were on, presumably in search of a pub to slake their thirsts and enjoy their utter lack of nerves.

On an associated theme, mixing with the fans before a show (for example, in the venue's bar) is something Olga has never done. It's partly to do with the pre-gig nerves, and also because he likes the idea of a bit of mystique before coming on stage. This contrasts starkly with bands like The Damned and The Wildhearts, who will generally be happy to sink a few pints and chat with people before disappearing to get ready for the show. I remember spotting a post-Buzzcocks Pete Shelley leaning on a pillar with a pint in his hand watching his own support band and almost not being recognised. After a show, though, it's a different matter: Olga reckons it's good to mix a bit then, partly to say thanks to the fans for coming to see the gig, and also to show that the lads are completely human and enjoy a drink and the chance to socialise.

One of the interesting things they did manage to rehearse in the short time available for such things was the amalgamation, for encore purposes, of 'Banana Splits' and 'Nellie the Elephant'. I recall this going down a treat at the gig I saw.

"Yeah, Leonard the singer said they wanted to do 'Nellie', and I wasn't keen, coz it was past and gone, you know? But he said they'd been doing 'Banana Splits' forever, so in the end we agreed to do a sort of joint version, singing together.

But yeah, it worked OK on stage. It was so enjoyable working with them, though – I loved every minute. I was playing bass guitar, which was what I wanted to be doing, it took the pressure off, and it taught me how to be something other than a front man, working just behind Leonard."

Olga has nothing but praise for the members of The Dickies:

"Stan and Dave are among the best guitarists I've ever seen. Stan's probably the creative one, even though on stage he might often seem just to go 'Kerrang!' while Dave's doing what looks like all the hard work. And I actually think Leonard is the best singer in the world. He's brilliant. He's a really clever front man, too – great at working the audience. Mind you, he's been doing the same banter with the audience for the last God knows how many years! The drummer Travis – who also plays for TSOL – is a dream drummer, and he made my bass-playing sound better than it really is. He was a great help. Yeah, it would be good to work with them again sometime if the opportunity ever arose."

The latter Dickies tour in 2002, as mentioned above, included plenty of gigs in Japan, Germany and the West Coast of America, so Olga was very much on familiar territory. What had become a very unfamiliar experience by this stage, of course, was playing live in the UK, but by the time the opportunity came, at the end of July, the band were playing out of their skins, were very relaxed, and frankly the Holidays in the Sun festival at Blackpool's Winter Gardens was an event to which Olga had been looking forward with anticipation, excitement and confidence. Again, as bass-player, the pressure was off:

"It was a fantastic festival, with a very polite audience – great people. The only sour point was when Leonard and I went out in the afternoon for a burger, and we saw one fight with some daft, groovedigging townie people – you know what I feel about townies – who were causing trouble with some mohican lads, guys with The Toy Dolls, The Dickies and The Adicts written on their backs, in fact all the main bands I'd played in! It took me right back to the beginning in Sunderland and all the 'Dig That Groove, Baby' sort of townie behaviour. But anyway, the audience was really respectful and respectable. I felt proud to be there, because the band put in a really good performance, for the final gig of the European leg of the tour, which was nearly 20 gigs back-to-back without a day off. And we played well – it sounded horrible on stage, but apparently out in the audience it was fine."

A year later, Olga was back at the same festival, this time held in Morecambe, not far from Blackpool, further up the same coast. This time, though, he was fulfilling a different dream, playing bass with The Adicts while their permanent bass-player was indisposed for a period. The chance had come about because The Adicts were in urgent need of a stopgap bassist, and had known Olga for years (they and The Toy Dolls had headlined and supported each other on previous tours), so he was the obvious choice for them, and he was delighted to learn their bass-lines and get out on the road with them.

Again, it was the final gig of the year for him, but this time, he had done a US tour in April, and the HITS festival was a one-off for The Adicts at the end of June. It went well, and once again Olga cherishes happy memories and a real sense of having done something quite relaxing and definitely worthwhile.

As 2003 dawned, and refreshed by a couple of years of leisurely bass-playing for bands other than his own, Olga felt that the time was right to start getting The Toy Dolls back together, and perhaps to think about a new album, too. Marty made it clear that, after one-and-a-half decades of association with the band, his priorities now were to spend time with his family and concentrate on his record shop in Sunderland, and Gary was out of the frame, too, having returned to a life of guitar coaching. (The amazing rate of Toy Dolls coincidences continues here, incidentally, as we note that Gary married Teddy's sister, Vivien.) Anyway, new recruits were therefore needed and, with the premise in mind that either the band would be at their best or the project would once again be shelved as unworkable, Olga had two people in mind to fit the bill.

David Nuttall, who grew up in Northumberland, studied at Lancaster University and stayed on in Lancashire to set up his own business – Jalapeno Drums – making high-quality kits for both professional and semi-professional musicians. His work is held up as exemplary in drumming circles, and has toured the trade conferences and shows with a great deal of success. He has known Olga for a number of years through a family connection, and the link became a bit closer when Marty used some Jalapeno gear towards the end of his reign on the throne of Toy Dolls drumming. As an excellent singer and fast, accurate drummer, David – or Dave the Nut, as he has since become known in Toy Dolls circles – was the obvious man to fill Marty's boots.

On the bass-playing front, another long-time acquaintance was in Olga's mind. Michael Rebbig – Reb as he was dubbed – was a big German bassist whose physical appearance hid a softer interior and a love of classical guitar, which he was studying at college in Germany. The geography of the thing wasn't ideal, but in terms of image and musical ability, Olga reckoned Dave and Reb would form the perfect rhythm unit to work alongside him. So by the end of the year, the trio were getting together for initial rehearsals, and plans were slowly taking shape to record a new album sometime in 2004 and set off around the world on tour once that was finished. All seemed well and, crucially, Olga was satisfied in his mind that, at least in principle, he now had the sort of line-up that could exorcise the ghost of the late 1990s and restore his faith in the band's capabilities as a top live act.

Personnel aside, Olga once again took out his notebook

and dusted down his recording equipment, and settled down for the lengthy, but ultimately productive, process of crafting The Toy Dolls' eleventh studio album.

While he was busy with this, he also got in touch with Ciaron Marlow, the technical wizard who built and continues to maintain The Dickies' website, and asked whether he'd be interested in setting up a site for The Toy Dolls. Ciaron jumped at the opportunity, and spent a long time with Olga discussing what sort of format and content would be required, and sifting through Olga's treasure trove of Toy Dolls memorabilia to see what would serve for uploading onto the incipient site.

So it was that, by the end of 2003, we were all able to enjoy a top site, which had replaced Ernie's Toy Dolls Fan Club as the primary source of contact and information for fans of the band. It started off getting about 8,000 hits per month, a figure that has (at the time of writing) risen to around 12,000, and there has been nothing but positive feedback about the content – particularly sections such as the popular 'Play With Olga' feature, in which guitar riffs and solos are explained – and the forum, in which fans from all over the world mingle with band members and exchange useful, amusing and often downright surreal information.

What the website has achieved, aside from the obvious aim of allowing fans to keep in touch with the band, is to prove what an approachable band The Toy Dolls are. Scarcely a day goes by without some band involvement in the forum – answering questions or supplying information or comments to widen our knowledge and enjoyment of their activities. With a new album and a world tour pending, this contact has been invaluable.

In mentioning a world tour, we think of all the previous tours that have taken place during the band's 25-year history. We can also start to marvel at how many countries The Toy Dolls have played in and loved, and how many nationalities of fans have become hooked by this most charismatic of bands. The next chapter widens our celebration to include input from fans across the globe, together with Olga's thoughts and memories of 25 years on the road.

The Toy Dolls – A Global Phenomenon

As we saw in an earlier chapter, British fans of The Toy Dolls have suffered a 20-year-old puzzle: whatever happened to the popularity of the band on their home soil in the UK? They built up a cult following for the first 5 years of their existence, had a massive UK hit with 'Nellie the Elephant', then no sooner had they appeared on *Top of the Pops* and, we might have thought, pocketed the cash from the lucrative record sales and made the video for 'She Goes to Fino's', than they were as good as finished in UK terms. Those of us who form the diehard fanbase back in Britain struggle to come up with a good reason why the British public should have rejected the band, but at least we can take heart from the growing stature of The Toy Dolls on the world stage. It's as much of an enigma for Olga, but I asked him what his thoughts were on the matter.

> "Yeah, it was weird. I remember playing to a sell-out audience at the Hollywood Palladium, then not too long afterwards coming back to Britain and playing in front of 3 people shouting 'bollocks' from the back at Adam & Eve's in Leeds. I dunno. It's a tricky one."

Was the success of 'Nellie' in the UK a factor, perhaps? Maybe the danger was that the band had been dubbed a novelty one-hit wonder? What else does Olga think was to blame?

> "Of the 600,000 people who bought 'Nellie the Elephant', 595,000 were just kids who'd never heard of the band

before then, and I think it went downhill from then. Also the line-up we had wasn't so good at the time, and we waited until we had a really good line-up before we played England again: we played in London in 1993 and that was really nice, even though 50% of the audience were Japanese girls, and the rest were members of The Wildhearts, Three Colours Red and The UK Subs and their mates, but it was still a very nice gig and we were really good, comparatively speaking. And then K'Cee, the bass guitar-player we had at the time of the 93 gig, left the band, and we've never really been good enough since to play in England. I say that because England's a very important place for me in my musical heart, if you see what I mean, because I live here."

I wondered whether the notoriously fickle British music press had had anything to do with the demise of the band in the UK. After all the early support of the local press and then people like Garry Bushell on a nationwide level, had the papers and magazines that mattered suddenly decided to turn their backs on The Toy Dolls?

"We would generally play in front of small audiences in England, so it wasn't a question of audiences getting smaller, but you're right, England's very cynical, especially in the music press. We played at the 100 Club in London in 1982 with the punk band Erazerhead supporting us, and they were all right, and the review said that we were a joke, and that Erazerhead were fantastic. Then we supported The Angelic Upstarts the same year at the Marquee in London. They put on the best show I've ever seen a band do, and the review said Heaven and Hell – it said that we were fantastic that night, and The Upstarts were crap, but in fact it was us who were crap. We went down that day on the bus with all our stuff, all the guitars and drums and everything, to do this Marquee gig and we were crap – we were knackered when we got there, and they said we were fantastic. I've got no faith in the music press, not in the British press."

Nevertheless, there are still plenty of Toy Dolls fans back in

Britain. I'd guess that the band could still sell out venues across the northeast, and maybe in London, too, but anyway, that's a debate for another day. A good number of fans got in touch during the preparation of this book to add their experiences, thoughts and comments for me to include, so here's a selection from the UK:

Kev Miller from Sunderland remembers getting into the band through the unusual angle of a case study he looked at as part of his law studies about 10 years ago. The teacher was explaining how spelling names incorrectly could help people avoid being prosecuted for defamation of character, and cited the example of 'Tommy Kowey's Car', before proceeding to discuss how the real Tom Cowie and his colleagues had been furious and had immediately sought to get the law changed. Kev's interest was aroused, and he has been an avid fan ever since, classing *A Far Out Disc* as his favourite album and 'James Bond Lives Down Our Street' as his top single.

Paul from Durham considers 'Tommy Kowey's Car' as one of the best songs he's ever heard.

> "It's pure class. It's catchy as hell, and very funny, and the best thing is that it's written about someone who was selling cars locally. That made it much more relevant to us as teenagers – there was someone you knew that you could take the piss out of."

Amanda Cummins (Manda 82) is quite a recent convert, but saw straight away why the band are so special to so many people. She'd heard The Toy Dolls mentioned in a Three Colours Red interview, so decided to check them out. Soon afterwards she was at a Three Colours Red gig with boyfriend Jonas and got talking to Danny from The Wildhearts (like you do), and hearing Jonas and Danny's warmth and enthusiasm for Olga and the boys, she got further into The Toy Dolls and quickly found herself hooked like the rest of us.

Outside of the northeast, the word spread, and gradually

real people – not specifically punks or skinheads or whatever – started to get into the band and enjoy the whole experience. Brian Martin, from Stafford, England, was a product of the 'Nellie the Elephant' period when, having seen the band on *Top of the Pops*, he rushed out to try and get his hands on everything they'd recorded. Looking back over 20 years of fandom, Brian can't choose between *Bare Faced Cheek* and *Idle Gossip* as his favourite album, but 'Yul Brynner Was a Skinhead' tops his list of singles by a hair's breadth. Brian's views are typical of many that people shared with me in the preparation of this book. It's not just the songs:

> "Being a bit skinny myself, it's always good to see someone even skinnier not afraid to strip down to his boxers on stage! It's very brave and very funny! Also I think Olga is one of the best showmen and guitarists our country has ever seen, second to none! I would like to take this opportunity to thank The Toy Dolls for years of musical enjoyment. I have every album so far and they remain the only band whose new albums still bring excitement to me when they are close to being released! Cheers to Olga and co, and thanks for everything!"

But, as we've established, the United Kingdom is now only a small corner of the worldwide reign of The Toy Dolls. A quick glance at the message forum on the band's website is proof that people from throughout Europe, the USA and South America are crazy about the band – some of them grizzly old punks in their 30s and 40s, others comparatively sensible music-lovers in their 20s, joined by enthusiastic Scandinavians in their teens. All share a love of the band and its music, and all praise the involvement and contact Olga, Dave the Nut and Tommy Goober manage to keep up with the fans via the website. In turn, all are welcomed and loved by the band, so what we're left with is a kind of global family. It is certainly a far cry from the early days back in Sunderland, when the horizons for the band must have seemed far more limited. We've seen in an earlier chapter how the 1984 American tours came about, for instance, but how did Olga feel when the opportunity first arose to play gigs abroad?

> "It was mad, but it was a great opportunity. Once the USA thing had happened as a result of good reactions to our first album, we then got the management set up with Dave Chumbley, and that opened doors across most of Europe – France, Switzerland, Germany, Austria, and so on – then eventually we hit Japan. It's always been hard work, but the chance to see so many countries and meet their people is a fantastic thing."

America was restricted in the early tours to just the West Coast (specifically California), which was where the initial interest had happened. But gradually the good news spread, and the band were able to make inroads into other states. Obviously the band were never going to 'crack America' in the way a huge, stadium-rock sort of band would, but does Olga feel happy with the way their profile in the States has developed?

> "Yeah. We can go over now and play the whole thing, really, but not massive places – maybe do 6 or 7 in California, plus Utah, Salt Lake City, Detroit, Chicago, and perhaps do a couple of nights at a small venue in New York, or something like that. So it's on a fairly small scale, and without any radio play or anything. But I'm completely happy with that – that's how I like it, and I really want to hang onto that, so why try to go massive?"

And the fans in the USA certainly seem to love the band.

> "Yeah, it's flippin' unbelievable. They've always given us such a great welcome. We've seemed to gel into what they want over there."

Phil and Tom wrote separately from California and agreed that The Toy Dolls kick ass both live and on record. Tom talked about the atmosphere at a Toy Dolls gig at the Hollywood Palace in 1998:

> "It's the complete show. I got a real excitement before the show, but I knew it was just going to be fantastic. The atmosphere was very safe but Olga and the guys really got you into it quickly – they were rocking the place within 2 songs. The best thing was that they really wanted to be there – you could see they were enjoying themselves and wanted us to have a good time too."

One of the first things most bands think about when they contemplate an American tour is the sheer size of the place. It's nowhere near as easy as doing a tour of a single country like, say, France, where the distances between cities and gigs is greatly reduced. I asked Olga to give us a flavour of life on the road in the States – how they dealt with the travelling.

> "I can confirm we didn't hitchhike! We've done it in nightliners and big vans and sleeper buses and all kinds of things, but in 1984 we had a little van or minibus thing, which was all right – not a big nightliner with videos – and then motels and so on. It was fine. On the road itself we usually try and sleep, but then we've got hotels waiting for us when we arrive. When I went to see Baz's band [the Stranglers] the other night, they had the proper big sleeper bus thing, but they didn't have hotels every night – only every now and again. It depends on who you are. Personally, I prefer to use just the little van to get there, then get to the hotel and have a shower. Actually I'd rather have a really flashy van *and* hotels. We've done the sleeper bus a couple of times, but it's so pricey. We did that just before the No Doubt time – this huge flashy sleeper bus with blacked out windows and video and disco, which held 15 people, and it was fantastic, it was as big as this pub. And we therefore had no hotels. But the bus only had one shower, and I want my own shower, in fact I'm happier with my own room."

What about the distances?

> "We were in the van all the time, never on internal flights.
> It was hard work. I remember being in the van and seeing
> this straight road in front of us, miles and miles, and I fell
> asleep, woke up 8 hours later, and it was still the same road.
> I thought, 'what's going on?' I asked the driver and he said,
> 'it's the same road. Keep going.' Unbelievable!"

Later on and further south, in 1988 the lads had the
opportunity to set foot on South American soil for the first
time. Thinking back to their origins in Sunderland, this must
have been an even crazier step to take. Was Olga nervous at
all about taking on Brazil and trying to make an impact
there? What memories does he have of that first Brazilian
tour?

> "That was four nights in São Paulo, and we had this support
> band called Cólera who were huge in Brazil. They had this
> huge coach that used to come and pick up Fat Bob every
> night from the hotel, just for him, at 5 o'clock, to take him
> to the gig so that he could put the guitar strings on and all
> that – then it would pick us up at 7.00 or something. But
> São Paulo is so big, and the first album they'd heard was
> *Bare Faced Cheek*, which is crap, and I just couldn't believe
> there were so many people there at the gig because of this
> crap album. But it was really nice, yeah. We had a great time
> and made a lot of friends. They treated us superbly there."

Brazil has now become an essential port of call on any Toy
Dolls world tour, because the fans are so unbelievably loyal
and mad. "Lovely people," as Olga puts it. The Brazilians'
fervour for the band is summed up by a couple of
correspondents from over there who got in touch with me.
Rafael Brito Kirsten was browsing through some records in
São Paulo's Galeria do Rock, when he heard some Toy Dolls
songs come on in the background and was directed towards
a CD of theirs. This turned out to be *Bare Faced Cheek* (not
one of Olga's favourites, but there you go – we all differ in

our tastes), which he quickly paid for and took home for a listen. As he listened, Rafael got hooked on the band, and realised, as he put it, that he "had made the best purchase of my life."

For another Brazilian, Vanessa Felipetto, the best Toy Dolls album is an earlier opus, *A Far Out Disc*, which also contains some of her favourite songs. But rather than distinguishing one album from another, Vanessa places the band's importance in their ability to perk up your mood with their "comic way of playing." For her, the songs get into your life, into your soul, and they're there for good. Her advice is straightforward:

> "If you are down, if you are feeling lonely and blue, just listen to a Toy Dolls song ... any of them! It's fucking great music!"

A thousand miles southwest of São Paulo is the Argentine capital of Buenos Aires, a city The Toy Dolls first visited in June 1995. Olga has happy memories of that date – which preceded four shows in Brazil the same week – and admits that it felt good to be expanding further into South America. Initially, he was a bit in awe of the venue, the Obras Stadium, which held around 12,000 people, which is quite a big ask to fill on your first gig in a new country. Reports before the show indicated that the place had sold out, and Olga recalls the rollercoaster conversation he had with the guy who'd arranged it all:

> "He told us it was a 12,000 venue, and we thought, 'brilliant, if we can fill this place, we've really cracked it. From Ashbrooke Launderette to 12,000 people!' Then the guy came up and said it was full, and we had the 12,000, which was fabulous for us, and he happened to mention that the Ramones had been there a couple of weeks previously. I asked him if they'd had 12,000 people, and he said, 'yeah, times four – they played 4 nights.' So that brought us back down to earth a bit. But it was a great gig – I just wish we could have stayed longer in the city, but we

had to be off to Brazil straight away for the next gig."

Dani Correa lives in Buenos Aires, and he sent me a great e-mail praising the band for their greatness and their style of playing, and explaining how they've taken over his life. He listens to *We're Mad: The Anthology* pretty much non-stop so as to get as wide a range of material as possible into his ears at the same sitting. *Bare Faced Cheek* is another favourite. Like so many thousands of other fans, Dani also sees The Toy Dolls' humour as being very important – like Vanessa in Brazil, he finds the music can liven him up and make him laugh. He finds 'I've Got Asthma', 'Fisticuffs in Frederick Street', 'James Bond Lives Down Our Street' and 'Florence is Deaf' particularly enjoyable in this context. His e-mail ends with a poignant hope that The Toy Dolls will carry on indefinitely, a hope we all share, wherever we live.

Gabriel Fumagalli (Gabriel from the website chatroom) lives in Tigre, close to Buenos Aires, and remembers listening to 'Harry's Hands' years ago and going on to be astonished at how Olga seemed to make the guitar speak for itself during his guitar solos. Gabriel judges *Orcastrated* to be the best-sounding of all the band's albums with the best collection of songs, though he also rates *Idle Gossip* and *Absurd-Ditties*. He is gutted at not being able to go and see the band when they were in Buenos Aires the last time – he was a bit too young to go to the gig alone and nobody was willing to take him – but he managed to get hold of an audio recording of the gig and he says it sounds amazing. You can bet your bottom dollar he'll be pushed right up to the front when The Toy Dolls hit Argentina in 2005!

Back on European soil, one surprise for many fans was that the band didn't play live in Italy until 1997 (a year which also saw 'firsts' in Russia and Finland). This was perhaps surprising, given the country's proximity to France, Austria, Germany and Switzerland, where their roots were firmly set, but the fact is that there was not enough evidence of a burgeoning fanbase in Italy until relatively recently. The decision to travel across and play the Made in Bologna festival was taken on the grounds that it would be an interesting experience and would allow the band to gauge how keen the public seemed to be. Since then, however, the fanbase has been growing. Danut Decaroli from Vestignè, close to Turin, describes The Toy Dolls as the best band he's ever come across. There's a touch of the Spinal Tap guitar volume in his comments as he assesses the band:

> "On a scale of 1 to 10, I'd have to say that The Toy Dolls are worth at least 11."

But what about the earliest gigs in continental Europe. The first such show was in Groningen, Holland on 31 March 1984, following dramatically on after the delights of a sunny Californian tour and the rainier depths of playing the Club in Shiney Row, a nondescript village on the road from Sunderland to Chester-le-Street. Holland has been a huge Toy Dolls country ever since, as a quick check of the craziness encountered on the website message forum will confirm. Olga is quick to nod and wax effusive about the band's history and experiences in Holland:

> "I love Holland, because it's unbelievable how you can just cross a little bit of water and sell out places, coming from a country where only the hardcore's interested. Mind you, there was a lovely moment once, very early on, when we were getting onto the North Sea ferry to go across and play in Holland, and there were 6 or 7 British fans, absolutely devoted and soaking wet in their Toy Dolls t-shirts, waiting to get on and travel over with us. I felt like crying, it was such a touching thing."

It is clear, talking to Olga, that the countries geographically closer to the UK are the nearest the band gets these days to playing on home territory. After so many years and so many gigs – plus the friendly, honest and open nature The Toy Dolls have always had – it's inevitable that some real friendships should have built up with people in places like the Netherlands and other countries nearby:

> "There are some places like Munich and Hamburg and most of Holland, too, where it feels like coming home, like coming back to your wife, so to speak. Even though it's physically hard work doing the gig, it's just so nice seeing the people again. You definitely build up a network of friends and familiar faces."

Travelling the world and meeting people from diverse cultures, the band have been interested to learn the different ways in which certain nationalities show their appreciation and manifest their fandom. Olga has always seen the Dutch (and the Scandinavians) as being quite liberal and open, and indeed the most likely to get involved with things like the website message board. Other cultures vary greatly, as we'll see.

Germany was the next continental European country to receive the band (the day after Groningen, actually, though there were no April Fools jokes as the band headed for Bremen). Germany has something of a reputation for efficiency and punctuality, and Olga has always been tickled by the prospect of playing somewhere in Germany then heading straight for a venue in southern Europe, where the concept of punctuality will be utterly different:

> "In Germany, you know that you're on at 9.00 or whenever, and you have to finish at a certain time, because of the curfew and all that, and you can be confident that the sound and the lights and everything will be ready and working in plenty of time. Then you go to somewhere like Spain, where things are so laid-back, and you see the difference. But it's pointless getting annoyed – the best thing is to enjoy the differences and relax with them."

In a conversation about favourite venues worldwide – not necessarily the biggest or the most spectacular, but places where the atmosphere is always at its best, and the venue has brought the best out of the band and forged the ideal contact between the lads and the audience – a place in Munich stands out in Olga's mind: the Theaterfabrik. It's the right sort of size, such that the band can have the right level of intimacy with the crowd and make them feel properly involved. The Alabamahalle in the same city is also great, though it's a great deal bigger.

The German press seems to love The Toy Dolls. An article in the *Süddeutsche Zeitung* on 29 March 1993 makes the fatal mistake of referring to their music as 'Punk-Light' and 'Fun-Punk' – terms Olga particularly hates – but goes on to describe the band's chaotic, breakneck stage performance and the heat and disorder of the moshpit down at the front. It is as if the whole show is programmed to deliver speed, noise, chaos and enjoyment, and the 'next generation' of punks – alongside polite young people wearing Benetton and politically correct slogans on their t-shirts – enjoy themselves just as much as their 1977 predecessors did watching The Clash or The Pistols.

Similarly to the Buenos Aires story, Olga remembers an incident when the band were first cutting their teeth in Germany in the early days of continental touring:

> "We played in Munich in the mid-eighties, and we sold the place out at 800 people or something, which was really good for us. Then we drove past this auditorium place on the way to the hotel, and I wondered what the place was, and the guy who was guiding us said, 'oh, it's where ZZ Top are playing, with 2,000 guests.' That's guests of the band! The audience was 37,000 or something. So it just shows you. Back to ground level!"

To the independent observer, Switzerland might seem something of an odd country for an English punk band to make an impact, but in January 1985 the lads took their first tentative steps into a country that welcomed them warmly and where they've continued to enjoy touring ever since, albeit at a limited range of small venues. But, as is well known, size isn't everything, and there's a venue in Switzerland that joins the Munich clubs on Olga's list of all-time favourite places to play live:

> "We play this place in Switzerland all the time because I love playing there, in Zurich – Winterthur actually, just outside Zurich – and the audience are right there in your face. Actually there's a story associated with that place: once when we were playing there I was leaning down playing the guitar and this guy with long hair got his hair wrapped round and round the machine head, and got stuck. So the roadie had to come and cut his hair – I couldn't believe it, man. But I like that close contact type of thing – it's important to us."

Switzerland is obviously a far richer country than many of its neighbours, but that doesn't stop it having had a thriving, ground-level punk and indie scene which has embraced The Toy Dolls for nearly 20 years. In this respect, it shares the warmth and enthusiasm shown towards the band by its neighbours France and Germany, and it is relatively uncomplicated for Olga and the lads to pop across the border into Switzerland during a longer tour close by. That's not to say that the touring in Switzerland is extensive – it's usually limited to a handful of towns and cities – but they do enough to make the Swiss fans happy. I'm interested in hearing more about the Albani venue in Winterthur:

> "It's a tiny little countrified kind of village, and the venue is small, but that's fine – as I said before, that's how we prefer it. The atmosphere it generates is superb, and maybe that's why loads of other bands have been to play there – Dr Feelgood and all sorts of people. Yeah, we've always been very happy there, and in Switzerland in general."

A report in the Swiss *Neue Zürcher Zeitung* from October 1997 chronicles how the writer was pleasantly surprised to see that the band, playing live at the Albani in Winterthur, surpassed all he had heard them play on record: "this crazy show was exceptionally good fun." It's often the case that a band are accused of not being able to match their studio capabilities when playing live, but with The Toy Dolls, seemingly this could not be further from the case.

In the early part of 1986, the band played in Scandinavia for the first time, moving from a gig in Olso up into Sweden for half a dozen shows then a first foray into Denmark. This was clearly virgin territory for The Toy Dolls, and it struck me that they must have been taking a bit of a risk financially, heading for such expensive countries without the kind of budget enjoyed by bigger bands. How did they get on?

"All the Scandinavian countries were really good – they always have been – and the people were so nice. We just about broke even on those gigs, but that wasn't the point – we didn't go there to make money. We'd been getting good feedback from those countries on our early albums, so we owed it to these new fans to go up and play for them. Maybe it had something to do with the Scandinavians' ability with the English language, I don't know (not that we sing in clear English!), but yeah, I remember having such a nice time there. It was fantastic."

The expense, though, is still a factor, as the band have a lot of things to take into account and to pay for. Accounting-wise, was it much of a shock in the early days to leave countries like Germany and Holland and move northwards into a different financial realm?

"Yeah, Scandinavia's a bit different from anywhere else – all you have to do is cross that border through from the north of Germany into Denmark, and it becomes so expensive: planning the journey there, plus the hotels and actually setting the gigs up. Then of course the beer's so expensive, and I think because of these things, and the weather, it makes people's attitudes different. With the Scandinavian people, everything's expensive, but it's not like Japan, where everything's expensive and the wages are high – in Scandinavia it's expensive but the wages are really not that high. It's 90% lads at the gigs up there. But we enjoyed it. And it's good to face the new challenge of a new country. It stops you becoming complacent, and keeps your feet on the ground. It's not like an Eastern Bloc kind of thing, where they were starved of any sort of entertainment, but it is a different kind of audience. Yeah, I found the Scandinavians to be really nice people, and I still do."

At around the time The Toy Dolls were first trying to break Scandinavia, a young boy named Jonas Wettmark – known to message forum fans as Maharadjan – was with some older friends who were listening to punk. He reserved judgement for the time being, but a few years later he discovered NoFX and Bad Religion, and was browsing in a record shop in Arvika in Sweden when he came across *Orcastrated*.

"The amazing guitar playing, the originality, the witty and cool lyrics and the mob vocals stunned me. I was trapped! I bought the albums one after the other and ordered the VHS tapes. Since lyrics weren't included in the majority of the albums I ordered lyrics sheets from the fan club. The Toy Dolls quickly became my favourite band and they still are. In 1997 I had the honour and pleasure of attending one of their gigs in Sweden. It goes without saying that it was the best gig I have ever seen!"

In addition to liking *Orcastrated* as it was his first purchase, Jonas shares Olga's preference for *Dig That Groove, Baby* and *Absurd-Ditties*, and also cites 'Charlie's Watching', 'She'll be Back with Keith Someday' and 'I'll Get Even With Steven (Steve is Tender)' as his trio of favourite songs.

But the music and the live performances aren't the only reason why The Toy Dolls are so special to Jonas: it was through the band's website – for which he has nothing but praise, like the rest of us – that he met his girlfriend Amanda (Manda 82) and finally got to see and photograph the landmarks in Sunderland that are both well known and tantalisingly distant to most fans across the world. And he met Marty. Hats off to Telly Addict, our beloved Admin man, for his skills not only as top technological wizard, but also as a faultless matchmaker and purveyor of love. A sort of Cilla Black with decent musical taste and without the facelift...

Another Swede with *Absurd-Ditties* as his favourite album is David Beijner (TD Addict in the chatroom). He's been listening to the band since he was 15, and counts 'Cloughy is a Bootboy' and 'You Won't be Merry on a North Sea Ferry' as special songs, along with 'Modern Schools of Motoring', which he confesses to having listened to over and over again at first until he was practically in a daze.

It's particularly pleasing to Olga and the lads that a younger generation of new fans has sprung up across the world. One fan who got into the band through a medium that would have been unimaginable 25 years ago is Ki Boy (Peter Andersson). The moment when he first saw the light occurred while he was listening to the soundtrack on a Tony Hawk video game in 2002, and heard 'Dig That Groove, Baby'. From then on he was hooked. Peter finds the band special because they encompass everything a punk band should: they play good music, they have both style and endurance, and they have fun when they are playing.

Robin Henricsson was another fan who came to the band via the Pro Skater 4 game, and recalls that he immediately set off on a mission to find information about the band and some way of listening to more of their music. Eventually he got his hands on *We're Mad: The Anthology*, and was quickly hooked. He feels the main reason The Toy Dolls are so successful across the world is that the songs have such a catchy quality, and is effusively thankful to the band for getting him into music properly in the first place. Before his eyes were opened, he'd scarcely found anything worth listening to, and now music is a huge part of his life thanks to one band. It's a great story.

Finally from Scandinavia, Jonatan Palmblad, a Swedish punk living in Gothenburg, wrote to say how much he likes the energy and the melodies of The Toy Dolls' songs. Having got into the band when his girlfriend played 'My Baby is a Battleaxe' for him, he now considers them to be like no other band on earth, and can't wait for the chance to see them for the first time on the forthcoming world tour.

1987 was the year when the band finally got round to playing live in France and Belgium. Again, there hadn't been enough concrete evidence before this to support the idea of a tour in either country, but since things had taken off so well in neighbouring Holland and Germany, the word eventually got out that there was a shit-hot live band out there playing just the sort of music they wanted, and eventually the combination of record sales and expansion of fanbase made some gigs in both countries possible. The Toy Dolls went down so well in Belgium and France that these countries have been an integral part of any European tour ever since.

Olga has always enjoyed playing in France, and has made some good friends there. He describes the French fans as quite a mixture, with old-style punks mingling with some quite stylish younger fans. (We're on our seventh pint by this stage, so we dedicate about 5 minutes to pronouncing the word 'chic' and pissing ourselves laughing at how it sounds. The French waitress recognises a vaguely familiar word, but is bewildered as to why we should find it so funny. It becomes Olga's official favourite word for the day.) How do French fans differ from other European Toy Dolls people, I wonder?

> "The French have always been very supportive and appreciative of our records and shows, but it's true to say that they're a bit more reserved, maybe a bit cool, if you like. It's the same with the t-shirts, as well: in a lot of countries, they want big, in-your-face designs and bright colours with the face logo and everything. If you go to France, on the other hand, they're generally keener on really designer things – black t-shirts with a tiny little logo, which we also do very well. So we can cater for all tastes."

It was a Frenchman who provided Olga with another of his growing number of Newcastle Airport anecdotes. Olga was arriving back in the northeast from a foreign trip somewhere, and a guy came up to him and said, "You're Olga from The Toy Dolls, aren't you? I saw you in concert." Olga asked him where, expecting him to say "Shiney Row Club" or somewhere, but the reply was, "Paris." Good for the ego. The guy then scuttled off to head for his girlfriend's house in Hexham, Northumberland.

The French newspaper *Le Monde* recorded a great little incident on 23 June 1999, during the Bayonne Music Festival. As loads of Basque youngsters roamed the streets drinking *kalimotxo* (a mixture of Coke and red wine), the journalist Davet Stéphane wandered deeper and deeper into the back streets, looking for the soul of the festival and trying to trace a pounding beat that could be heard on the night air. Eventually, the source was revealed in the back room of a dingy bar: a band of radical Basque rockers were playing Toy Dolls songs with all their hearts, and the joint was sweaty and rocking to the foundations.

On 6 October 1987, *La Nouvelle République* described the band's songs as "full of humour, mockery and rebellion," the same week as the Breton listings magazine *Loisirs*, advertising a forthcoming gig by the band, invited the public to "come along and sing, dance, cry, jump about, drink, laugh, cry again, stamp your feet, pogo, and generally have a ball with The Toy Dolls." Lively affairs, these Toy Dolls gigs. Oh, yes.

Koen Velleman from Belgium, a fan from 1987 onwards, has had the fortune to spend quite a bit of time with the band, and went to extreme lengths to catch as many European shows as possible in the early 1990s. Koen's moment of seeing the light came with a first hearing of 'I've Got Asthma' in 1987, then 2 years later came the glorious moment of seeing the band live for the first time. The journal I received by e-mail is quite a document, and really gives a flavour of life on the road with The Toy Dolls, but what were Koen's first impressions of The Toy Dolls live?

"I thought, 'wow, this must be the best live band ever.' All my favourite songs just kept coming and the crowd went mad. After the show I got the opportunity to meet the lads, and there I found out that not only was the music fantastic, but also the people behind the music were the nicest, kindest people I've ever met."

After travelling to Holland and Germany to see the band later on, in 1991, Koen got a real hunger to get immersed in Toy Dolls life, and decided to follow the band to as many gigs as possible on the 1993 tour. Here's an edited account of Koen's tour diary:

"From that moment on it all went crazy for me. My tour started on 3 March 1993. Early in the morning I packed my bags, grabbed my motorcycle and off I went to Arnhem to meet with Olga and the others. I arrived half frozen, but that was put right by the Belgian chocolates I'd brought along. That night I slept outside. It was freezing cold, and it was a stupid thing to do – obviously I wasn't so world-wise then as I am now!

"The next day they had to be in Enschede at the University, where the gig would be in the sports-hall. I felt terrible but that didn't stop me from helping them set up the stage. I remember they marked the front of the stage with arrows that said 'stagedive', and I recall thinking what a funny thing to do that was. So Olga played the whole set standing in between kids diving up and down the stage. It was a great night. And for me there was some good news, too – I got to share a room supplied by the band. In the morning we had breakfast and everything. That was a lot better than sleeping outside.

"The 2nd gig I went to was in Utrecht, Tivoli. Fantastic! The place was packed, the atmosphere, the sound, the night was unbelievable. I sat beside Ernie the whole time while he was doing the lights. The harmony between the public and the band was amazing. It was so much fun to see my favourite band every night that I didn't mind sleeping outside, but I still had a long way to go.

"The 3rd show was on March 6 in Noordescharwoude. That was funny – Olga lost it for a second and said, 'I've got asthma and I can't breathe. I went to the dentist...' You should've seen the looks on John and Marty's faces when Olga continued with, 'and he sent me to the doctor and he gave me one of these.' It was hilarious!

"After the next gig in Amsterdam we were off to Ubach Palenberg, Rockfabrik, which is situated in an industrial area in the middle of nowhere. Again the place is packed and the party starts. Olga's playing dazzling solos, and doing great jumps. Even seeing them night after night doesn't become boring at all. Once in a while I found myself dancing in the pit. Can you ever get tired of this? I also became friends with Olga and the others.

"When we arrived in Munster at the Odeon on March 9 they decided to let me sleep in the van. This was also good for them because now they always had someone to watch over the van. And for me no more sleeping outside! March 10, Zeche Carl, Essen. March 11, a day off. That was the first time for me, hanging around with them, watching other people rush to work and it was a very beautiful day. Marty, of course, went to all the record shops he could find.

"March 12, everybody back on stage, filled with energy. They were at their best. The next day was in Hamburg at the Markthalle. A rough area, the gig was rough as well, but the band was top.

"March 14 was in Berlin at the famous Loft. An unbelievable gig! The crowd was packed together, joining forces with fans of the support band Big Boy Tomato. The people there sure knew how to party: there was a lot of singing and dancing and afterwards a goodbye party for Big Boy Tomato. I thought Big Boy Tomato were really good and they were a lot of fun to hang around with. At that party everyone had a lot to drink, which was a real killer the next day. Then we had to drive a long way, from Berlin to

Frankfurt. I rode my motorcycle for 6 hours and felt like I was dying, but I had to go on because after that I had to go back home. I took all the energy I had left for my last gig and danced in the pit. The sound wasn't that good but the fun just never ended. And then it was time to say goodbye, but not for too long...

"Time flew by and a few months later I was back on the road. May 28, Reims, France. Very nice backstage passes they had there. Once again I noticed that wherever The Toy Dolls play, there's always a party. That's what makes the trips so much fun.

"On May 29 the lads played in Paris, Elysée Montmartre. A big stage gave them the opportunity to put on a very big show that covered the whole stage. The lights were brilliant. Afterwards the promoter took us to a nice Chinese restaurant. Everyone drunk sake – it burned like hell, but no harm was done. It was another great night out.

"A couple of days later we drove to Holland to perform at the Paard in Den Haag. This was a few days before the end of the tour and the band was still fresh. The way they played was very fast and smooth, like a well oiled machine, without losing their sense of humour and the contact with the fans.

"On June 8 they played in Rotterdam, the city of Carlo. Carlo is a big fan, a great dancer and he has a heart of gold. They played in Trier the next day. That gig took place in some kind of wine cellar. It reminded me of a documentary I saw of the Beatles when they played in Liverpool at the Cavern Club. It was very small, but I danced too much and had no time to take any pictures. 12 June 1993 was scheduled to be the last gig of the tour. We spent the day in Cologne, at the Luxor. A lot of funny things were happening on the stage: a condom over the Lambrusco wine bottle, shaving cream on their bodies, water splashing around, real madness. Aside from that they pulled off a great show.

"And just when you think, 'this is it,' they announced

one more gig thanks to the Waldrock Festival in Holland. A very strange festival that was. Apart from The Toy Dolls and Bad Religion there were only Death Metal bands playing. Picture this: a whole lot of noise from Deicide stopped, there was silence for a few minutes and then suddenly you hear, 'Hello!' from Olga's squeaky voice. It was hilarious! But it seemed as if everyone at the festival had come to see The Toy Dolls. As soon as they started playing, people packed up together at the front. Olga was playing faster than usual – he even broke a string – all because they couldn't play the whole set, as there wasn't enough time. A festival, though, is so much more relaxing. After doing your own act, you can watch other bands play or hang around and drink, smoke and talk about music. Of course this wasn't the end of my craziness to see the band live. By now we were good friends. They were already talking about a new tour for 1995, and I became determined to follow them again across Europe. But that, as they say, is another story."

Spain is a country where The Toy Dolls – since their first performance there in 1986 – have always been rapturously received. Aside from the laid-back thing we mentioned earlier, it's also true to say that Spanish fans stand out for a couple of their characteristics: firstly, they're fiercely loyal, even though the band are scarcely if ever on the TV there, and there is only a limited amount of radio play; and perhaps more importantly, they behave like absolute nutters at live gigs. It may be something to do with the Mediterranean temperament, or the fact that, by the time The Toy Dolls finally appear on stage, it's usually well after midnight, and plenty of San Miguel, Estrella or *kalimotxo* has been consumed, but whatever the reason, gigs in Spain absolutely rock, and the atmosphere – to put it politely – may be termed 'boisterous'.

Olga remembers the scene outside the band's first-ever Spanish show, at the Zeleste in Barcelona in December 1986. The Barcelona Zelestes have joined Olga's list of favourite venues, again because of their size, their feel, and the sort of atmosphere and audience contact they can offer. That first night was a belter:

"It was absolutely unbelievable. We played the Zeleste Club in Barcelona, which held about 500 in those days. That was a smallish crowd, but again, it's the sort of size we like, especially in a new country where you're still gauging the level of support. But I remember them bending cigarette machines and smashing things up outside the venue and going absolutely crazy. It was incredible. Then later on you get the newer version of the Zeleste, which holds about 2,500 or something like that, and it's just the perfect size of place for the combination of big show (I mean you can get the big backdrop up, great lights, great sound, you can do a great show, and everybody can see) with a good feeling of the crowd being involved. There's something good about that place. I love it."

Smashing cigarette machines, eh? That's your respectable Catalans for you! But Olga loves Barcelona as a city, and has fond memories of the Ramblas and the port area and the beaches at the bottom, as well as other Spanish cities such as Madrid and Valladolid (which we're both too drunk to try and pronounce by this stage). He finds the Spanish people quite similar to the Brazilians: warm, friendly, and "absolutely mad – brilliant people."

An article in the Spanish daily newspaper *El País* on 13 October 1997, in effect advertising the band's forthcoming gig at the Zeleste, referred to The Toy Dolls as:

"... veterans, revellers, uninhibited hooligans, noisy, fireproof and punker than punk. This is a band that doesn't have to bring out records in order to tour. They don't need promotional baggage to sell records, nor do they need interviews to say daft things. They are The Toy Dolls, and their gigs are a guarantee of chaos."

What better recommendation could you ask for? Two years

earlier, Kike Buitre, writing in the influential Spanish rock magazine *Ruta 66*, described the band as:

> "… simple but rebellious, charming, fun-loving little devils, naughty troublemakers in the face of an adult world."

In the same article, Olga is amusingly quoted as saying that his objective in bringing out a new album is crystal clear: to keep a handful of drunkards pogoing happily for an hour and a half.

Gradually, the band's domination of Europe spread, and as we reach the present day, in addition to the countries mentioned above, they have also played in Russia, Finland, Estonia, Hungary, Poland, Croatia and the Czech Republic. Each country has produced a new excitement in the minds of the lads as they've travelled there, and Olga repeats his views about every country being both a new challenge, and an opportunity to see new cities and meet different types of fans. When they first played in Prague – which was in 1991, when the city was still part of the former country of Czechoslovakia – a memorable incident happened at the gig:

> "Prague was unbelievable, absolutely unbelievable. At one point in that first gig, two-thirds of the lights in the city went out, all the electricity, so we played 'Glenda and the Test-tube Baby' with acoustic guitars, and they all had their cigarette lighters out. It was a memorable occurrence. It was flippin' class. And I wondered what was going on, so I was shouting to 2,000 people, 'we're going to do "Glenda" now,' trying to make them hear. And they all got their lighters out. And because of that, everybody talks about that gig. Had it been a normal gig, and had we been a better band, it may not have been quite so memorable, but there you go. We played in Prague 3 or 4 times after then, and the last time we played there, we supported Sinéad O'Connor, in a kind of festival, and Erasure were there, and loads of other bands. I remember knocking on the door of Erasure's dressing room, because the singer looks the same as our

sound man. And I said, 'you've got to get a photo together, you look exactly the same.' So I knocked on the door, and he came out and I said, 'Andy Bell?' And then I pointed out the sound guy, and he knew straight away what I was getting at. And he said, 'another ugly bastard.' It was really good, coz he understood he looked the same. But yeah, I have great memories of Prague – a fabulous place, and great memories for the band."

We find ourselves chatting about Russia, and Olga makes a neat comparison between the types of audiences the band have had in Russia and Hungary. He was astonished to watch a video of a show the band had done in Moscow, where the entire audience was singing along to every word of every Toy Dolls song. He tells me that it had struck him at the time how weird it was – writing a song as a teenager in his bedroom in Sunderland, then 20 years later hearing thousands of people singing it alongside him in a country whose language and culture are about as far removed as it is possible to be from what you find in Sunderland. The same thing happened in Hungary, where the band played three huge festivals, with something like 30,000 people singing along and seemingly knowing every word, but without having a clue who Tommy Kowey was. Those were magical times for the band.

Festivals offer mixed feelings for Olga. He'd never choose to go to one himself as a fan, because there can be too many people there and there's no guarantee you're going to see your favourite band giving of their best. As an artist, it can be a let-down, as you often have to use whatever equipment you're given, which can compromise the quality of your sound and your performance. The upside is that you sometimes have time to relax and spend time with other bands, whereas other times again you have to rush straight off to your next engagement. At the festival in Croatia, for instance, Olga managed to have something of a conversation with Shane MacGowan from the Pogues and understand most of what Shane was saying (which is more than most people can manage), but in Estonia the experience was very different:

> "That was a big gig. It was for about 10,000 or something. We flew straight in, got changed, straight on stage, did the gig, then straight back to the hotel, and flew out the next morning. But they were really nice – the people there all were. And the gig was good – we did well. But it was a big rush for only 45 minutes on stage. I can't remember who else was playing – there were a number of groups that flew in from London. But again, it was different from Shiney Row Social Club, back near Sunderland."

Further afield, perhaps the most surprising corner of the world for The Toy Dolls to have experienced unbridled success is Japan. Geographically and culturally, that's about as far as you can get from Grangetown in Sunderland (apart from Australia, about which more later). I ask Olga to give us the background to how the link with Japan was originally made:

> "1986, with the first shows in Japan, was the turning-point for us. Our manager, Dave Chumbley, who was on board by this stage, was managing New Model Army and King Kurt, and he said he'd like us to go to Japan just before our Californian tour. And I was shocked – I didn't know whether they were all going to be in kimonos, you know? (Typical northeast thug that I am.) But he said, 'no, your first album has really taken off,' so we went there and did 3 nights – 2 nights at the Tsubaki House in Tokyo, and 1 in Kyoto at the Vibra Hall. It was unbelievable! It was tremendous – the number of people at the airport just for us, and the train station, everywhere. And the girlfriend of the drummer from The Wildhearts was at our very first gig, and I didn't even meet her until 2 years ago, when I moved to London! We couldn't do a thing wrong, what with the thousands of girls in the hotel, and all that kind of thing. We flew straight from there on 17 January 1986 to do a gig in Hollywood on the same date. We were so jet-lagged we were

crap. The Dickies were the support group, and they blew us off the stage. They were absolutely fantastic. But we still went down really well, although we were very complacent because of the reception we'd got in Japan. We did the whole Californian thing so complacently because of the high we were enjoying from Japan, where everyone had been screaming and we couldn't do a thing wrong. So yeah, that was the first time in Japan – we went back later that year."

I can't help asking Olga more about his reception and his profile in Japan. It's common knowledge that he's always been popular with the screaming female fans over there, and I figure it will do his ego no harm whatsoever to regale us with a few stories from his time there:

"The fan thing in Japan was unbelievable, it was just out of this world. We went back to Japan in the middle of 1986, only for a week and only to do television, and there were kids in the street screaming for us. Then I remember we arrived straight from a European tour in 1991, and arriving at the hotel and there were 200 girls, and I said, 'what are they waiting for?' and I was told, 'they're waiting for you.' And I said, 'you what?' I couldn't believe it! And they're all checking into the hotel where you're staying, putting little notes through your door and all that. Aye, it was an experience all right..."

One of the things that always made Japan stand out from other countries (apart from the vast cultural differences) was the gender make-up of the audience. Olga reckons that it's now maybe 60-40 female-male, but in the early days of Japanese touring it was 99% female. I put it to Olga that this must have made for a very different dynamic between the audience and the band at gigs:

"Yeah, you're right. Also, the Japanese are very, very conservative, especially in the audience. If you play Japan, the place might be sold out, but they won't make any sound until the end of the song, then they scream, and then stop to allow you to play the next song. Japan's a different planet. It's not like going to another country; it's like going to a different planet completely. It's changed over the last 15 or 20 years – when we first went there we used to be playing at 4.00 or 5.00 in the afternoon, and a bell used to go, like for last orders, and it would be 5.00, spot-on, lights down, and at the end of the gig it was, 'right, everybody out,' and now it's 8.00 or 9.00, or maybe 10.00. It's become a lot more westernised now, but that was something we had to get used to at first."

There's a strange contradiction between the screaming in the street and a more restrained kind of behaviour in Japan. Can Olga put his finger on what makes Japanese fans tick in this respect?

"Yeah, it's weird. There doesn't seem to be a single Japanese person getting involved with the website chatroom, for instance. There's a much more reserved philosophy about things like that over there. But then, I remember being on a train with the band in Japan, and there was a famous Japanese singer, the most famous singer ever, and 7 people and me there, then there was Metallica in the next carriage. They were big over here but there they were unheard of and were playing 2 nights in a tiny little place in Tokyo, and we were playing 4 nights in this flippin' massive place. And there were so many people at the station to meet us – media and fans and people to look after us – and Metallica just kind of disappeared out of a side door. That's how it was – we just had to get used to it. Now, of course, Metallica play to 50,000 people."

Once the band were established in Japan, a number of lucrative sidelines presented themselves. The story of the Lolita No. 18 involvement is dealt with in another chapter, but Olga was also asked to lend his patronage to various products in the Japanese TV advertising industry. After much thought, he turned the offers down. It's easy to see how, back in the UK, endorsing products would lead to an immediate slagging-off by the music press and the newspapers in general, with suggestions that the artist had sold out, or had reached such a low ebb that he was 'reduced' to seeking money from the world of advertising. Over in Japan, though, Olga found the whole business of being approached by advertisers much more straightforward, and refreshingly honest:

> "In Japan, if you're good, the press will say you're good; if you're bad, you're bad. And you'll get a punk band that's doing an advert for shampoo, and you'll have the name of the band in the corner of the television, and Japanese people think, logically enough, 'they'll sell more records,' not fewer, as would happen in Britain. And I tend to think, 'yeah, why not?' Unless it's against your principles, or what you believe in, or it's promoting animal testing or it's some kind of war thing that you don't believe in, in which case that's different. But when it's shampoo or soap or something, so what? Why is that a sell-out?"

But I suppose that any media exposure – particularly in the early days – must have helped greatly in getting the band a bigger profile and making them more money (it's no secret that Japan was been by far the most lucrative country for the band over the years – whereas in some countries they'll tour and break even, there's always a profit to be made in Japan, even after all their heavy expenses and so on are taken into account). Record sales have helped, too: *Dig That Groove, Baby*, the band's first album, has sold about 150,000 copies worldwide since its release in 1983, and something approaching 70,000 of those sales were made in the Tokyo area. Did Olga ever get to feel like a household name in Japan?

> "Would you believe I was once voted Japan's sexiest male! Can you imagine that? Me? I couldn't believe they were serious!"

But you kept the newspaper cutting?

"Aye."

Such a sexy male must have expected to attract the attention of particularly keen female fans, and before long, Olga started going out with a girl who ended up coming over to England to live with him in Sunderland. As I've detailed in another chapter, she became the inspiration for 'My Wife's a Psychopath'. It was an experience, but, one assumes, not one to be repeated. A lot later, when he was over working with Lolita No. 18, Olga met Mihoko, with whom he's now very happy, living in London and sharing a love of Japanese food, culture and good times. The food was also an eye-opener for him – at first, he couldn't stomach it, but as the years went by his palate adapted, and now he wouldn't be without it, especially all the fresh fish.

Before we complete our world tour of Toy Dolls fandom and look forward to the real thing in the autumn of this year and the first half of 2005, let's spare a thought for fans in whose countries the band have never played. It took a long time for The Toy Dolls to reach South America, but they did finally play there, and the fans' thirst was temporarily slaked. The Portuguese, Russians and Croats similarly had to wait a good few years, but gradually they were included. But what happens if you live in the largest English-speaking country in the world, 24 hours away from Sunderland by plane, and nevertheless your only contact with the band is your precious CD collection? Our final story comes all the way from Australia, from Alec Wendleman, who lives in a small town in Victoria State called Bacchus Marsh. You've heard 'Alec's Gone' and 'Alec's Back' – now here's Alec's story:

> "Me and my girl were out for a Sunday drive and we stopped in a town called Daylesford. After getting some lunch, I knew of a good second hand book/CD/record/tape store around the corner and as my Kiss tape busted just as we were about to stop we were jiveless in the car. Entering

the store, in a rack by the door a catchy tape cover caught my eye. I had a second look and at first I thought it was just another kids' tape. But then I looked again. There were two Marshall stacks in the background. And I thought, 'damn, this ain't no kids' tape!' It was on sale for 4 dollars. What the hell. I'll take it. Man, am I glad I did! I put it in my tape player in the car and the first thing that hit me was a sickeningly good guitar solo that just about blew me out of the car. To cut a long story short, I listened to that album – *Wakey Wakey* – non-stop for the next 4 weeks until our local CD store finally got me a copy of *10 Years of Toys*. I now own 5 CDs and the DVD, but still think *Wakey Wakey* is the band's best work. I'm 23 years old right now and Olga's guitar-playing has inspired me to dust off the old stick, rip out the amp and try to play a few of these songs. Olga is one of the best guitar-players I've heard in such a long time, and has been a real inspiration."

An inspiration indeed! Thanks to everyone who shared their experiences with me, and here's hoping both *Our Last Album?* and Our Last Tour? help us all – wherever in the world we live – to celebrate 25 glorious years of ToyDollism in appropriate style!

Top 25 All-time Toy Dolls Rhymes

Before we launch into the final chapter, as a personal tribute to The Toy Dolls on the occasion of their 25th anniversary, I thought it would be a good idea to pick out my favourite rhymes conjured up by Olga's fertile brain over the last two-and-a-half decades. (No inclusion of any lyrics from *Our Last Album?* has been possible since, at the time of writing, the album has not yet been released.) They are set out alphabetically by the title of the song in which they feature, so there's no 'number 1' on the basis of merit – they're all winners in my book.

1. From 'A Bunch o' Fairies' (*Fat Bob's Feet*)
    You can commit any crime you please
    You won't get nicked in Sunderland, the coppers are softies

2. From 'A Bunch o' Fairies' (*Fat Bob's Feet*)
    They hide when there's a thief or rogue at large
    When they get hit they run and tell the sarge

3. From 'A Diamond' (*Bare Faced Cheek*)
    She used to have a thousand fans that really used to spoil her
    Until they found out that Anne's a dodgy boiler

4. From 'Audrey's Alone at Last' (*Anniversary Anthems*)
    It's a tragedy but

When she spied Alfie's nut
Drooping down on top of his gut

5. From 'Audrey's Alone at Last' (*Anniversary Anthems*)
    Left in debt
    She won't forget
    The greedy get

6. From 'Bitten by a Bedbug' (*Fat Bob's Feet*)
    A nit in need of nourishment
    It got inside the bed and went
    for me

7. From 'Bored Housewife' (*One More Megabyte*)
    She's a bored, bored housewife – in the cul-de-sac
    She's a bored, bored housewife – she's a
    nymphomaniac

8. From 'Dorkamania' (*Anniversary Anthems*)
    It's dorkamania, he's goininsania
    I never met a moron who is more mundania
    Dorkamania, he's gotta be brainia

9. From 'Fat Bob's Feet' (*Fat Bob's Feet*)
    Fat Bob's not cleaned his socks yet
    He's not been to the launderette

10. From 'Fat Bob's Feet' (*Fat Bob's Feet*)
    Spray Fat Bob's feet with fungicide
    He's wiped out two-thirds of Tyneside

11. From 'Firey Jack' (*Dig That Groove, Baby*)
    Firey Jack, Firey Jack, it's red hot on your back
    Firey Jack, Firey Jack, believe me, it does knack

12. From 'Geordie's Gone to Jail' (*Idle Gossip*)
    He never takes any drugs, only penicillin

When he's got a headache.
The fingerprint wasn't Geordie's – Geordie's never been
a villain

13. From 'Ivy's Lurid Lips' (*Orcastrated*)
Ivy's lips are a bleedin' disgrace
Ivy's lips gotta chipmunk's face

14. From 'I'm a Telly Addict' (*Absurd-Ditties*)
Sh-sh-sh-shakin' like a jellyfish
I need a satellite dish

15. From 'I'm a Telly Addict' (*Absurd-Ditties*)
And with a telly in the bog
I never miss the epilogue

16. From 'I've Had Enough o' Magaluf' (*Anniversary
Anthems*)*
But tell me why did she have to pick Charles Atlas?
… Or did the bastard teach her gracias?

  * Note: the title itself is probably worthy of inclusion here.

17. From 'I've Had Enough o' Magaluf' (*Anniversary
Anthems*)
I've been a mug, I might o' known, the scheming
skunks
… Coz she had her hands inside his swimming trunks

18. From 'Kids in Tyne and Wear' (*Fat Bob's Feet*)
Whitley Bay across to Cumbria
You'll be broke if you come 'ere

19. From 'Lester Fiddled the Tax Man' (*Wakey Wakey*)
Lester's accountant was a daft clot
He made a mockery of Ascot Ascot Ascot

20. From 'One Night in Moscow (& We'll be Russian Home!)' (*Wakey Wakey*)
    We had the flu and caught a Russian cough
    We said we would complain to Gorbachov

21. From 'Ron Dixon Dumped D-D' (*Orcastrated*)
    The most repulsive sight on earth, too ugly to discuss
    How could anyone give birth to a bird so hideous?

22. From 'Ron Dixon Dumped D-D' (*Orcastrated*)
    The chance that Ron had waited for, he gave D-D the push
    This was the last time Ronny saw D-D's monstrous mush

23. From 'Taken for a Mug' (*Orcastrated*)
    A lovesick nut, easily misled
    He's always infatuated

24. From 'The Ashbrooke Launderette' (*Bare Faced Cheek*)
    They say my clothes are cleaner, but I'm not a lunatic
    They should be shot, they have not got Persil Automatic

25. From 'The Coppers Copt Ken's Cash' (*Fat Bob's Feet*)
    Ken, Ken, who's he again?
    A disappointment to the Diddymen

History 2004-2005

Our Last Chapter? The Present and the Future

2004 began – like so many other years before it – with viciously cold English weather, and with Olga shutting himself away in his spare bedroom to complete the writing of the new material for *Our Last Album?* This time, of course, things were made far easier with the addition of the Pro Tools recording gear, but it was still a hell of a task. With the website up and running, fans were now able to keep in almost daily contact with the great man, who would come up trumps by providing updates on how things were going, how tired he was and how much he was looking forward to escaping for a few days to get some rehearsals done.

The nature of the band's rehearsals was soon to change when it became apparent that, despite fitting in really well and being an excellent bass-player, the geography of Reb living in Germany and Dave and Olga living in England was not going to work. With great regret, the decision was taken for Reb to leave the band, which was a great shame as he hadn't lasted long enough to put his skills to work on stage. It was still on Olga's mind as we talked:

> "Yeah, the Reb thing was absolute hell – such a shame as he's a really nice guy and a great bassist. We were auditioning and playing a bit with Reb, learning songs, going to and from Germany, and I thought it wasn't working out, and it was costing me a fortune, so we had to do something."

Tommy Goober – top bassist with Vanilla Pod and The

Goober Patrol – had worked as Olga's bass roadie during the Dickies tour (a job he got through his housemate, who is The Dickies' European tour manager), and the two had developed a good working relationship. When the situation with Reb was starting to become unworkable, Olga asked Tommy if he wanted an audition, just as a stand-by, and he came down from Norwich to London and, as Olga puts it:

> "... he was flippin' excellent, as good as Reb. You could see that straight away. He had really good plectrum work. We get on really well, too. Tommy seems to be the real, stereotype sort of punk, with his spiky red hair, and he's a big feller, looks the part, you know?"

Tommy (real name Thomas Blyth) is a native of the county of Norfolk, in eastern England, and has been playing the bass for about 15 years, the last nine of these with The Goober Patrol – who were boosted by being signed by Fat Wreck Chords in 1996 – and he's also recently been working with Vanilla Pod, as well as completing a degree in Animation. Busy man. Taking his nickname from an American word for a hillbilly who makes his own moonshine, Tommy was influenced in the beginning by Stiff Little Fingers, The Clash, The Sex Pistols, Minor Threat, The Dead Kennedys and Poison Idea, and counts Matt Freeman (Rancid), Paul Simonon (Clash), Chris Bauermeister (Jawbreaker) and the late John Entwistle (The Who) as his favourite bass-players. He uses a Fender Precision for most of his work (for its looks as well as its sound), has enjoyed the hard work of rehearsals and the recording studio, and is looking forward to the world tour. He admits that with The Toy Dolls he's doing more singing than he's been used to with other bands, but is rising to the challenge like a star.

I asked Tommy whether, as someone who's joined the band only recently, and with the website up and running, he felt that there was a good vibe and sense of community around The Toy Dolls, and he said that his reception by the fans and his incorporation into the band musically had both been amazing. He feels really at home, and is attacking the experience with relish.

With a powerful three-piece restored, the early months of this year were spent with Olga working 16-hour days on the album, and Dave and Tommy spending what spare time they had learning the drums and bass respectively for as many Toy Dolls songs as were required. Occasional rehearsal weeks were held up in the wilds of Lancashire, where Dave has made his home since taking his degree in Community and Youth Work at Lancaster University, and these periods served to make the band tighter (in the musical, as well as the drunken, sense of the word), and to confirm in Olga's mind that he now had 2 top-class performers working alongside him, which must have come as something of a relief. It's interesting to note that the new line-up also serves to exorcise the ghost of the late 1990s when, in Olga's opinion (though not so much in the mind of the fans), the band was simply not good enough to tour successfully. Let's remember that Olga's primary objective is to put on the best show possible for the fans who buy the records. I asked him, six months before the tour was scheduled to kick off, what his thoughts were about this latest trip around the world:

> "I've got no aspirations this time, other than to have a good show. If I wasn't ready to put in a top show, I'd call the whole thing off and call it a day. I'll not do it unless it's absolutely fantastic. What's the point? What's the point in life? OK, I need the money, but I could get a job in the little fruit shop across the road there. It wouldn't matter how crap I was working there, but I wouldn't have to put on a performance. But I don't want to be crap with my band, which I've built up over 25 years. I want us to be the best, and the audience to be blown away by the show."

With that in mind, we can look forward to good things this autumn. During the spring, we also started to try and guess which countries the lads would be visiting on the world tour, and to hear rumours of a possible live album and/or DVD to be recorded during the tour. The latest I have on this is that one of the early Dutch dates in October – probably Utrecht – will be the scene of this multimedia feast. What price a ticket for that gig!

But before they could think in earnest of the tour, of course, they had to get the album written and recorded. We know all about Olga's songwriting technique, and how much energy and time he puts into it, but I wondered whether it was hard to get himself back into his stride after what was a relatively long gap since *Anniversary Anthems*:

> "Aye, it was hard to sit down and discipline myself again. I think there were some good, fresh areas for songs, which I'd derived from the usual places, like friends and acquaintances, incidents, and soap operas. To be completely fresh, the first album needs your life beforehand for input, which might be 20 years, so that album always stands a better chance, and there's never going to be that much time to draw on again. But this time round the gap's been long enough for me to be happy with what's forthcoming. It should be good."

At the end of April this year, the lads went into the studio up in Newcastle, for a process scheduled to last between 5 and 6 weeks. Why the choice of city? Was it to do with getting back to the roots or, more likely, a financial decision?

> "Yeah, we're recording in Newcastle. It's partly to do with the cost. There are recording studios around this part of London where all the greats have recorded, but you're looking at a thousand pounds a day. You can imagine that we haven't got that sort of budget. So in Newcastle we can do it for around £200 a day, and there's not going to be a lot of difference in quality. So yeah, we're doing 5 weeks. Also, the engineer is a former Penetration man, so that should be good, working with him."

Tommy and Dave were only in the studio for a relatively short period of time, as the bass and drums were quite straightforward, then they were released to taunt us on the website with what might and might not be the cover versions. Eventually, the tension was broken when we learned that 'The Final Countdown' and 'She's So Modern' had been chosen. Meanwhile, Olga had drafted in some of the lads from Loaded 44, Crashed Out, Red Alert, Because We Can and Decca from The Angelic Upstarts to help out on mob vocals and kazoos. That would have been a difficult one to predict back in 1979!

As I put the finishing touches to this book, the schedule of tour dates is starting to take shape nicely. Most of the traditional Toy Dolls countries in northern, central and eastern Europe are covered before Christmas 2004, with the southern part (Spain and Portugal, principally, plus France) plumbed in for the early part of 2005. It is then anticipated that dates in Japan, the USA and South America will follow, plus as many festivals as can feasibly be worked in for the remainder of the year. Regarding a show or shows in the UK in 2005, I kept my eyes and ears open for hints while talking to Olga, and it proved inconclusive. Maybe we can hope for a single show in London, but I think the dream many of us share of the band playing somewhere in Newcastle or Sunderland to close the delicious 25-year circle is just that: a dream.

After that, what?

If I knew the answer for sure, I'd be a far less nervous man than I am now. It seems to hinge on how Olga judges audience reaction during the tour, how he feels himself about being back on the road again (and at an older and wiser age, which is also a factor), whether he feels the new line-up is giving the fans the top show he always says we deserve, and what he then concludes at the end of 2005. Maybe there will be no more world tours of the type we were used to before 2000. Perhaps they'll just do a handful of big festivals each year, to keep up the excitement of playing live. Or there's just a chance that this new album and world tour will go down a treat and spur the lads on to big future projects. In short, we don't know and, in the words of Stiff Little Fingers, we'll have to wait and see.

Aside from working with The Toy Dolls, what future might there be for the lads? We know that Dave has his drum-making business, and Tommy has his other bands to record and tour with, and is qualified in animation. But what of Olga? In the course of this book we've seen that he has worked as a guitar tutor and a record producer, and there will surely be continued work for him in both or either of these areas (though he states, quite rightly, that getting frequent production work is hit and miss). He has a number of properties rented out, that he's bought over the years as investments for the future, so maybe he could return to that and make a go of it. One place he probably wouldn't go back to, however, is the world of stocks and shares, where he got his fingers nastily burned a few years ago.

Olga has also had the offer of spin-offs from his fame. The BBC music quiz programme *Never Mind the Buzzcocks* asked him to do a guest appearance once for the 'line-up' round, but he wasn't keen, as it would have been far preferable to have been a bona fide contestant. A couple of one-hit-wonder-style TV shows – and a book of the same nature – have approached him to see if The Toy Dolls fancied being included, but in each case there was little the band could realistically have gained from participating. There was even an occasion when some amateur singer 'did' Olga on a *Stars in Their Eyes*-style show on British TV. Did he see it?

> "No, I never saw it. But it's frightening to think there was another skinny, anorexic toilet brush with glasses knocking about!"

But surely his first love of music will continue to provide him with his main means of making a living. There is always the thought of collaborations with the vast who's who of friends and contacts he's built up over 25 years in the music business. Interviewing Olga is a process that's delightfully peppered with names from famous and not so famous bands, punk and otherwise. He drinks with The Vibrators, eats with The Wildhearts, jams with Mr Big and goes backstage with The Stranglers. He has toured as bassist with The Adicts and The Dickies. The Toy Dolls and NoFX are mutual fans (there was a great moment when Olga met the singer from NoFX: the two approached each other and, almost simultaneously, each gushed that the other was a great influence on his work). Even No Doubt know and love Olga. He has musical knowledge, technique and inspiration coming out of his ears; business sense; drive and determination; and above all, an infectious personality that has always won him friends. With a CV like that, you can't fail.

25 years on from their humble beginnings, The Toy Dolls are at the crossroads. The next 12 months will, I'm sure, give us all the answers to the questions we're forming in our minds, but for the moment, we'll have to live with the butterflies of waiting for the tantalisingly entitled *Our Last Album?* to come out, and count the days until Our Last Tour? is finally a reality.

Questions and answers... Sham 69 had a hit with that very phrase the same year The Toy Dolls were formed. Whatever solutions Olga and his merry men provide for us over the next few months, we'll at least have the certainty that they've given us 25 years of pleasure – on stage, on vinyl, on CD, on video, on DVD and online. No music fan could ask for more, though we can always dream...

25 years of The Toy Dolls. From Fulwell to Fukuoka, we wouldn't have missed it for the world.

About the Author

Ronan Fitzsimons was born in Newcastle upon Tyne in 1964, and got hooked on The Toy Dolls in 1980. In his younger years, he played bass and drums in a number of bands (punk and otherwise) in the north of England, none of which reached the dizzy heights of mediocrity. He now has a sensible day job but wishes he hadn't.